Econ

ALSO AVAILABLE IN THE BANKING CERTIFICATE SERIES:

ECONOMICS AND THE BANKS' ROLE IN THE ECONOMY

REVISED SECOND EDITION

GEOFFREY LIPSCOMBE

Series Editor: David Palfreman

PITMAN PUBLISHING
128 Long Acre, London WC2E 9AN
A Division of Pearson Professional Limited

© Geoffrey Lipscombe 1988, 1991

First published in Great Britain 1988
Second edition published 1991
Reprinted with revisions 1992
Reprinted with revisions 1993
Reprinted 1994, 1995

British Library Cataloguing in Publication Data
Lipscombe, Geoffrey
    Economics and the banks' role in the economy.–(Banking certificate
series)
    2nd ed.
    1. Great Britain. Banking
    I. Title   II. Series
    332.10941

    ISBN 0-273-03250–X

Printed and bound in Great Britain by Clays Ltd, St Ives plc

Contents

Preface

In many ways this book, and the syllabus it covers, is a 'quart in a pint pot', comprising basic economics and basic elements of banking. Obviously, a lot of detail on the banking side and many aspects of economics have had to be omitted. Because most students work in branch banking, the economic content has concentrated perhaps on the micro- (or branch) side rather than the macro- (or whole bank) side, in order that students may relate theory to local practice.

It is hoped that the result is still a very interesting, job-related book, which should help young bankers to understand how economics affects our daily lives at home and at work. Because it is job-related and not too academic, the syllabus is suited for group learning in projects, some of which are mentioned in the questions at the ends of the chapters. Examinations are lonely experiences for candidates but there is no need for learning to be a similar one-to-one relationship between teacher and student. Much of it should be a group process, so that we have the benefit of specialisation, with each student researching a different part of the project, and drawing upon the wider experience of the members of the group.

This second edition has been expanded to include additional chapters on microeconomics and banking. It describes the economic and banking scene as at 30 June 1992. Factors which will have an impact in the near future are a decision on the location of the European Central Bank and the publication of the Bingham Report on the supervision of BCCI.

I would like to thank everyone who helped in the preparation of this manuscript. Finally, my apologies to Jill, Andrew, Clare and Sophie for neglecting them so much in writing and revising this book. Without the cooperation of family and colleagues the book would never have been written. Thank you all.

1 What is economics and why do we study it?

OBJECTIVES

After studying this chapter you should be able to:
1 **To define economics;**
2 **To contrast the economic systems throughout the world;**
3 **To look briefly at the factors which affect economics.**

■ INTRODUCTION

Most books on economics for students begin with a definition, but we need to discuss what economists study and how economics affects us all.

Economics is concerned with:

- the production of goods and services,
- the distribution of these goods and services from the producer through the wholesaler and the agent to you and me;
- the exchange of goods and services, usually for money.

In brief, we can say that economics deals with *production, distribution* and *exchange.*

Organisation of the economy

Rules and practices concerning production, distribution and exchange differ according to the country in which we live. In the USA and other western industrialised countries (the 'First World') the system is still very different from that in what was the USSR and many of its former allies (the 'Second World'). In many poorer countries in Latin America, Asia and Africa the system is different yet again; these countries (the 'Third World') have a large subsistence economy, not using much money and using, not selling, most of their crops.

Sometimes, countries come together to harmonise parts of their rules: the European Community (EC) is the leading example of this type of economic grouping. The world's most important industrialised countries, including the USA, Japan, Canada, Australia and the countries of the EC, have formed the Organisation for Economic Co-operation and Development (OECD), which acts as a sort of club for the richer, industrialised countries.

Distribution of income

Although the richest countries are in the Arabian Gulf, they cannot be compared in size to the industrial giants of the USA, Japan and the European Community. Some countries are very poor indeed – an example is Chad where the inhabitants have, on average, about £2 a week each. When we

1

consider that some of the inhabitants have more, and that many have less, we can appreciate to some extent the rigours of life there. Just as economists study the distribution of income between individuals in one country, so they also study the differences between the average income levels of different countries.

Employment

Another topic of interest to economists is how people earn their living and what they are paid for it. Not everybody in the world earns their living from a job. Some of us are too young, too old, too ill; others work in the family as housewives; or work on the land to feed themselves and their families (rather than to sell their crops or animals for cash at a market); some are self-employed, working for themselves as farmers or craftsmen rather than working for an employer; some are unemployed. Economists are concerned, like everybody else, with the problem of unemployment, although they often disagree as to how jobs can be created for the jobless.

Levels of income

To return to a favourite subject – income, yours and mine. Many of us will earn less than the nation's average wage, and many will earn more – for that is one meaning of an average. But most of us earn less than our bosses and nearly all of us earn less than pop stars or international footballers. Economists study the reasons for these disparities in income.

Most of us do not have the ability or luck to become top-class athletes. Our physical abilities vary in much the same way as our financial resources – some are strong, others are weak. Similarly, nations differ in their natural resources: the USA, Russia, the Ukraine, Canada, Brazil, China and Australia are richly endowed with materials and farmlands, Japan and the UK, being much smaller in area, have fewer natural resources. But not all countries with rich natural resources are wealthy: Angola is one example of a poor country with many natural resources. Japan is an example of the converse: a wealthy country with so few natural resources that it imports nearly all its raw materials.

■ A WORKING DEFINITION

Resources are limited to a greater or lesser extent, but the uses to which we could conceivably put these resources are limitless. For instance, the world's food is unevenly shared by its people. In the EC and the USA there are surpluses, while millions go hungry in Africa and other less developed regions. Some countries produce surplus stocks, while others have acute shortages. The nations of the world could conceivably alter these arrangements, so as to even out the distribution of their food. It is doubtful whether this would succeed in alleviating hunger but at least it would mean that the quality of life would be higher for more people.

Another example of a resource, this time created by heavy industry, is steel. Steel can be used for bridges, for building hospitals, for pipelines and for tanks and guns. It is currently used for all of these.

Economists study the way in which decisions are taken on matters such as how to allocate the uses of steel and to allocate the food production for consumption or for storage. These decisions can be taken by governments, businesses, families or individuals.

In brief, we can define economics as the *science of studying the allocation of scarce resources between competing uses.*

■ THE LANGUAGE OF ECONOMICS

Economics is concerned with facts, some of which we discussed at the start of this chapter. Facts can be grouped together in large numbers to produce statistics and we can then use these statistics to establish various relationships – e.g. the average incomes of people in different occupations. But we shall not be using a lot of statistics or mathematics in this book. Apart from some diagrams and some bank balance sheets, we shall be using words to communicate. We use words to communicate at work, especially to motivate people, and good bankers (as well as good economists) need to be as proficient with words – both spoken and written – as they are with figures. That is why some of you studied Business Communications and Business Calculations last year.

However, one of the difficulties we shall encounter is that economists use words in special ways, somewhat like the Mad Hatter in *Alice in Wonderland.* A Swedish economist once remarked that an economist would rather use another economist's toothbrush than use that economist's definitions!

Saving and investment

Bank staff will come across one of these conflicts very early on in their study of economics. To bankers, *saving* is much the same as *investment* – think of high interest cheque accounts, building society deposits, unit trusts, stocks and shares, endowment policies and pension schemes. They might say, 'Buying your own house is the best investment you can make'.

To economists, saving and investment are very different concepts. To them saving means not consuming or spending (i.e. not using all your income to buy goods and services), while investment means the purchase of *new* assets such as roads, hospitals, houses, industrial and commercial plant and machinery. It does not mean the purchase of stocks and shares or any of the things investment brings to the mind of bankers.

Margin

Another word much used in economics is *margin*. To business people it usually means the difference between costs and receipts – their *profit margin.* But to economists, the margin means the *additional* unit of sales to be bought or of output produced. This margin must be considered where the decision whether or not to buy or produce an extra unit of the product is about to be taken.

For instance, if the cost is 40p a unit and the demand is for 10,000 units at that price, the *marginal* unit would then be unit 10,001. The *marginal cost* of that unit would be the *addition to total costs* caused by the production of that extra unit. As we shall see in Chapter 4, this marginal cost should also be 40p under certain conditions.

Elasticity

This is another term which we shall look at shortly. However, it has nothing to do with underwear!

Factors of production: land, labour, capital and enterprise

Three other terms often used by economists are *land*, *labour*, *capital* and *enterprise*. Together they comprise the *factors of production*, i.e. those goods and services used to produce other goods and services. An economist regards *land* as all the natural resources of our planet, on and under the surface, and in the oceans. *Labour* comprises all mental and physical human effort. We all occupy a bit of land to do our jobs and most of us sell our labour to our employers.

Capital is a bit more tricky. The economist regards capital as those goods which are used to produce more goods rather than being consumed by their purchasers. A good example of capital is a wood-working lathe, used to manufacture chair legs. The economist considers a lathe to be part of capital, using that term in a somewhat different sense than an accountant uses it. The accountant regards a lathe as an asset, which is on the opposite side of a balance sheet to capital.

Enterprise is a fourth factor of production, involving the organisation of the other three factors, land, labour and capital, into a managed structure such as a limited company, and bearing the risk of failure.

ACTIVITY 1.1 * (Outline answers to Activities marked * begin on p217)

Write a letter to the Head of your old school, suggesting that the fourth and fifth years should study some economics. Your reasons for this should be very convincing. ✓

ACTIVITY 1.2

Draw a plan on a piece of plain paper, in the form of a rectangle, with 21 squares – 3 squares wide and 7 squares deep. These are 'time boxes' and will form the basis for your study plan.

Write the seven days of the week down the left-hand side. Write along the top above the 3 squares 'a.m.', 'early p.m.' and 'late p.m.'. Write your major activity in each appropriate box. Ten of the boxes should have 'work' written in them. Others may have activities, such as your sports or hobbies written in them.

The next task is to find spaces for study – three or four, including the evenings you attend college. You might be able to squeeze in some early morning study if you 'rise with the lark' or you may prefer to study in the evening.

This will be your *operational plan*.

Distribution

The term distribution has three meanings:

1 The physical transport of items from manufacturer to final consumer, and the firms organising the flow of goods. This is the meaning to most people.

2 The shares of income between the various factors of production:

- labour – wages, salaries;
- land – rent;
- capital – interest;
- enterprise – profits.

3 The shares of income between people. For instance, a few people receive large incomes, while far more receive very small incomes.

■ HOW TO STUDY ECONOMICS

First, do not rely entirely or even largely on memory. Obviously, it helps if you can remember facts and use them sensibly and in the right places to back up your arguments. For instance, nobody really supposes that the Bank of England's recent history is influenced much by the fact that it was founded in 1694. More important is the fact that it is very old – nearly three hundred years old – and that it has developed a wide range of functions very gradually.

Again, the digits of the year when the Bank of England was founded can be changed round to give us the year (1946) when it was nationalised. Examiners see hundreds, if not thousands, of students' answers with this date correctly given, but few ever comment that this date shows the Bank of England was considered so important that it was the first private company the post-war Labour Government nationalised, even before the coal industry.

Here we're allowing politics to creep in. As our definition stated, economics is a science, and so we must be dispassionate. We must avoid allowing our personal prejudices to affect our arguments. We use this word 'argument' a great deal because economics is concerned with choosing what to do with our scarce resources and we need to convince other people that our choices are right. Many economists are employed in an advisory capacity and they need to be able to convince their employers that their recommendations are sound and will be beneficial to the firm or government department for which they work. A list of unrelated or unsupported facts would be no good.

We do not want to stress too much the avoidance of memory work, but nobody ever learnt to swim or ride a bicycle by using their memories. We learn by practising until we are proficient; similarly with economics, which should be regarded as a way of *analysing problems*, such as prices, output, unemployment, poverty. The two most studied economic problems in banking are interest rates and exchange rates, which are important to our large corporate (company) customers. Interest rates, because they were very high in 1989–91, have also been a problem to house-owners with large mortgages.

■ HOW TO ENJOY STUDYING ECONOMICS

First, regard it as a way of thinking and of asking questions such as: Where?

Why? How? For instance, study the price of petrol, and who sells it in your town or village. Where is it sold? Have any garages closed recently? If so, can you find out why they closed? Closures could be difficult to explain, because the number of cars on the roads is still rising. Thus, relating the local market for petrol to the concept which you will study in the next two chapters should help you see economics not as an abstract set of theories to learn parrot-fashion but as a live subject of vital importance to you and your friends.

Second, always try to relate what is in the book or in your class notes to everyday life – at home, in the bank (remember the rules about confidentiality, however) and in the High Street. We shall discuss in Chapter 6 a difficult concept called gross domestic product (GDP), which is the total output of a country. However, it is possible to imagine the gross domestic product of a country by just driving through it – and you have probably all driven through parts of the UK! The farmland, factories and shops are all producing part of our gross domestic product. The world famous economist, Milton Friedman, once remarked that, having driven across England, he was amazed at how high the gross domestic product seemed to be! If he can estimate GDP by looking about him, so can we!

ACTIVITY 1.3

1 Buy a big diary, with at least a page for every week and rule each page down the middle.

2 Head the left-hand column 'Economics' and the right-hand one 'Banking'.

3 *Pencil* in likely dates such as the following:

	Economics		Banking
a Tuesday in March 1993	Budget for 1993	end-February	Profits declared for previous calendar year
a Friday in the middle of every month	Inflation figures?	end-July	Profits declared for first half-year
December 1993	Budget for 1994		

4 When important events occur, enter them in the diary. In this way you will have a good record of recent events to help your studies. Make a note also of the important regular economic statistics about which you will be told in the following chapters of this book.

5 To make your record easy to read, do not put too much in the diary. For instance, in the Banking column put such items as major purchases or sales of subsidiaries, e.g. the successful bidder for Midland Bank. However, if a local branch closes, then record that, because it could affect your daily life.

6 Enter the date of the examination, which for this subject is usually the second or third Monday in May or in October (and add a reminder to send in the application form well before the deadlines of 28 February or 1 September).

7 Then divide your time between now and your examination date by 13 – to give yourself a study plan covering all the chapters in this book and a period for revision before the examination. It could be you will be starting a new chapter every fortnight,

with about six weeks left for revision. Don't forget to have time for relaxation and any holidays you have planned.

Strategic plan

This is your strategic plan, which you must use weekly to insert the information as it occurs and to check your progress. You should use it with your operational plan.

■ SUMMARY

1 Economics deals with the problems of production, distribution and exchange.

2 It may be defined as the study of how scarce resources are allocated by different countries, businesses and people to the unlimited uses to which they can be put.

3 Economics is also a way of analysing problems.

4 It has a vocabulary of its own; it often uses words in a different sense to their everyday meanings.

5 Studying economics is much more than memory-work and involves questioning and reasoning.

■ SELF-ASSESSMENT QUESTIONS

Some of the following questions can be answered with a 'yes' or 'no'; others require more lengthy answers, while some are best tackled by groups of students working together and others will need a little research. They are designed not just to test your memories but to set you thinking about the High Street and the industrial estate, about our customers' problems and the banks' problems. Answers to many of these questions and those at the end of every chapter begin on p 196.

1 Which of the following is regarded as investment by a banker and by an economist:

   (a) the purchase of shares in the privatisation of a nationalised industry?

   (b) the purchase of a new house (not an existing house)?

2 Name some of the member countries of the OECD.

3 What does the term 'Third World' mean?

4 Explain, in ordinary language, the economist's meaning of the word 'margin'.

5 Explain how business people use the word 'margin'.

6 Why was the Bank of England the first privately-owned company to be nationalised after the end of the Second World War?

7 Name some of the world's richest countries.

8 Name some of the world's poorest countries.

9 Why does Japan import so many raw materials?

10 Name the member countries of the European Community.

11 What is understood by the term 'distribution'?

12 What are stated in the chapter as being the two most studied economic problems which concern bankers?

13 Do these problems also concern our customers?

14 How do economists define 'saving'?

15 Explain in a few words the meaning of the term 'gross domestic product'.

2 Prices and output – market clearing price

OBJECTIVES

After studying this chapter you should be able to:
1 Explain two major influences on price – demand and supply;
2 Appreciate that demand must be supported by the ability to pay the price;
3 Understand the various influences affecting demand;
4 Explain why a demand curve usually slopes downwards;
5 Understand some of the influences on supply;
6 Explain why a supply curve usually slopes upwards;
7 Demonstrate that the price of an item moves to the level at which the amounts demanded and supplied are equal.

■ INTRODUCTION

Prices are the sums of money we pay for the goods and services we buy – for instance, our food, clothes, rent, stereo, bus fares or petrol. One of the first questions economists try to answer is: 'How are prices determined?'

When demand for something exceeds its supply, price rises, and when there is excess supply then price falls. You may think this is obvious but there is more to it than that for an economist, who attempts to answer such questions as:

- What *exactly* do we mean by demand and supply?
- Why has demand risen or fallen?
- Why has supply changed?
- By how much have prices risen?
- By how much has the quantity bought and sold changed?
- How do prices change over periods of, say, three months or 30 years?

Economists analyse *supply* and *demand*. It seems better to discuss demand first because someone will always try to supply goods or services where there appears to be a demand, however small. This chapter, therefore, will examine first demand (using the concept of the margin), then supply, and move on to show how both interact to determine price.

■ MARKETS

Markets can be described as places where buying and selling take place. This includes the high street shops, the Stock Exchange, and the dealing rooms of banks.

With modern communications, buyers and sellers do not have to be in face-to-face contact. For example, they may buy goods by mail order, or on the foreign exchange market. What is important is not the physical contact but the decision-making process.

An economist defines markets as the *decision-making processes between buyers and sellers*.

Markets can be:

- *wholesale* dealing in large amounts between a few buyers and sellers;
- *retail* where many buyers and sellers deal in small amounts.

Whatever their size, however, markets are all ruled by the same principles of demand and supply.

■ DEMAND

Our wants are unlimited, but our capacity to demand the goods and services is limited by our financial resources and the *physical* characteristics of the goods and services. Salt is very cheap but we need very little of it – too much will ruin our meals and our health. Hence, we don't spend much of our money on salt, although it is so cheap. Caviar is very expensive and so most of us can rarely afford to have it. Not much of our money is therefore likely to be spent on caviar, but for a different reason.

When economists talk about demand, they mean *effective demand*, i.e. *wants backed up by the financial ability to buy the goods and services desired*. Many of us might want a Rolls Royce or a private swimming pool, but we can't afford them, so we shall never have them. Many starving people in Ethiopia need food desperately but they can't afford to buy anything, so they will die. Thus, neither the greed to own a Rolls nor the need of the Ethiopians are the same as effective demand, since there is no effective ability to pay.

This identifies two factors which influence demand for a good or service – *price* and *physical attribute*.

- Price is crucial and we shall return to it in the next section and in the next chapter.
- The physical attribute in a good is the material used in the product and the people involved in producing and selling it. In a service it is the human element – the person or organisation performing the service for you.

Utility and diminishing marginal utility

Utility is a third influence on demand. The utility of a good or service is the satisfaction people get from consuming or using it. However, the utility is not constant – for instance, the second 'bite of an apple' may not be as good as the first, and the twentieth may be too much. Economists call this tendency the *law of diminishing marginal utility*. This states that the extra (marginal) units consumed of any good or service usually yield less and less additional utility.

To give an example of how this principle affects a service, many people will go to the hairdresser from time to time, but only a film or TV star needs to have their hair done every day before going in front of the cameras. The principle of diminishing marginal utility is extremely important – with the notable exceptions of addictive goods such as drugs and alcohol, where consumption tends to increase. Because our resources are limited, we resent having to pay the same price when we obtain less satisfaction from each extra unit. So, to buy more, we have to be enticed by a lower price.

Other influences

- *Income* is a another influence determining demand. As people's incomes have risen in the UK (and other western countries) since the 1950s, so people can afford not only one car per family but often two cars. In famine-plagued Africa, however, incomes are falling and people have to walk miles just for food and water.
- *Habit* or *custom* is another influence – and beverages are a good example. Coffee is the customary hot drink of the USA and continental Europe; tea is the customary hot drink of the UK and, importantly, of India.
- Closely allied to habit is *fashion*. A British pram is different from a German one; German ladies wear hats quite different to those an English lady would wear.
- *Religious beliefs* can affect the demand for goods such as food and drink. Members of certain faiths may be obliged to eat specially-prepared foods, such as Halal meat, lamb or fish, while other goods may be forbidden, e.g. pork and alcohol.
- *Advertising* aims principally to increase the demand for an item. (There are other aims – such as corporate image-building, as you may discover in 'Customer Services – Marketing and the Competitive Environment'.)
- *Population* is a further influence. To give an example from the UK: East Anglia is one of the few areas whose population is rising substantially, with the result that demand for roads, houses and services is rising. This is a demographic inluence (i.e. an influence to do with population).
- *Age distribution* is another 'demographic' influence. From 1964 until 1983, the number of children born each year tended to fall, so that the demand for school teachers has fallen. But the numbers of elderly people have risen, and enterprising business people have created new products to help the elderly – such as sheltered housing and battery-powered tricycles for use on the pavement.
- *The price of other commodities* is also an influence. For example, a sharp rise in coffee prices could cause some people to switch to drinking tea – a situation where the products compete with each other. On the other hand, a sharp rise in fish prices could cause the price of fish and chips to rise and this could lead to a decrease in demand from fryers for potatoes.

Demand schedules and curves

Of all the factors affecting demand which we have discussed above, price is

Table 2.1 Demand schedule for petrol

Price per litre (pence)	Quantity demanded per week (million litres)
10	90
15	80
20	72
25	66
30	62
35	59
40	56
45	54
50	52
55	50
60	49
65	48
70	47

crucial. *To see how demand is affected by price, economists assume all other influences except price are unchanged.* They then list the various possible prices of the item in a schedule, showing against each price the total number of units which will be demanded at that price, for a certain period of time.

A typical example of a demand schedule is shown in Table 2.1. As the price rises, so the quantity demanded falls.

These figures can be plotted on a graph (*see* Fig 2.1). Price is shown on the vertical scale (remember price usually goes *up*!) and quantity on the horizontal scale (remember output has to be moved *along* the ground).

In Table 2.1 and Fig 2.1, only two elements change – the price of the good and the quantity of the good. Everything else – such as tastes, income and other prices – remains constant. In the next chapter we shall see how we take into account changes in these other influences.

The slope of demand curves

This demand curve (Fig 2.1) slopes steeply downwards from left to right. Although most demand curves do slope in this direction, this one is very steep, showing that the amount demanded does not change greatly in comparison to price changes. In other words, the buyers need their petrol very badly, in comparison perhaps to other items such as haircuts. If hairdressers raised their prices by 600%, which is the percentage price increase for petrol from 10p to 70p a litre, they might lose most of their customers! Thus, a demand curve for haircuts would have a more gentle slope, but it would still be downward from left to right. Usually, demand curves for essentials slope more steeply than demand curves for less essential items, reflecting our dependence on buying essential goods at almost any price.

By now, you ought to be asking: 'Why does the demand curve slope in this particular direction?' The answer comes from the law of diminishing marginal utility. This tells us that the more we consume of a good or service, the less

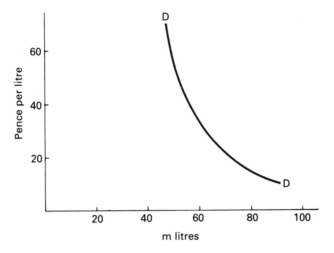

Fig 2.1

we desire more of it. Hence, we have to be enticed or attracted by a lower price to buy more of it. And a lower price means that to buy more of the cheaper item, we have to surrender less of all other goods and services where prices have remained unchanged. As a result of this fall in price we now achieve greater satisfaction from all our consumption than we did before.

In general, if sellers want to sell more *units* i.e. a greater quantity of the product, they usually have to reduce their price, as we shall see later.

■ SUPPLY

Economists define supply as *the quantities of a good or service which people are willing to sell at various prices.* As well as price, technology is an important influence in determining the quantities offered for sale.

At low prices, only the smallest quantity of goods will be offered because only the suppliers with the most efficient manufacturing processes will be able to offer their goods very cheaply. As price rises, so other and dearer producers find it possible to enter the market and sell their output. So, price rises should cause an increase in the quantity supplied, but producers may find their costs rising more rapidly when output increases.

Diminishing marginal returns

This principle refers to the extra output arising from using more of one factor of production – land, labour or capital – while holding the amounts of the other two constant. At first, output should rise – and this is very important – but there comes a time when the extra or marginal output gets smaller and even becomes negative.

In most inductries it is labour which is the variable factor and this can be very unpleasant for those workers sacked when demand for an industry's product falls and output must be reduced. However, when over-time is worked and more workers are employed to achieve a greater output then pay packets will be bigger!

The best example of this law is the old poser – if it takes 12 men a week to build a house then how long would it take 36 men to build the house? Arithmetic says 7 x 12/36 days = 2 1/3 days, but common sense should tell us that the 36 men would get in each other's way and that trebling the number of men might effectively only reduce building time to 5 days. In other words, the last six men add very little to the marginal product (the house) and certainly far less than the 13th man.

This phenomenon is called the law of *diminishing marginal returns* and is as important to supply as diminishing marginal utility is to demand.

Returns to scale

This principle refers to changing *all* factors of production to the same extent, keeping their proportions the same. Often, output will rise by a larger percentage than the increase in the factorss of production employed – say by 70% when the factors are increased by 50%. This extra growth is known as *increasing returns to scale.*

Sometimes, however, an across-the-board increase in the use of all the factors of production may not result in a similar or greater increase in output, because the firms and businesses which comprise an industry may become too unwieldy to control. This is known as *decreasing returns to scale.*

Hence, the existing firms in the industry, even in the long run, may be unable to increase output substantially. But more firms should be able to enter the industry and supply the extra output needed.

Factor prices

Firms must buy factors of production when they start to supply goods and services. The prices which they pay for their land, labour and capital will influence the quantity of the product they are able to supply and the prices they must set, in order to pay the costs for their factors of production and also to make a profit.

Short run and long run

In this analysis of price, economists define the short run as the period during which at least one factor of production is *fixed*. The long run then becomes the period when *all* factors can be varied and firms enter or leave the industry. We shall meet this distinction again when we discuss individual businesses rather than a whole industry.

Taxation of goods

Other influences on supply, apart from price and marginal productivity, include government action. Governments quite often tax goods – such as petrol, tobacco, and new motor cars – and also levy taxes such as VAT on the *sale* of many goods and services, including petrol, tobacco and new cars.

In the UK VAT (value added tax) is levied on many items, e.g. telephone calls and certain bank services, at a standard rate of 17.5%. Additionally, some goods need to be imported and hence many have to bear a tariff on their price. A tariff is a tax on imported goods: it is not levied on domestic output.

We will leave taxation until the next chapter. So, the *supply schedule* for petrol (Table 2.2) ignores the taxes placed on petrol sales, which is why the prices are so low! The schedule lists the amounts which will be supplied at various prices.

Supply curves

From Table 2.2 we can draw the supply curve, which slopes upwards from left to right – the opposite to a demand curve.

Table 2.2 Supply schedule of petrol

Pence per litre (excluding tax)	m litres supplied
10	20
15	30
20	40
25	50
30	60
35	70
40	80
45	90
50	100
55	110
60	120
65	130
70	140

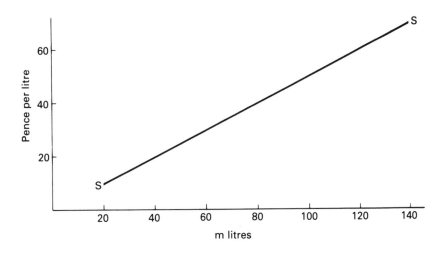

Fig 2.2 Supply of petrol

■ PRICE DETERMINATION: MARKET CLEARING

If we place the demand and supply schedules side by side, we can show, by simple subtraction, how many surplus goods will be left unsold at each price and also how much unsatisfied demand there will be at lower prices. Table 2.3 shows the supply schedule alongside the demand schedule.

Table 2.3 Supply and demand for petrol

Price pence/ litre	Supplied m litres	Demanded m litres	Excess demand (–) excess supply (+)
10	20	90	–70
15	30	80	–50
20	40	72	–32
25	50	66	–16
30	60	62	–2
35	70	59	+11
40	80	56	+24
45	90	54	+36
50	100	52	+48
55	110	50	+60
60	120	49	+71
65	130	48	+82
70	140	47	+93

* Equilibrium price 30.8p.

At low prices, there will be a large, unsatisfied demand and the unsatisfied people will bid up the price of petrol: the suppliers, of course, will be only too pleased to raise their prices to everybody and not just to those unlucky not to have got petrol at a lower price. At high prices, there will be a lot of unsold petrol in the tanks and so the sellers will be willing to reduce their prices, increase sales and reduce their unsold stocks. Somewhere in the middle, the pressures to raise and reduce prices will even out, at what is called an *equilibrium* or *market-clearing price*.

In the example in Table 2.3, the market-clearing price is somewhere between 30p and 35p a litre. More exactly, it is just under 31p a litre when the amount supplied is 62m litres. Have you asked yourself why this amount? You should have! The answer is that if we look closely at the supply schedule the amount supplied increases at a constant 2m litres for every penny increase in the price – 62m litres at 31p, 64m at 32p and so on.

Demand, however, does not change at a constant rate because, as price rises, so the proportionate fall in the litres demanded gets smaller. A 5p rise to 30p a litre causes 4m litres less petrol to be demanded, but another 5p rise to 35p causes only 3m litres less to be demanded.

After some trial and error then the price appears to be about 30.8p a litre when there are no extra sellers pulling the price down and no extra buyers pushing it up. Price should then be in equilibrium. The market is cleared of

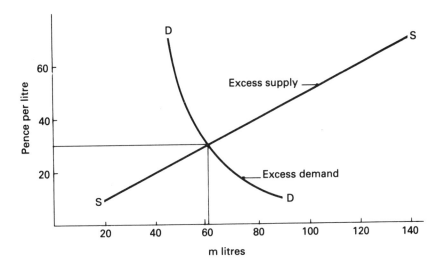

Fig 2.3 Price of petrol

excess buyers and sellers. However, with some goods, these can be last-minute price reductions to get rid of excess stocks. An example of this price-cutting to get rid of unsold stocks occurs in supermarkets on Saturday afternoons, when prices of perishable food on the shelves are reduced. Otherwise the goods would rot over the weekend. So it is better to sell at a loss at 3.45 pm on the Saturday than to get nothing for them on the Monday morning. However, this is the only 'clearance' sale we are likely to see in supermarkets.

Some supermarkets do sell certain goods cheaply – and advertise these reductions – in order to entice buyers into their stores to buy their other produce. Goods with such price reductions are known as 'loss leaders'. Supermarkets are not like department stores, or clothing or furniture shops, which have regular new year and summer sales in order to empty their shelves and warehouses.

The scissors diagram

We can now plot the schedules on the same chart, using DD for the demand curve and SS for the supply curve. (*See* Fig 2.3.)

Figure 2.3 combines the supply curve with the demand curve we examined earlier. At prices above 31p a litre there is more supply coming into the market than there is demand to take it off the market, so price moves downwards until supply and demand are equal. At prices below about 31p a litre, the opposite occurs and the excess demand bids up the price until supply and demand are equal.

At the equilibrium price of about 31p per litre where the two curves intersect in Fig 2.3, there is neither excess demand nor excess supply; the market is cleared. Diagrams like Fig 2.3 are sometimes called 'scissors' diagrams, because many have smooth demand and supply curves shaped like the blades of a pair of scissors (*see* Fig 2.4).

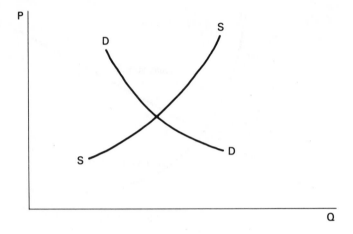

Fig 2.4 Scissors diagram

Now, in order to introduce more reality into the theory, we must begin to vary those other influences which have remained constant until now. However, you may have found this chapter difficult, so we will break here and consider this in the next chapter.

ACTIVITY 2.1

Compile a table, listing any price reductions which you notice, either from your observations in shops or in the news media.

Against each reduction note the time of year when it was announced and any reason given.

We will return to this table at the end of Chapter 5.

ACTIVITY 2.2

Take your own or your family's weekly grocery shopping list and code against each item the reasons why it was bought.

Suggested codes might be:

A Essential, e.g. bread.
B Preference, e.g. wholemeal bread.
C Income, e.g. the best quality wine you can afford.
D Price, e.g. the cheapest 'own brand' on shelf or a special offer.
E Moral/religious views, e.g. vegetarian, frozen meal.
F Inessential – you could get by without it, although you might have to buy something else.
G Seasonal, e.g. a turkey for Christmas.
H Advertising, e.g. it's been advertised on television.

If you say, 'We like it' or 'We're running out of it', then you need to be more precise! And don't forget that there can be more than one code against an item.

ACTIVITY 2.3 •

Draw up a list of regular television and radio programmes of special interest to economists and other business people.

■ SUMMARY

1   In economics, demand means effective demand – need plus purchasing power.

2   Demand for an item is influenced by:

- the *price of an item;*
- people's incomes;
- habits and customs;
- population – its size and age/geographical distribution;
- advertising
- prices of other goods and services.

3   In this chapter we concentrated solely on how demand changes as the price of the item changes.

4   A demand schedule shows how much will be demanded at each price.

5   Usually more will be demanded as price falls, because we get less satisfaction from each successive unit we buy. We therefore need a reduction in price in order to induce us to buy more.

6   A demand curve is a demand schedule plotted on a graph – price on the rising vertical axis and quantity along the horizontal axis. (A demand curve usually falls from left to right.)

7   Supply comprises the amounts of an item people will sell at various prices.

8   Costs, which we shall study in detail, are very important in influencing the amount supplied for any range of prices.

9   Costs depend on many influences – technology, other prices, people's abilities, etc.

10   At higher prices, suppliers with higher costs can enter the market.

11   Costs also depend on the quantity of the good being produced; they can fall as this output rises and can then rise again as bottlenecks occur.

12   Taxation is an important influence on costs and supply.

13   Supply curves usually slope up from left to right.

14   When there are more buyers than sellers – strictly, more is being demanded than is being supplied – then the extra demand will bid up the price.

15   When more is being demanded than supplied – excess supply – price will be forced down.

16   When there is neither excess demand not excess supply, the price should be stable. At this price, the market is cleared and the amount demanded equals the amount supplied.

■ SELF-ASSESSMENT QUESTIONS

1   Demand must be

(a) efficient; or (b) effective? ✓

2 Fill in the blanks.

(a) Wants are ... *UNLIMITED*

(b) Resources are ... *LIMITED* .

3 Describe in everyday language the law of diminishing marginal utility.
SECOND BITE THEORY.

4 Why are drugs and alcohol exceptions to this law?
ADDICTIVE.

5 Apart from its own price, name five influences on the demand for a product.
PRICE OF OTHER COMMOD, POPULATION, UTILITY, RELIGION,

6 Does religion affect demand for food and drink in the UK?
YES HALAL MEAT ETC

7 Which parts of the UK, if any, have a growing population?
EAST ANG

8 If the price of coffee rises, what might happen to the demand for tea?
INCREASE .

9 Give a way of remembering that price is plotted on the vertical scale of a demand/supply curve. *PRICE GOES UP.*

10 Give a way of remembering that quantity is plotted on the horizontal scale of a demand/supply curve. *QUANTITIES ARE MOVED ALONG THE GROUND.*

11 Why do demand curves, as a rule, slope downwards from left to right?
LESS IS DEMANDED AT HIGHER PRICE.

12 Define the terms *short run* and *long run*.
S.R. WHEN ONE OF THE FACTORS OF PRODUCTION IS FIXED) L.R = ALL VARIABLE .

13 Define the terms *returns to scale* and *diminishing marginal returns*. *= TOO MANY COOKS SPOIL THE RETURNS T.S) = INCREASE IN LABOUR = INCREASE IN OUTPUT (CAN INCREASE OR DECREASE)*

14 What is meant by *increasing returns to scale*?
MORE EFFICIENT TO INCREASE ONE OF THE FACTORS OF PRODUCTION.
Insert the words omitted from the next three questions.

15 When supply exceeds demand, price *FALLS* .

16 When demand exceeds supply, price *RISES* .

17 When demand equals supply, an ... ∧ ... price exists. *MARKET CLEARING*

18 Why do supermarkets often sell some goods very cheaply after 3.30 p.m. on a Saturday? What sort of goods have the price reduced?
PERISHABLE / SOMETHING IS BETTER THAN NOTHING .

19 In what sense do you, as bank employees, sell your services to your employers? *?*

3 Prices and output – shifts in demand and supply curves

OBJECTIVES

When you have studied this chapter, you should be able to:
1 Assess the effects on price and quantity sold of changes in non-price influences such as: incomes; taxation; tastes; population; advertising; and of changes in the prices of competing goods and services;
2 Understand that rising prices usually lead to a fall in the quantity demanded but not necessarily to a fall in total sales revenue;
3 Explain the concepts of price elasticity and the other elasticities of demand;
4 Give practical examples of these concepts;
5 Understand what is meant by elasticity of supply;
6 Understand what is meant by joint demand and joint supply;
7 Describe how banks and building societies cross-sell products.

■ INTRODUCTION

In the previous chapter we saw how in a scissors diagram the demand and supply curves cross at one point; this shows the balancing point where demand and supply are equal. The price is an equilibrium or market-clearing price, a price at which all the goods will sell because demand and supply are in balance. All other influences – incomes, taxation and tastes, for instance – remain unchanged.

Now we are going to change these influences and watch the effect on demand and/or supply and, most important, on price and quantity. We are also going to examine how far price will change as compared to quantity, because rarely will only one of them be affected. For example – has anything ever really been taxed out of existence?

■ CHANGING DEMAND

Suppose that all other prices remain the same but that we all get a 10% rise in our income. This means we can decide whether to spend or save all or part of this extra income and it may be that we all decide to do some more motoring. The demand for petrol will increase at each price on the demand schedule and so the new demand curve will be to the right of the old one.

Let us look at a schedule for both the old and new demands.

Table 3.1 Demand for petrol

Price/litre	Quantity demanded before income rise (m litres)	Quantity demanded after 10% rise in income (m litres)
10	90	108
20	72	86
30	62	74
40	56	67
50	52	62
60	49	59
70	47	56
80	45	54
90	43	52
100	41	49

To make it easy, a 10% rise in incomes has led to roughly a 20% rise in the demand for petrol at each price. The two demand curves look like those in Fig 3.1.

Next (Fig 3.2) we draw on this diagram the supply curve, which is unchanged and is the one we met in the previous chapter.

Immediately we see that the increase in demand has been converted by a shift along the supply curve into a rise in both price and quantity. If the supply curve is very gently sloping upwards, the increase in quantity sold will be much greater proportionately than the rise in price.

However, if the supply curve slopes sharply upwards, the relationship is reversed, with the price bearing most of the change and the quantity supplied remaining relatively constant. The scissors diagram would be as shown in Fig 3.3.

Now let us vary another influence − population. Suppose that the population of a country falls by 10%, perhaps because of emigration. With 10% less people, it is likely that less petrol will be demanded at every price. So, the scissors diagram might appear as in Fig 3.4, with the demand curve moving to the left.

ACTIVITY 3.1 •

Your manager teaches economics to young bankers and has asked you to help prepare a lesson on 'prices and output − shifts in demand and supply curves'. Examples are needed of how changes in the weather affect the demand for food and clothes, i.e. where there are two demand curves and one supply curve.

Construct a table, in two parts, giving examples of where:

(a) demand increases (the curve shifts to the right);
(b) demand decreases (the curve shifts to the left).

Which seems to be affected more by the weather − the demand for food or the demand for clothes?

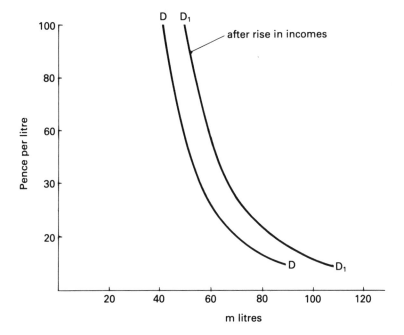

Fig 3.1 Increase in demand

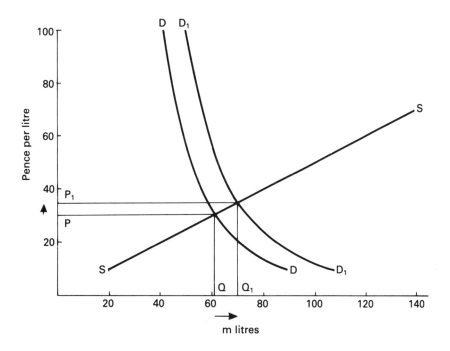

Fig 3.2 Gently sloping supply curve

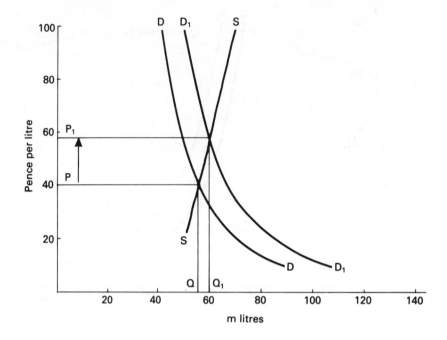

Fig 3.3 Steeply sloping supply curve

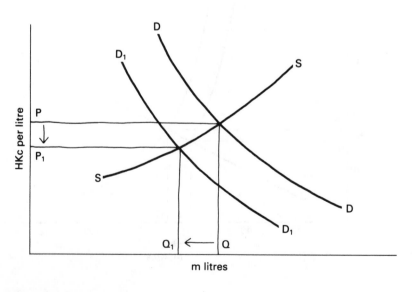

Fig 3.4 Fall in demand

■ CHANGING SUPPLY

Suppose that large reserves of cheap oil have been discovered near the river Rhine. The market is 'flooded with oil'. The supply schedule would then change, increasing at every price. It might look like that shown in Table 3.2.

Table 3.2 Petrol supply schedule

Price pence/litre	Amount before Rhine discoveries (million litres)	Amount after Rhine discoveries (million litres)
10	20	20
15	30	35
20	40	50
25	50	65
30	60	80
35	70	95
40	80	110
45	90	125
50	100	140
55	110	155
60	120	170
65	130	185
70	140	200

However, we must remember that this supply schedule tells us *nothing* by itself about the price of oil. All it tells us is what the supply will be at various prices. So many students forget to draw the demand curve! We must not make this mistake. So, let us take the demand schedule and curve we used in the previous example, placing it on the same diagram with the two supply curves.

Immediately we can see by how much the price falls and how much extra petrol is sold as a result of the coming on stream of 'Rhine oil'. The two prices – before and after – and the two quantities are read off against the price axis,

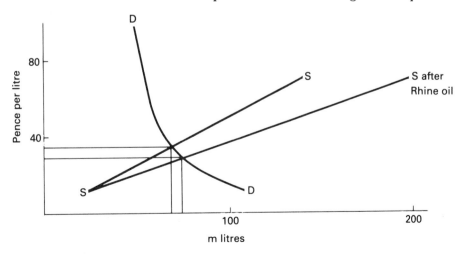

Fig 3.5 Demand, new supply and price of petrol

and the quantity at the two intersections of the demand curve with the two supply curves. The new price is about 25.9p a litre, and the quantity is nearly 76m litres.

Taxation

Do you remember that, in the previous chapter, we mentioned that taxation affects the supply curve? Well, this is another point to be noted: a tax on a good or a service may affect its supply. The supplier pays the tax to the government, and so tries to pass on the tax to the buyer by raising the price. Demand might be so weak, however, that the higher price causes buyers to turn away.

First we will look at the supply schedule when the government places a 20p per litre tax on petrol. We will take the schedule after the Rhine oil has begun to flow.

Table 3.3 Petrol supply schedule

Price (pence/litre)	Before tax (million litres)	After 20p a litre tax (million litres)
10	20	(it is now impossible
15	35	for petrol
20	50	to be sold
25	65	at these prices)
30	80	20
35	95	35
40	110	50
45	125	65
50	140	80
55	155	95
60	170	110
65	185	125
70	200	140
75		155
80		170
85		185
90		200

Remember, please, that this schedule tells us nothing about the price, except that suppliers would like to charge an extra 20p a litre in order to pay the tax without suffering any drop in profits. Can they do this? Well, they may try, but we must look at the demand curve to see if they can succeed.

By inspecting the diagram in Fig 3.6, we can see that the price of petrol has risen from 25.9p a litre to about 44p a litre, with sales falling from about 75.5m litres to about 64m litres.

Let's look at the tax revenue: 64m litres at 20p a litre – this comes to £12.8m. So, the tax brings in revenue to the government. But the suppliers are hit. At 44p a litre they sell 64m litres, which brings them in total sales revenue of £28.16m. Of this, £12.8m has to be paid to the government so they are left with £15.36m. They have been able to pass on 18.1p of the tax, bearing the

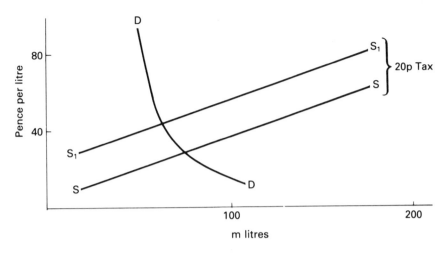

Fig 3.6 Who is affected by the tax?

other 1.9p themselves. Their sales have fallen by about 11.5m litres.

Now let's see what happens when the demand curve is a lot less steep than this one, as in Fig 3.7. S_1S_1 is the supply curve after tax has been imposed.

Price rises, but the quantity sold (and bought) falls more, relative to the price rise, so that the government will still gain revenue from the tax, but not as much as it might have wished, because the quantity sold has fallen so drastically. The effect of the tax has been to reduce our consumption of the good from Q_1 to Q_2, with a less pronounced rise in price from P_1 to P_2. The total outlay (or sales revenue), measured by multiplying price times output, which was the rectangle $0Q_1$ x $0P_2$, has actually fallen to $0P_2$ x $0Q_2$.

From the government's point of view, it still gets the tax per unit it wanted (the vertical distance between the two supply curves) but the number of units taxed has fallen from Q_1 to Q_2. Suppliers are badly hit, with greatly reduced

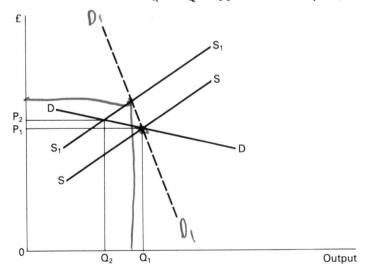

Fig 3.7

27

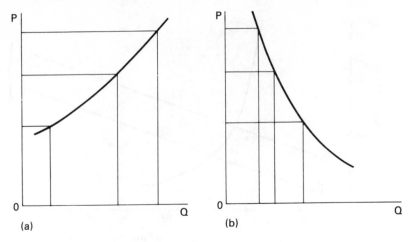

(a) (b)

Fig 3.8 Price elasticity of demand and total revenue

sales, and there is less tax revenue.

In Fig 3.7, there is a dotted demand curve with a much steeper slope than the continuous demand curve DD. If this dotted demand curve really existed, instead of the continuous curve DD, then the tax would have caused the price to rise considerably and the output to fall only slightly, with the result that the government would receive much more in tax revenue. Try it for yourself in pencil, so that you can rub it out before revising.

ACTIVITY 3.2 •

Your previous table was a success with your manager, who has now asked you for a second list. This time it relates to examples where the *supply* of food and clothes is affected by the weather.

■ PRICE ELASTICITY: SENSITIVITY TO PRICE CHANGES

You will remember that in the previous section we mentioned total revenue (or total outlay), measured by multiplying price by the units sold at that price. Graphically, we show it by the rectangles between the demand and the two axes in Fig 3.8. Note that we refer to revenue, not the quantity sold. We know that usually a price rise causes the quantity sold to fall (and supply to rise) but it is not so clear as to the effect on total revenue, because each case must be examined individually.

Let's take a steeply sloping demand curve and draw two total revenue rectangles (*see* Fig 3.9). To make it realistic we'll discuss it in terms of price rises – for falls you just reverse the arguments. A rise in price from P_1 to P_2 will cause demand to fall (it almost invariably does) but, with this steep demand curve, demand does not fall all that much, so that it is apparent from Fig 3.9 that the box showing total revenue (outlay) at the higher price is very much larger than the total revenue (outlay) at the lower price. In everyday language the price rise frightened few customers away.

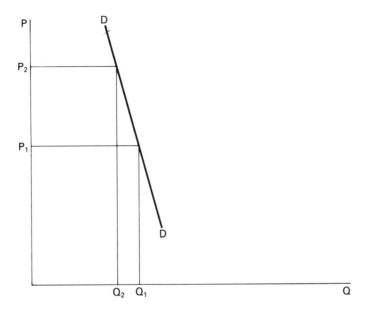

Fig 3.9 Price inelastic demand

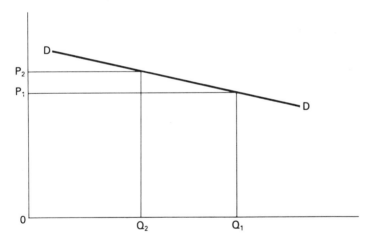

Fig 3.10 Price elastic demand

Now let's have a look at a more gently sloping demand curve in Fig 3.10, again with two prices. Here a price rise from P_1 to P_2 has caused a massive reduction in sales (by nearly 50 per cent) to Q_2, so that total revenue (outlay) is smaller at the higher price. In everyday language, the price rise frightened almost half the customers away.

Economists prefer to be more precise, however, and they have conceived the concept of *price elasticity*: when total revenue is greater at the higher price, demand is said to be *price inelastic*; when total revenue is greater at the lower price, demand is said to be *price elastic*. If total revenue is unchanged between the two prices, price elasticity of demand is said to be *unitary*.

Put in another way, price elasticity of demand shows whether total revenue (outlay) is greater or smaller following a price change. It measures the sensitivity of output to changes in price or, less frequently, of price to changes in output. For instance, if there is a sudden flood of goods supplied to a market then if demand is price elastic there will not be a substantial fall in price. But if demand is price inelastic then the price will fall drastically and certainly by more than the percentage rise in the quantity sold.

Put in yet another way, price elasticity of demand enables economists to know *how much* of the effect of a price rise will be borne by the almost inevitable fall in the quantity sold. If the quantity sold changes, as a percentage, by a great deal – and it will be a fall – and the price had risen by only a relatively small amount, then demand is said to be price elastic.

Measuring elasticity

It can be cumbersome to calculate total revenue each time price changes, so a rule-of-thumb is to use the percentage changes in price and output, and to remember that a fall in price usually causes a rise in sales. There is a simple formula:

$$\text{price elasticity of demand} = \frac{\% \text{ change in quantity demanded}}{\% \text{ change in price}}$$

If a 1 per cent change in price leads to a more than 1 per cent change in sales then demand is said to be price elastic. If a 1 per cent change in price leads to an exactly 1 per cent change in sales then demand is said to be of unitary price elasticity. If a 1 per cent change in price leads to a less than 1 per cent change in sales then demand is said to be price inelastic.

If total revenue is (say) £100m and price £100 so that sales are 1m, and a 1 per cent fall in price from £100 to £99 leads to a 2 per cent rise in sales, demand is said to be price elastic: total revenue rises to £99 x 1,020,000, which is £100.98m. Total revenue is £980,000 higher at the lower price, so demand is elastic.

Practical examples

All business people have an instinctive feeling for the price elasticity of demand for their products: they may not be able to express it in numbers but they have a gut reaction as to how far they can push up their prices. Sometimes they may be able to increase advertising or even improve their product at the same time, so as to mask the effect of the price rise. Extra advertising will shift the demand curve to the right. For instance, a motor car manufacturer may introduce car radios as standard accessories to the basic models of its cars, in order to soften the effect of a price increase.

Governments also have a need to take price elasticities into account. The first instance is when they are considering *tax changes* on various commodities – in particular the taxes on petrol, tobacco and alcohol – as we saw above. Second, governments must assess the price elasticities of demand and supply when considering whether to make *changes in the exchange rates* of their currencies, as we shall see in Chapter 12. Third, governments have to consider price elasticities when deciding whether or not to impose a *tariff* (a tax on imports) on a commodity. In the case of the UK and other EC countries, tariffs are now handled by the European Commission in Brussels and so it is the 'Eurocrats' who have to consider the elasticities.

Bankers have to consider elasticities in connection with pricing decisions for such products (services) as taxation calculations, administration of trusts, travellers' cheques, etc.

In general, if an item is a necessity or if there are no readily available substitutes, it will have a price inelastic demand. Luxuries tend to have price elastic demands.

ACTIVITY 3.3 •

Write a short playlet, on price elasticity in banking. (Some of the lines are put in to help you.)

Senior colleague: There are very few substitutes for travellers' cheques, so we might to be able to raise our commission charges quite a bit. But the pattern is that every time we raise them we end up selling fewer cheques – so maybe there are substitutes after all.

Student: Let's take your last point first ...

Senior colleague:

Student:

Senior colleague: Well, I've learnt two things. First, aren't there a lot of products we can sell instead of travellers' cheques. Secondly – and this is remembering rather than learning – I've remembered about price elasticity of demand. You've brought back memories of studying for my ACIB, and you haven't blinded me with science. I'll buy the cakes!

Other elasticities

There are other forms of elasticity. Of these, the most important to a banker is *interest elasticity of demand*, i.e. the sensitivity of the demand for a good or service to changes not in its own price but to changes in the rate of interest. Export finance is particularly sensitive to interest rate changes, because a rise in the rate of interest might well turn a particular export transaction from being slightly profitable into making a small loss. But, for most of us, the supreme example is the demand to buy houses. A rise in interest rates could, to use journalese, choke off the demand for houses, as happened in the late 1980s.

Income elasticity of demand is also very important. As our incomes rise, after allowing for inflation, our expenditure on such items as overseas holidays, hi-fis and videos, compact discs, camcorders, dishwashers, etc. tends to rise faster than our incomes. This is important to the manufacturers and importers of such products and to banks (who can provide us with the finance with which to buy them).

Cross-elasticity of demand is another variant. An example is fish and chips. If the price of fish were to rise sharply (perhaps because the fish have moved away from their usual part of the sea) the rise in price could affect the sales of potatoes to be used as chips. The demand for such potatoes could well fall, because fewer people are buying fish and chips.

Price elasticity of supply

This is measured by the percentage change in the quantity supplied divided by the percentage change in price. As price rises, so existing suppliers increase their output but, as we shall see in the next chapter, sometimes this increase can be achieved only by working longer hours so that the cost of a unit of output rises. These rising costs may not now be a problem for such firms, because the price has risen. Also, other firms with higher costs may now deem it worth their while, in view of the higher prices, to enter the market. This is because the higher price now offers them a chance of making a profit, in spite of their higher costs.

So, the price elasticity of supply depends on the costs of existing and potential suppliers. It also depends on the ease with which the potential suppliers can actually enter the market. For instance, if very large costs are involved in purchasing expensive new plant and equipment, potential suppliers will need a very large price increase for them to enter the market, so that they can soon recover their expenditure on these fixed costs.

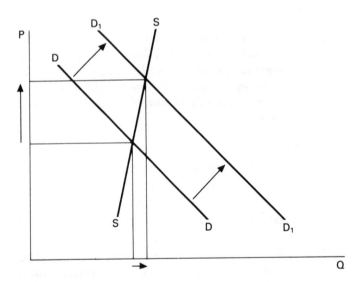

Fig 3.11 Inelastic supply

■ SHIFTING DEMAND AND SUPPLY CURVES

Equipped with the concepts of price elasticity of demand and supply, we can now begin to analyse how price and quantity sold change when the underlying conditions of demand and supply change. Briefly, the answer is: it all depends on the price elasticities.

If demand increases but supply is relatively price inelastic, the likely effect will be to bid up price, leaving the quantity relatively unchanged. Fig 3.11

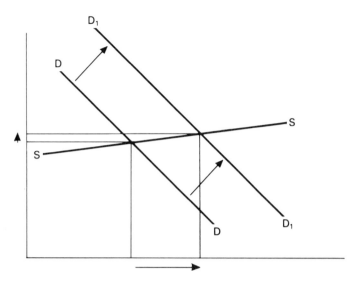

Fig 3.12 Elastic supply

shows this. If supply is relatively elastic, price will not rise much but quantity will. This is illustrated in Fig 3.12.

When it is supply that is changing, the effects vary according to the price elasticities of demand. Here is the classic tax example again, with price inelastic demand – *see* Fig 3.13.

When demand is price elastic, imposing a tax can be a disaster for the industry (we must remember that the government will prosecute traders who do not pay the taxes levied on their goods, so that the government does not lose out).

The suppliers have to pay the light shaded area (in Fig 3.14) in tax to the

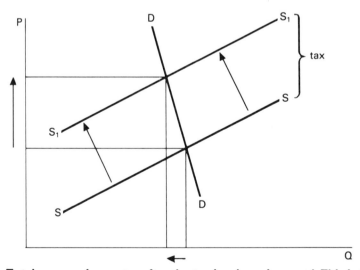

Total revenue is greater after the tax has been imposed. This is in spite of the fall in sales, which is quite small.

Fig 3.13 Inelastic demand

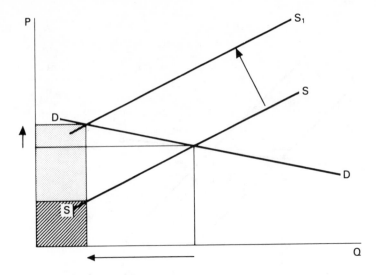

Fig 3.14 Elastic demand

government, leaving only the dark shaded area to cover their costs. As a result of the tax, price has risen by only a small amount, but the quantity sold has fallen by a percentage five times larger than the rise in prices.

You must be aware whether an event affects the demand curve or the supply curve. At the beginning of the last chapter we described some of the non-price influences on demand: incomes, tastes, population, season, other prices. All these change the demand schedule and the demand curve. Supply can be affected by: technology, a strike in the industry, the weather (as with water in recent hot summers), taxation, price rises or raw materials. Sometimes an event can affect both demand and supply:

1 A cold snap will ruin the vegetable crop so that supply decreases and prices rise. however, if the weather is so cold that people do not go out to buy the food, living on tinned food from their kitchens, then demand will decrease and the demand curve will shift to the left.
2 A strike can have unusual effects. In 1989 a series of BR and tube strikes meant that sales in Sock Shop kiosks in railway stations fell sharply, because the demand fell as there were no passengers to buy from the kiosks.

■ JOINT DEMAND AND SUPPLY

This brings us to those goods and services which are demanded or supplied jointly. Fish and chips are an example of joint demand, mutton and wool an example of joint supply.

The typical textbook example of joint supply is a manufacturing or agricultural process in which a number of separate products are produced in fixed proportions. Meat and skins (hides) are one example. However, we are no longer living in an agricultural society and better examples of joint supply are to be found in the many products produced by modern oil refineries, ranging from kerosene for aviation fuel to heavy heating oils. Examples of joint supply in service trades are more difficult: one might be hairdressing, which produces human hair as well as personal service. But the amount of hair per customer is not fixed, depending on the wish of the customer.

In banking and finance, perhaps the best examples of joint demand are connected with insurance. If you buy a house you need to insure it and you usually need to borrow on a mortgage to pay for it; if you buy a car you must insure it and often need a personal loan.

Cross-selling

Because banks and finance companies are very flexible, at least when compared to a manufacturer, they can quickly adapt and jointly sell the products (services) needed. Thus, home loans and the insurance for structure and contents can be sold together, as can a personal loan for a car and car insurance. Another example is travel insurance and travellers' cheques/ foreign currency.

These examples of 'financial footwork' are not really joint supply but rather 'cross-selling'.

■ EXAM TECHNIQUE: THE THREE-CURVE RULE

In the previous chapter, we had only single demand and supply curves which told us what the market-clearing price would be under the conditions of demand and supply shown by the two curves. But this two-curve diagram tells us little about *changes in the conditions of demand and supply* caused by taste, income, technology and a lot of other influences. This is what we have been studying in this chapter.

If these influences change, then we need to draw a new demand or supply curve, making three curves in all. An exam question often requires you to decide whether to change demand or supply by drawing this third curve, but it does not usually say so outright. For instance, if taxes on goods change, then a new supply curve must be drawn; if incomes change then we need a new demand curve.

In most examination questions requiring demand and supply curves the examiner expects to see at least three curves. One curve, and movement along it, will not bring more than a solitary mark. The examiner will be seeking to test how you tackle either:

(a) a shift in the supply curve to a new curve leading to a new price;
(b) how demand reacts to this new price, by moving along its curve (*see* Fig 3.15);
or:

(a) a shift in the demand curve to a new curve, leading to a new price;
(b) how supply reacts to this new price, by moving along its curve (*see* Fig 3.16).

Let us look at a possible question.

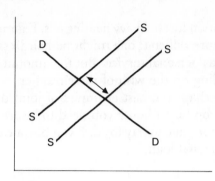

Fig 3.15   **Fig 3.16**

Show by means of demand and supply curves (or just 'diagrams') the effects on the demand for motor cars as a result of:

(a) an increase in VAT charged on purchases of motor cars from 17.5 to 25 per cent
(b) an increase in the basic rate of income tax from 25 to 30 per cent.

Let us go through the answer.

(a) (This is the 'tax on the good or service' type of question.) With a rise in tax on the item, the *supply curve* shifts to the left, with the new curve showing that a supply of X cars cost 8.7 per cent more at the new VAT rate than at the old. A car costing £11,500 will rise to £12,500 if the seller can pass on all the extra VAT. The new supply curve will not be parallel to or equidistant from the old one but moving away from it slightly.

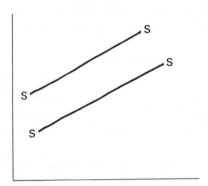

Fig 3.17

We then draw the two supply curves as in Fig 3.17 and then add a demand curve. To get better marks, we could draw two demand curves but, for clarity, not necessarily on the same diagram (*see* Fig 3.18).

And away we go with what should be a high scoring answer! But please note it is the supply curve which shifts, so we need two of them and at least one demand curve. We need to argue that this is likely to be price inelastic.

(b) This one is tricky because we have not mentioned income tax. Income tax reduces take-home pay – that is what it is meant to do! So, changes in income tax affect income and hence shift the *demand* curve.

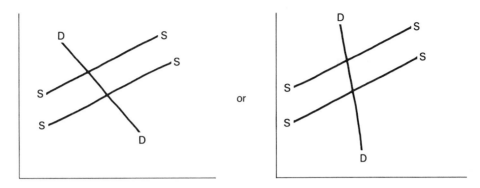

Fig 3.18

We need, therefore, two demand curves, the 30 per cent tax rate one being to the left of the 25 per cent rate curve, and at least one supply curve. Also, because the two parts of the question deal with the same product, it makes good sense to use the original demand and supply curve as in Fig 3.19.

We also need to argue that the demand for cars is likely to be fairly price inelastic and supply fairly elastic. We could draw a diagram with an inelastic supply curve (*see* Fig 3.20) and show that the fall in demand affects mainly the price, so that the quantity is relatively unchanged.

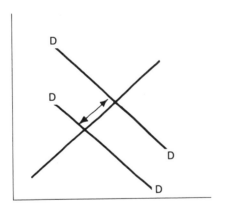

Fig 3.19

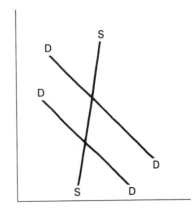

Fig 3.20

■ SUMMARY

1 A single demand curve and a single supply curve show us how price is determined while everything else is unchanged.

2 When one or more of these other (non-price) influences change then we must change either the demand or supply curve, or sometimes both.

3 We need a new demand curve for changes in:

- income;
- fashion, taste, habit;
- advertising, because this affects our demand for the product advertised;

37

- prices of other goods, because these affect how much we may wish to spend on this particular item;
- population and its age structure;
- income tax.

4 We need a new supply curve for changes in:

- taxation of the items supplied;
- technology, making it cheaper to produce.

5 With three curves – two demand, one supply or vice versa – we not only have a movement or shift of one type of curve but also a movement *along* another.

6 This movement along a curve – reading the price and quantity axes – is linked to the concept of price elasticity.

7 Price elasticity shows how much the quantity demanded or supplied changes as a result of a small change in price.

8 Price elasticity of demand (PED) is measured by the following formula:

$$PED = \frac{\% \text{ change in quantity demanded}}{\% \text{ change in price}}$$

If PED is more than 1, then there is price elastic demand.
If PED is less than 1, then there is price inelastic demand.

9 When demand is price elastic, total sales revenue will be greater at the lower price.

10 When demand is price inelastic, total sales revenue will be greater at the higher price.

11 Price elasticities are important for businesses and governments.

12 Other types of elasticity are price elasticity of supply, interest elasticity, income elasticity and cross-elasticity.

13 Joint demand occurs where goods are demanded together, often in fixed proportions. In finance, insurance is usually demanded when money is borrowed to buy an asset: the asset should be insured.

14 Joint supply occurs where goods are demanded together, usually in fixed proportions as a result of nature or in processing. The many oil-based products available from refining oil are modern examples, meat and skins are an older one.

■ APPENDIX

If you have found this long chapter rather 'hard-going', don't worry. The ideas are complex and you need to think about them quite hard. You may find useful the following article (by the author) from the spring 1989 issue of what is now *The Banking Cert* (published twice yearly by the Chartered Institute of Bankers for all Banking Certificate students).

Having trouble with economics?

Do you find economics difficult? Some senior bankers admit that they never really liked or understood the subject when they were younger. Perhaps the problem lies in the theoretical approach needed to study demand, supply and price at the beginning of the course. Does this 'switch you off'; particularly if you've been used to a lot of memorising for your studies? Well, if this is so, let's see if we can switch you on again!

Let's make a comparison. Most of us know something about isobars on weather maps. When they're close together we're in for a windy time! But we can't actually see the isobars when we look at the weather, only the trees bending in the wind. Isobars only appear on weather maps. Similarly, supply and demand curves can usually be seen only in economics textbooks. However, where they intersect tells us two very important facts – the *price* and the *quantity* of the commodity or service traded. We read the price on the vertical scale of the diagram and the quantity on the horizontal scale. It's the equivalent of predicting the effect of the wind from isobars.

The curves also tell us something more important – what is likely to happen when one of them *shifts*. Let's look at a practical example of this. 1988–9 saw substantial shifts in the demand curve for houses. In the South East of the UK, the demand for houses has fallen after the heady days of the summer of 1988. This is mainly due to rises in interest rates making mortgages more expensive. On a diagram, this means that the demand curve has shifted to the left. The effect of this shift is that sellers needing to exchange contracts to complete a chain of sales and purchases may well have to take a cut in their asking prices. The diagram looks something like this, the shift being represented by a move from D to D¹. (*See* Fig 3.21.)

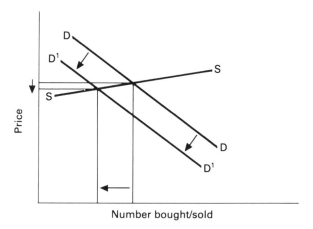

Number bought/sold

Fig 3.21

House prices don't fall by very much but the number of completions (sales) drops significantly, with a large number of sellers looking for buyers. For a time, even more 'For Sale' boards are erected, while other sellers withdraw their homes from the market. Moreover, potential sellers think twice, or even three times, about putting their houses up for sale. In this way, the market moves to a new *equilibrium* with prices falling only slightly, but the numbers of houses bought/sold falling sharply. At this new equilibrium price, the number of houses for sale will match at least in theory over the market as a whole, the number of people wanting to buy.

'What's this got to do with banking?' you might ask. Well, we [banks] sell home loans, insurance policies, personal loans and budget accounts when people buy houses. The shift to the left of the demand curve means that there will be less opportunities for us to sell these products in 1989. In addition, banks which own estate agencies will find these agencies generating less profits while the housing market is stagnating.

Unfortunately, there isn't space to discuss the questions you should now be asking, e.g. 'Why did the demand curve shift and will it move back again?' We really need a whole year to show how and why economics is so useful! Of course, you'll also discover this for yourself as your experience of banking grows – you'll appreciate that understanding the basic theory is a big help. We hope we've shown you just one simple example of why.

■ SELF-ASSESSMENT QUESTIONS

1 Which of the following events will shift the supply curve, and which will move the demand curve, for the product(s) specified?

(a) Copper miners' strike at the world's largest producer, on

- *copper*
- *fibre optics* (a competitor with copper wire in industry).

(b) Arctic weather in Europe on *fresh vegetables.*
(c) A rise in the basic rate of income tax from 25 to 30 per cent, on the demand for *most goods and services.*
(d) Severe frost in Brazil for several years running, affecting coffee crops and depleting stocks of beans to zero, on:

- *coffee*
- *tea.*

(e) Bumper sugar harvests – with stores overflowing – on *sugar.*

2 If vast quantities of oil are discovered in, say, the Sahara desert, and if the oil can be transported to and sold on the world's markets, what is likely to happen to the price of crude oil?

3 Name some goods and services with a low income elasticity of demand.

4 If the price of oil were to rise to $60 a barrel, why would you expect oil fields on the mainland of the UK to be brought on stream?

5 Sales quantities fall when price rises because:

(a) demand is price elastic;
(b) the demand curve slopes downward from left to right.

Which is correct, (a) or (b)?

6 You and a colleague are discussing the branch's sales of travellers' cheques last year, after a 20 per cent rise in commission charges on 1 January. He/

she comments 'The number of travellers' cheques issued fell by 10 per cent because demand was elastic.' *Was* demand really price elastic?

7 Which of the following goods/services might enjoy an increase in their demand as a result of a rise in average incomes?

(a) large cars;
(b) small cars;
(c) summer holidays abroad;
(d) mini-holidays in the UK;
(e) winter holidays in the UK;
(f) butter;
(g) margarine;
(h) alcohol;
(i) petrol;
(j) bus journeys;
(k) dishwashers;
(l) launderettes.

8 What bank products (if any) are involved with the purchase of the items mentioned in Question 7?

9 Why does a can of fizzy drink sell for 60p to tourists in the West End when it can be obtained for perhaps 22p in a 'cash and carry'?

10 Visit a theme park, where the admission price is high, but all the rides are free. In this 'market' of free rides, how is demand satisfied? How do people allocate their priorities? How is the 'market' regulated and 'cleared'?

11 How many employers likely to purchase your services as a bank clerk are there in:

(a) the Scilly Isles?
(b) Jersey, Guernsey and the Isle of Man?
(c) a large city such as Birmingham?
(d) the City of London?

12 Why do governments try to impose taxes on goods with an inelastic demand and supply?

13 If you were an inhabitant of a country with one major product – such as Zambia (copper) or Mauritius (sugar) – and demand for it was inelastic, would you favour exporting as much of it as possible? How would you attempt to maximise total export revenues from such products?

14 If VAT at 17.5 per cent were levied on new houses, what effect is it likely to have on the prices of existing houses? What are likely to be its effects on the demand for the following bank products:

(a) home loans?
(b) insurance (structure)?
(c) income from estate agency subsidiaries, which is a percentage of the price of houses sold?

15 Why do banks usually lend only about 50 per cent of the value of unprocessed commodities with an inelastic demand but a higher percentage of the

value of manufactured goods which have a more elastic demand?

16 Assess the influence of, first, fashion and, second, custom/habit on the demand for these bank products:

(a) non-interest-bearing current accounts;
(b) unit trusts.

17 Why do restaurants on top of mountains charge sky-high prices for meals and drinks?

18 What bank products are likely to be sold by banks in towns such as Worthing, Eastbourne and Rhyl, where many customers are retired?

19 What bank products are likely to be sold by banks in new towns and suburbs with a high proportion of 'young marrieds'?

20 Now try a couple of exam questions: Question 3 on pages 224–5 and Question 2 on page 235. The answers are on pages 228 and 237–239 respectively.

4 Prices and output – firms and industries

OBJECTIVES

When you have studied this chapter you should be able to:
1 Understand the nature of fixed and variable costs;
2 Define marginal and average costs;
3 Appreciate the limits to specialisation, especially the size of the market;
4 Show why average costs fall and then rise, as output rises;
5 Describe the various economies of scale;
6 Explain why large and small firms can co-exist, although not necessarily in the same market;
7 Give examples of the location of industry;
8 Explain what is meant by marginal and average revenue.

■ INTRODUCTION

'Combien?' 'Was kostet?' are words we soon learn when we go to French- and German-speaking countries, because costs are important. In this chapter we shall examine how costs vary with output, and see why some firms are large and others small. We shall see how people and areas specialise and the drawbacks associated with such specialisation. It is a part of economics where you can learn as a team, sharing your knowledge with one another.

Note, please, that economists use 'firm' to mean limited company, sole trader and nationalised industry, as well as the banker's narrow meaning of partnership. Confusing, isn't it?

■ COSTS

Economists use the term *cost* in what seems to be two senses, but, on closer examination, they are two ways of looking at the same principle. First, they often use it just as the person-in-the-street does, to mean the outlays or expenditures undertaken in order to manufacture a product or provide a service.

Second, they also regard cost as what is termed *opportunity cost* – the opportunity (to produce something else) which is given up when we produce a particular commodity. One example is the lack of motorway service areas on the M25, because the government would not sacrifice the crops which could be produced from the land on which they would have been built.

However, there is no real conflict between the two concepts because the money value of the expenditures or outlays is merely the result of bidding

43

against people who have alternative uses for the factors of production purchased. If steel can be used to make both cars and lawn-mowers, then the lawn-mower manufacturers must pay at least the same price for their steel as the motor car manufacturers would pay. The opportunity cost of a motor car is then a number of lawn mowers – the alternative use for the steel.

ACTIVITY 4.1

Use the principle of opportunity cost to show what you will have to do without if you decide to:

(a) leave the bank and go on a world tour;
(b) start a family;
(c) buy a second-hand car with:

- cash;
- a bank or building society loan.

Justify your decision to go ahead with each of these actions (assuming that the benefits are greater than what you have to do without).

Fixed and variable costs

Fixed costs change only when the firm begins or ceases production and do not vary with the level of output. The premises of a bank branch are a reasonable example – not the best, because premises can be extended and rents may rise every five or seven years. The insurance of the property and the uniform business rate are other examples. The important point, however, is that as output increases, there are more units to bear these *overheads* as fixed costs are sometimes called. Overheads *do* increase as a result of inflation, however, but not as a result of extra output.

Variable costs vary directly with output: labour and materials are obvious examples. A branch bank takes on more business, so its staff numbers rise, along with costs of postage, telephones, etc. But in banking the greatest variable cost is the *cost of funds*: if a bank needs more deposits it must bid for them, either by paying interest or providing better current account services.

Marginal and average costs

Here the business person and the economist again part company, having been in agreement over fixed and variable costs, because the economist uses marginal in the sense of 'extra', or 'incremental' or 'additional', and most business people do not. They usually use it to denote the difference or 'mark-up' between cost and selling price: their profit margin.

Marginal cost is the economist's way of measuring the *extra* cost of an *extra* unit of output. The marginal cost of the first unit will thus be very high because it includes all the fixed costs. If we add all the marginal costs for the first ten units of output and divide by ten, we get the *average cost* of these ten units. Now, if the marginal cost of the eleventh unit is *above* the average cost of the ten, the new average cost of the eleven units will also be higher than for ten units. Try it on a piece of paper: average cost of ten units is 12p (total cost 10 x 12p

= 120p); the marginal cost of the eleventh is 15p (total cost 120 + 15 = 135; divide by 11 and the new average cost is ...).

So, to get average costs down we must keep marginal costs down, or, possibly, pare the fixed costs, e.g. move to cheaper premises or try to negotiate a lower rent.

■ SPECIALISATION

Specialisation is found in many aspects of social life: in clubs and societies for our hobbies, in many team sports – football, cricket and hockey – and in business. Not all shops sell everything, not all factories make everything. Even banks and insurance companies specialise to a certain extent. For instance, Hambros is a merchant bank with extensive Scandinavian connections, while Lloyds Bank has wide-ranging operations in South America. Building societies are an example of specialised financial institutions which, since the Building Societies Act 1986, are trying to sell a wider range of products.

Economists often refer to Robinson Crusoe: specialisation was virtually impossible for him – a single person on a desert island must do everything.

As the population of an area increases, so specialists can develop. Thus, many hamlets do not even have a shop; if they grow large enough to be a village they may have a church, shop and post office. Larger villages may have a full-time vicar, doctor and a primary school, although the secondary schoolchildren will still be 'bussed' to school several miles away, in the nearest town. Here there should be at least one bank, a fire station and a health centre, as well as a wide range of shops. Each of these – banks, shops and public services – will regard the population of the town and the surrounding villages and hamlets as together comprising its 'market', i.e. its customers. The larger the market, the greater the amount of specialisation possible. In England, London is the classic example, with a population large enough to support three universities (London, City and Brunel), eight polytechnics and several large teaching hospitals, to give examples from just education and medicine. And, in the arts, London has several orchestras and dozens of theatres.

Division of labour

In Chapter 1 we met the factors of production – land, labour, capital and enterprise – and here we will show how they too can become specialised. Land is usually capable of supporting only one activity at a time, e.g. grassland for animals, cultivated land for crops, land for housing, shops or factories. Capital, which we will define as machinery and buildings, is similar. A bulldozer cannot harvest grain and offices cannot easily be converted into factories.

Labour is different. We are flexible and can be trained to do a number of different tasks, although re-training is harder as we grow older. It was Adam Smith, known as the 'father of economics', who first set out the principles of the division of labour over 200 years ago. He took the example of pin-making, identifying eighteen different processes on which workers could specialise.

Instead of a worker making perhaps ten pins a day doing everything, when eighteen workers each specialised in one process average output could rise to 4800 per person per day – a 480-fold increase in productivity. In other words, marginal and average costs have both fallen dramatically.

The modern-day counterpart to the soul-destroying pin manufacture is perhaps the assembly line of a motor car factory; the 'track' as it is known. Here, each worker used to be responsible for perhaps only four or five nuts but, recently, robots have begun to do the work instead of humans.

Obviously, to use such processes in manufacturing requires a large number of customers: it is the volume car manufacturers, such as Austin Rover, Ford and Vauxhall, which use robotics, rather than manufacturers of custom-built cars such as Lotus. In other words, the *division of labour*, which is that part of specialisation applying to workers, *is limited by the extent of the market*, just as with all forms of specialisation.

Specialisation could not really develop before exchange and, of course, transport. It also needs a well-developed form of money to help people exchange goods and services, as we shall see in the chapter on money.

Earlier in this chapter we mentioned that banks can specialise, so what about the division of labour in banking? Does the principle still apply? The answer is, as you will realise, 'yes', but it is limited by the size of the market, which means the size of your branch because the larger the market the larger the branch. In a small village sub-branch open once a week, the cashier will do many things: taking orders for foreign currency, travellers' cheques, statements and cheque books. These would next be processed by the foreign clerk or one of the enquiries clerks at the main branch. A branch might need to have a staff of, say, twenty to have a full-time foreign clerk, but even he or she might not be expected to handle documentary credits. These might be opened or advised by the regional overseas branch, up to 100 miles away perhaps and serving over 100 main banking branches.

Economies of scale

Economies of scale is economic jargon for *lower average costs when production is on a large scale*. There are two main classes of economies of scale:

(a) *internal* economies, which occur *inside* a firm as its output rises;
(b) *external* economies, which occur outside a firm as *the industry's* output rises.

Internal economies

There are as many as ten different kinds of internal economies, available to a firm only as its output increases.

1 *Specialisation*. As we saw in the previous section, when workers are given separate, specialised tasks, their output increases. Accordingly, we can reverse the argument: when there is a need for greater output, managers can in many cases achieve it by making greater use of specialisation. Managers themselves can specialise, e.g. into marketing, cost control, etc.

2 *Indivisibilities*. Some goods just cannot be produced on a small scale. Steel-

making is a good example, where a 'small firm' produces 100,000 tons a year. There are no 'one-man firms' in steel! Yet coal-mining is different, because small 'drift mines' can continue with a handful of workers, operating under licence from British Coal.

3 *Lower average overheads.* As output rises, the average fixed costs per unit will fall, because they are calculated by dividing the increasing total of output into a fixed amount – total fixed costs. For the aircraft and space industries, this can be very important, because the development costs of a new type of aircraft can be very high, so that a large number of sales must be made if there is to be a profit. Concorde is an outstanding example. Very few were ever sold, so the development costs of the handful made were very high and had to be paid for by the British and French governments. Medicinal drugs are another example.

4 *Increased dimensions.* If we double (multiply by 2) each dimension of a three-dimensional object, its capacity increases eightfold (is multiplied by 8). If that's baffling, here's an example: a tank 2 metres by 2 metres by 2 metres has a volume of 8 cubic metres (2 x 2 x 2 = 8); doubling the dimensions to 4 metres by 4 metres by 4 metres increases the volume to 64 cubic metres (4 x 4 x 4 = 64). Hence, cargo ships are getting larger.

5 *Linked processes.* Steel-making is a good example of this type of economy. The cost of transferring molten iron to an adjacent plant is far less than the cost of reheating it after transporting it to a separate location. To produce iron and steel at the same plant, however, requires a very large complex to operate at low average cost. At Scunthorpe, for example, there are four blast furnaces to 'feed' one basic oxygen steel plant, which produces about 4m tonnes of steel a year.

6 *Commercial.* Larger firms can obtain lower prices when they purchase goods and services. These often take the form of discounts for bulk purchases or for bulk loads. 'Bulk buying' is the phrase used to describe such economies.

7 *Organisational.* Delegation of authority is often possible in a large organisation, thus relieving senior managers of the burden of day-to-day operating decisions.

8 *Financial.* Large firms can achieve financial economies in several ways:

(a) negotiate lower rates of interest from their bankers;
(b) take longer to pay their trade suppliers;
(c) use sources of finance not available to smaller firms.

Raising finance by issuing shares to the general public is a classic example. Another is to issue sterling commercial paper, as we shall see in Chapter 7.

9 *Risk-bearing.* Large firms are able to quantify their risk of loss, because it is easier for statisticians to predict events which occur in large numbers. Again, with a number of factories, a firm is unlikely to be affected by fire or accident, as would one with only one factory.

10 *Diversification.* Not only can a large firm diversify its sources of supply, but it can move out of its mainstream industry altogether, to avoid placing 'all its eggs in one basket'.

All these 'economies' are achievable *within* the firm, as it grows bigger. They are related to increasing returns to scale but are not exactly the same. Economies of scale are falling average total (fixed and variable) costs, expressed in money. Increasing returns to scale show how physical output increases in comparison to physical changes in the input of factors of production.

External economies of scale

These economies arise as an industry grows bigger, i.e. *outside* the firm, and are enjoyed by all firms in the industry, large or small. There are three types.

1 *Economies of information.* For instance, a trade paper may begin publication to provide more up-to-date information to firms in the industry.

2 *Economies of disintegration.* Software houses may begin to write computer programs specifically for the industry, for example. Alternatively, subcontractors may develop, as with contract harvesting for farms and farm secretarial agencies.

3 *Economies of concentration.* Specialist firms may be founded to help the industry. In London, for example, there are one or two specialists who advise foreign banks on some of the problems in setting up a London branch or representative office. Sometimes, the industry has become localised – as with cotton textiles in Lancashire and wool in Yorkshire. This facilitates further specialisation within groups of towns and enables technical colleges to help to train the employees. A pool of skilled labour can develop.

ACTIVITY 4.2 •

As part of an initiative course, you are to take a group of visitors around firms operating in each of the following industries and services, giving a commentary on the operations: farming, motor car manufacturing, hairdressing, solicitors and banking. For each of these tours, prepare notes on the scope for economies of scale.

Diseconomies

Costs do not continue to fall, mainly because the management problems become much more difficult as the firm becomes larger. Bureaucracy may stifle initiative in the drive to ensure the co-ordination of the various parts of the firm. Also, the original factory may be incapable of being expanded, so that it is cheaper to relocate to a new site and close down the old one rather than to run two factories simultaneously. Eventually marginal costs, and later average costs, will begin to rise.

Integration

Sometimes firms expand not by establishing new operations but by purchasing firms in the same industry – their local rivals perhaps or, more frequently, those operating some distance away. Economists term this expansion *horizontal integration*. It nearly always involves purchases of other firms operating at the same stage of the production or distribution process. An example was the purchase of British Caledonian by British Airways in 1987.

Vertical integration is another form of expansion. It involves a firm beginning to operate at a different stage of the industry. A steel manufacturer, for instance, may buy a coal mine; the Milk Marketing Board owns Dairy Crest, which supplies milk to shops and homes and which is likely to be privatised soon. The Kuwait Petroleum Company owns filling stations in the UK, which operate under the name Q8! Vertical integration does not necessarily have to involve a purchase, but buying an existing operation is quicker than trying to set up a new one.

In banking we have seen horizontal integration when two banks merge; as when the Royal Bank of Scotland merged with Williams & Glyn's in the early 1980s; the purchase of Midland Bank is a topical example. Vertical integration is exemplified by banks buying estate agencies (which introduce new customers for loans) and, in advance of Big Bang in 1986, buying firms of stockbrokers.

Small firms are important

In the 1980s small firms made a come-back for several reasons. First, personal computers became available for less than £1,000. Secondly, the government launched several schemes to help small firms become established as part of its programme to contain unemployment. Thirdly, service trades grew faster than manufacturing, and small firms are better at many service trades than large ones. Is there a national chain of hairdressers or solicitors? Banks, too, have striven to help small firms.

However, small firms are not increasing their share of retail trade. Here hypermarkets and supermarkets are able to achieve considerable internal economies of scale.

Location of firms and industry

As we saw earlier, some localities become very specialised: textiles are a classic example, not only in Lancashire and Yorkshire but in Nottingham, Leicester, Macclesfield, Belfast and Dundee. More recent examples are 'high-tech' areas with large numbers of computer and bio-chemical firms in the M3–M4 corridor from Heathrow to Reading and Basingstoke, and the area around Cambridge.

An industry may move to an area by chance. For instance, in 1859 a guest at a shooting party rediscovered the long-lost local ironstone at Scunthorpe, which led to the British Steel plants there today.

But areas can become over-dependent on a particular industry which, if it begins to decline, will cause acute problems. Chatham was very dependent on its naval dockyard until it closed in 1984 and it has taken a great deal of effort to establish new enterprises there to provide employment for former dockyard workers.

In general, there are two main forces determining the location of industry: the pull of *resources* (mining is a classic example), including *fuel* and the pull of the *market* (brewing is a popular example). Obviously, mines must be where the minerals are, and beer, because it is bulky, is expensive to transport to its markets. Hence, many local breweries still exist, even in these days of bulk tankers and brewing under licence from another brewer.

Banking is an example of the pull of the market; London is the big one, here. You may ask: isn't it also the pull of all the bank clerks in London? The answer is that a trained labour force does help but then, to clinch the point, look at Jersey. Here, the pull of the market (which is a tax haven) is so strong that the banks wish to *import* labour from the mainland. Labour shortages, as in London and Jersey, demonstrate the pull of the market because banks set up there in spite of the difficulties of recruitment.

ACTIVITY 4.3

Obtain a street plan of your nearest town. Plot on it the locations of:

(a) banks and building societies;
(b) estate agents;
(c) petrol stations;
(d) chemists;
(e) supermarkets;
(f) public houses/hotels;
(g) garden centres;
(h) confectioners, tobacconists and newsagents (known as CTNs – they usually sell all three types of goods).

Which groups of retailers tend to cluster together in the centre? Which are strung along the roads leading out of the town? Which are located on the outskirts?

(*Note:* in a large city, such as Birmingham or Newcastle upon Tyne, it may be possible to plot such specialists as musical instrument shops or second-hand book shops. Book shops may be found close to a polytechnic or university – the pull of the market.)

■ AVERAGE AND MARGINAL REVENUE

So far we have concentrated on costs, but we must not neglect sales revenue. In Chapter 2 we saw how a demand curve usually slopes downwards from left to right, so that a price reduction is necessary for the *industry* to sell more goods. Does this principle apply to individual *firms*?

The answer is 'Yes and no'. In many cases a firm may have to reduce its price to sell more goods but it may first increase advertising expenditure in order not to reduce the price of all its output of that product, i.e. the firm tries to move its demand curve to the right. In some cases, however, the firm is so small and the industry so big that it can sell all its output without having to reduce its price.

This brings us to two new concepts – average revenue and marginal revenue.

Average revenue

Average revenue is the total revenue from sales divided by the number of units sold. It is the same as the demand curve *for that firm*, because the demand curve plots sales at each price, with total revenue being the the units sold at each price multiplied by that price. If a firm is so small that it can sell all its output at a constant price, then *its* demand curve (not that of the industry) is horizontal.

Marginal revenue

Marginal revenue is the addition to total revenue caused by an increase in sales. If sales can be increased without lowering price then marginal revenue will be equal to price. However, if price has to be cut, the reduction must apply to all the output; marginal revenue will thus be the price of the extra unit sold, less the total price reduction on *all* the other units sold. In other words, marginal revenue will be less than price, falling as more output is sold.

The relationship between marginal revenue and marginal cost

In the next chapter we shall come across the theories of the firm but, no matter how many firms there are in an industry, economists usually assume that each one wants to maximise its profits. It will do this by increasing output until marginal revenue equals marginal cost. In other words, each firm produces that output at which the extra revenue from the last unit of output is equal to the extra cost of producing that unit. Since marginal cost is usually rising, once the economies of scale have been achieved, and marginal revenue cannot rise (at best it is constant) then any further output will result in a smaller profit. Because the firm seeks to maximise its profits, it will not produce that extra output. However, in the next chapter we will come across some exceptions to this principle of profit maximisation, where firms limit their profit – at least in the short run.

■ SUMMARY

1 Costs mean (a) outlays or spending on factors of production to produce a good or service; (b) the alternative uses to which factors could have been put.

2 Fixed costs change only as a result of inflation; they do not vary in relation to output. Variable costs vary directly with output.

3 Marginal cost is the additional cost of producing an extra unit of output.

4 Average cost is the total cost of a certain level of output divided by the number of units produced.

5 Specialisation is widespread in industry, commerce and social activities. It is limited by the size of the market – there can be little specialisation on a small island.

6 Specialisation applies to all factors of production.

7 When specialisation occurs in the labour market, it is called division of labour.

8 Economies of scale occur in a firm when average costs fall as output rises.

9 Internal economies occur inside a single firm.

10 External economies occur in a whole industry and are available to all firms in that industry, irrespective of size.

11 Economies of scale are roughly the same as increasing returns to scale.

12 Diseconomies of scale occur when average costs rise. They are roughly the same as decreasing returns to scale.

13 There are two types of integration (one firm buying another):

(a) horizontal, when competitors merge;
(b) vertical, when manufacturers purchase suppliers or retail outlets.

14 Location of industry within one particular area can be caused by the pull of:

(a) new materials and fuel; or
(b) markets.

15 Average revenue is total sales revenue of a firm divided by the number of units sold.

16 Marginal revenue is the increase in total sales revenue of a firm resulting from the sale of an extra unit.

17 One major assumption of economists is that firms seek to maximise their profits, selling that quantity of their product at which marginal cost equals marginal revenue.

■ SELF-ASSESSMENT QUESTIONS

1 Which of the following are considered to be firms by (a) economists, (b) bankers?

Sole traders, partnerships, limited companies, nationalised industries (public corporations).

2 Define: (a) cost; (b) opportunity cost.

3 Give four examples of fixed costs.

4 Give four examples of variable costs.

5 Define marginal cost and average cost.

6 Explain the relationship between marginal cost and average cost.

7 Using a hospital as an example, explain the meaning of 'specialisation is limited by the size of the market'.

8 Show briefly how specialisation requires exchange of goods and services.

9 What are economies of scale?

10 Give five examples of internal economies.

11 Give three examples of external economies.

12 What are diseconomies of scale?

13 Why were small firms increasing in numbers?

14 Give examples of location of industry other than those in this chapter.

15 What are the two main 'pulls' in determining where an industry is located?

16 State the three main factors of production.

17 Give examples of specialisation from all three types of factors.

18 Is a small firm or a giant (such as ICI) better able to react to a change of demand?

19 Which has the higher fixed costs – a ladies' hairdresser or British Steel?

20 Have you thought about starting a business on your own? If so, identify the banking products which you may need.

5 Prices and output – competition

OBJECTIVES

When you have studied this chapter, you should be able to:
1 **Understand why some firms can sell all their output at a fixed price and why others have to reduce their price in order to sell more;**
2 **Demonstrate the importance of market share;**
3 **Describe some of the strategies available to businesses;**
4 **Know how economists classify the structures of different industries;**
5 **State the ways in which the government tries to control monopolies.**

INTRODUCTION

Economists have an array of theoretical models of firms and industries, ranging from *perfect competition*, where there are thousands of firms, none of which is able to influence the market price at all, to *monopoly*, with one firm in the industry.

PERFECT COMPETITION

Perfect competition theory rests on the following assumptions:

1 Every firm in the industry is so small that it cannot influence the market price by its own actions; the effect of this is to make every firm a price-taker rather than a price-maker.
2 Firms are free to enter and leave the industry if they so wish; the result is that supply becomes fairly elastic.
3 Factors of production are also mobile, thus adding to the elastic nature of the supply curve.
4 There are no transport costs, i.e. no local monopolies and no differences in price due to distance from the factories.
5 There is no ignorance in the market as to prices, so that all buyers buy only at the market price.
6 Each firm's product is similar to the products of its competitors, so that there is no need for any firm to advertise the uniqueness of its products.

Now we come to the crux of the theory. If each firm accepts the market price and cannot affect it by its own actions then each firm must be able to sell as much of its output as it wishes at the constant market price. In economists' language, the demand curve for each firm is infinitely elastic, being flat and parallel with the horizontal scale, while marginal revenue always equals price.

But this doesn't mean that each firm can sell at a profit as many goods as it can produce, because the theory has no special assumptions about the cost structures of firms. As we saw at the end of the previous chapter, each firm will expand output until marginal cost equals marginal revenue. Now, marginal revenue is fixed and equal to price, so marginal cost becomes crucial as the sole determinant of each firm's level of output.

Notice, too, that the theory does not say that all firms in the industry are of the *same* size – only that all are so small that none can influence the price. As we saw in the previous chapter, marginal costs will eventually rise so the key to profitability is cost. Assuming that the output is of sufficiently high quality to be sold, costs will determine profits.

Where do economies of scale fit into the theory of perfect competition? The answer is they don't! Under perfect competition the firms are very small, so that economies of scale have only a minimal effect on costs and hence on permitting the expansion of firms. Expansion soon becomes unprofitable because marginal costs rise rapidly to exceed price (marginal revenue).

Perfect competition – in practice

If you bear in mind the importance of costs in determining profitability under perfect competition, together with the virtual absence of economies of scale, you will be able to see the relevance of the concept in helping us to understand practical examples. To some extent only, farming is a fair example of perfect competition, because most farms are so small that their output cannot have any effect on price. Dairy farmers are a classic example: under the EC's former dairy price regulations they could sell all the milk they could at a fixed price, determined every year by the EC.

The UK Ministry of Agriculture used to give advice to dairy farmers as to how to increase output and reduce costs. However, the EC is now imposing quotas or limits on milk production, and countries and their farmers producing more than their quota have to pay a fine, called a *levy*.

Suddenly, that wonderful elastic demand curve for each farmer has begun to slope downwards very dangerously!

Also, when we look at the other assumptions we see that in many ways farming is not really a good example of perfect competition. It is not easy to become a farmer – lengthy training is necessary and farms are still very expensive to buy. Movement in the industry is one way – outward, as farm workers leave and more land is used for other uses such as roads and housing. So factor mobility is limited. Also land is not very mobile – you can't grow cereals on hill farms.

Let us now turn to a market where banks play an important role – the foreign exchange market in the world's leading currencies, such as the US dollar, the Deutschemark and the Japanese yen. Massive as some of the world's largest commercial banks are, it is still difficult to imagine that any one of them could alter the exchange rate by its own purchases and sales of a particular currency. Yet, the market is not perfect in the economist's sense because central banks such as the Bank of England – which act to protect their economies and their currencies – frequently intervene in the market for the very purpose of altering the rate. This 'foreign exchange management' obviously precludes the existence of perfect competition.

To take a second banking example, the London discount market is not a perfect market because the Bank of England acts as lender of last resort, usually to influence interest rates, as we shall see in Chapter 13.

■ MARKET SHARE

Under perfect competition, producers are not really interested in finding out their share of the market; it is very small and an irrelevant fact. Much more important is the need to reduce cost.

However, once we leave perfect competition and move to markets where the suppliers can influence the price of their product (and their competitors' prices) by their own actions, then market shares become increasingly important. Competition among the few can involve intense struggles to capture a larger percentage of total market sales. Yet, when we reach the other end of the spectrum from perfect competition – monopoly – we find that market share is again of little interest, because the monopolist has 100 per cent of the market.

Outside the limiting case of perfect competition, suppliers are faced with downward-sloping average revenue (demand) curves and somewhat steeper marginal revenue curves. Not only must they watch their costs but also make decisions about prices.

Let us return to market share, because we need to do a few percentages. At the time of Big Bang in October 1986, when banks were able to own stockbrokers and jobbers, there were 28 *market makers* (combined brokers and jobbers) in the gilt-edged market. On average, the market share of each would be $1/28 \times 100 = 3.6$ per cent. However, some were much bigger and better established than others and were probably aiming at a market share of 10 per cent. This would depress the average of the market share available to the others (about 25), so that they could expect to have perhaps no more than 3 per cent of the market. Thus, some firms left the market in the late 1980s because their small market shares made it impossible to achieve the number of deals necessary to obtain the economies of scale possible from their expensive new computers. In other words, they failed to cover their overheads and ceased trading.

When we look at retail (high street) banking, petrol stations, breakfast cereals and volume car production, we are dealing not with 25 or 30 suppliers but with perhaps six or seven. Consequently market shares are that much larger, with perhaps an average in the region of 15–17 per cent.

Under the Fair Trading Act 1973, the critical market share is 25 per cent controlled by a single firm or by a proposed merger of two firms. Such firms and merger proposals can be investigated by the Monopolies and Mergers Commission, as was Lloyds Bank's bid for Midland.

Concentration ratios

Economists have a way of measuring the degree of *concentration* in an industry, by ascertaining the combined market shares of the leading firms in that industry. The ratios can be calculated for the three leading firms, the top five, or for any number. The 'five-firm concentration ratio' for the gilt-edged market makers might be (a pure guess) 35 per cent, but for retail banking it could be 70 per cent, i.e. the total market shares of the 'Big Four' clearers and Royal Bank of Scotland. For an industry like cement making the 'two-firm concentration ratio' could approach 80 per cent.

Market strategies

As firms grow they become increasingly concerned about their market share. Some firms will make a conscious decision to maintain their market share or even to increase it wherever possible. The latter strategy is vital when the total market is not growing and the firm seeks to increase output and thus profit. Other firms may strive to become a market leader, e.g. in design, technology or in price setting. They wish to be the firm to which their competitors look for guidance. Many would say that Barclays Bank strove for many years to be the market leader: first with a credit card, first with students' gift schemes, a leader with cash dispensers in the late 1960s and, in the 1970s, frequently the first to change its base rate, the price of its main product – loans.

This need to protect market share and, therefore, to continue to enjoy economies of scale was the reason Lloyds Bank became, in January 1989, the first of the 'Big Four' to launch a current account that paid interest on all credit balances, no matter how small. Its market share had been diminished by the interest-bearing current accounts introduced in 1987 and 1988 by two major building societies.

You may say that this suggests that firms do not pursue profits all the time. To a certain extent this is true, because firms must always consider future as well as current profits. For instance, if a manufacturing firm does not invest in research now for future products, it may find its market share falling and so face a reduction in future profits. Extra profits today, achieved by cutting back on research, may cause profits to fall in, say, five years' time. It therefore has to decide which is more worthwhile – £1m of profits today or more than £1m in five years' time.

■ OLIGOPOLY

Oligopoly is a term derived from the same Greek word as *oligarchy*. It refers to competition among the few, in industries where there are perhaps five or six major suppliers. Retail petrol distribution is a classic example, with seven major companies – Shell, BP, Exxon (Esso), Mobil, Texaco, Socal (Chevron in the UK) and Gulf. There are also minor companies, such as Bulldog, ICI which is found only in north-east England, and Q8, to name but a few.

Oligopoly is remembered by students chiefly for its *kinked demand curve*, as will be seen in the diagrams in economics textbooks. In other words, no oligopolist can raise prices independently because this would drive away all the customers, so oligopoly has a relatively flat demand (average revenue) curve for price *increases*. Worse, however, is the effect of a price *fall*, because this would attract so many customers from the rivals that their market shares would fall. To protect their market shares they would virtually simultaneously reduce their prices to the same extent as our oligopolist did, so that the final result is not much different from before the fall was precipitated. The oligopolists are thus faced with a steep demand curve for price *decreases*. The kink in the demand curve occurs at the prevailing price, where it changes from a gentle to a steep slope.

Our oligopolist still increases output to a point where marginal revenue equals marginal cost. The unique feature is that the cost structure is such that economies of scale result in marginal cost equalling marginal revenue at such a high level of output that it comprises perhaps 15 per cent of the total market.

Oligopoly – in practice

The peculiar shape of the demand curve entails oligopolists being 'locked in' to the current price. They have to move in concert with their rivals if their market shares are to remain intact and their cost structures protected – we must remember that the industry's economies of scale are such that the oligopolists need to operate at about 15 per cent of total industry production for marginal cost to equal marginal revenue.

So, how do oligopolists compete? The answer is in many ways except price. Examples are:

(a) location: petrol filling stations and high street banks cluster along the main road;

(b) heavy expenditure on advertising, designed to increase brand loyalties among customers;

(c) emphasising quality or uniqueness: NatWest advertises itself as 'the Action Bank', the Midland, as 'the Listening Bank', while Lloyds claims to be 'the Thoroughbred Bank';

(d) gift promotions: many of us have collections of mugs and wine glasses from our usual petrol station. Gifts are also now featuring in banks' marketing tactics.

As well as petrol and oil, and retail (High Street) banking, brewing is now another oligopolistic industry and has been the subject of several Monopolies and Mergers Commission reports. Breakfast cereals are another.

ACTIVITY 5.1 •

When in the country or the side streets of a town, look out for petrol stations selling little-known brands, e.g. Bulldog or Anglo petrol. Is their petrol cheaper or dearer than that of the majors? Why are such stations rarely found on main roads?

■ MONOPOLY

The monopolist enjoys, if that is the right word, being the sole producer of a commodity or a service. British Telecom used to be a monopoly supplier of telephone and telex services, with the exception of Hull. Now it has competition on inland and international lines from Mercury plc. The Post Office used to have a monopoly of all mail: now it faces competition from courier companies on international services and in large towns.

Monopolists have to make a crucial decision on pricing and output policy. They can control one but not the other. Which is it to be? If they force up the price they may frighten away too many customers so that they cannot take full advantage of the usually large economies of scale. If they aim to sell all they can produce, the price may be too low.

Monopolists follow the same great rule that other producers do and equate marginal cost and marginal revenue. However, they are unique in that marginal cost and revenue are inter-dependent. If they change output they must change price in order to be able to sell the output. You must remember that they cannot force everybody to buy their product. Nothing in the theory says that monopolies enjoy a completely inelastic demand. Their demand is certainly inelastic but most consumers will be deterred from buying the same quantity of their product if they raise their price.

Nevertheless, monopolists do try to group their customers to see if the demand curve (and hence marginal revenues) differ. For instance, public utilities such as gas, electricity, water and telecommunications charge differently if the consumer is running a business. The rental of a telephone line costs more for a commercial user than for a private person. A better example of this *price discrimination* comes, surprisingly, from prices changing according to where the customer sits – in theatres, cinemas, concert halls, trains, ships and aircraft. Another example is at a Spanish bull ring, where spectators pay more for seats in the shade than seats in the sun – yet the cost of building and servicing the seats is the same. A third example, partly of discrimination but also of product development, is at the soccer ground, where you can stand on the terraces to watch the same match seen by the business people wining and dining in their executive suites. Obviously, it costs more to provide an executive suite than it does to provide standing room on the terraces, but the marginal revenues are very different.

One danger monopolists have to watch for is the possibility that by maximising short-term profit they will cause another firm to enter the market and try to share some of the profit. If this is likely, they will not raise prices to the point where MC = MR and profits are maximised but will limit them below that level. The *limit pricing* will reduce profits now but should ensure that they continue at that level for some time to come. It is another example of the need to take a longer view than maximising today's profits, similar to the need for research expenditure which we saw earlier.

Monopoly – in practice

As you probably realise, pure or 100 per cent monopoly is as rare as perfect competition, but there is always the possibility that suppliers will come together to fix prices or output. The economist's term for such an agreement is *cartel*, derived from the German 'das Kartell' because of the development of the practice by German chemical companies. The American word is *trust*.

Perhaps the most notorious recent cartel is the Organisation of the Petroleum Exporting Countries (OPEC), which raised the price of crude oil dramatically in 1973 and again in 1979/80. Since then, however, other producers such as Mexico and the UK have undercut OPEC while Russian exports of natural gas have begun to provide further competition for OPEC crude in Western Europe. Consequently, OPEC has taken the defensive and begun to limit output rather than control price. Remember, as a monopolist it can't do both. By fixing output, which it can monitor more easily than prices, the cartel hopes to discourage price-cutting by its members.

Cartels used to be found in banking and finance. Until 1971, the London clearing banks had an interest rate structure related to the bank rate announced weekly by the Bank of England. Whenever the bank rate changed, the clearing banks' interest rate structures moved together, for both advances and deposits. As part of the wide-ranging changes known as Competition and Credit Control, this practice ceased and each bank has since announced its own interest rate structures, usually linked to its base rate, upon which rates for many of its loans and advances are calculated.

Until 1983 building societies followed a similar practice, adopting the Building Societies Association's recommended rates for deposits/shares and home loans.

Cartels were not known as such in Adam Smith's time but he was fully aware that business people seldom meet together without conspiring to raise prices. Indeed, the medieval guilds of tradesmen or merchants were, in effect, cartels. Certainly, meetings do provide the opportunity for tacit (hidden) rather than open collusion. Tacit collusion often takes the form of price leadership. Usually this is *dominant-firm* leadership, as with Barclays Bank in the 1970s, when it competed with National Westminster to be the first to announce a change in base rate. Other banks frequently became passive and merely followed Barclays to protect their market shares.

Sometimes, however, the price leadership comes from a smaller aggressive firm. Thus, Williams and Glyn's, before it merged with the Royal Bank of Scotland, led the way in price-cutting as interest rates rose in the 1970s. It also seems that some of the independent petrol companies (such as Jet) led the majors in trying to curtail price increases when crude oil prices rose in line with OPEC policy, so that pump prices were not as high as the majors would have wished. Such price leadership is termed *barometric*.

Monopoly – government intervention

In the face of the potential power of monopolists to restrict output and so raise prices, it is not surprising that governments in many countries regulate monopolies. In the USA the policy began almost a century ago and was known as *trust-busting*. The EC, too, has its regulations, under a number of articles of the Treaty of Rome.

The UK has two important pieces of legislation: the Monopolies and Mergers Act 1965 and the Fair Trading Act 1973. The latter created the post of Director-General of Fair Trading, whose office can refer monopolies and proposed mergers to the Monopolies and Mergers Commission for close examination. As we have seen, the guideline as to a monopoly situation is if 25 per cent of the market is controlled by a single seller or buyer. The guideline could apply in cases such as the pay of civil servants, where there is only one purchaser of the labour in question but, not surprisingly, the Commission's work does not extend to the labour market. Prior to 1973 the critical level of market share was 33 per cent.

Once an industry or proposed merger has been referred to it by the Director-General of Fair Trading, the Monopolies and Mergers Commission will prepare a report. The Secretary of State for Trade and Industry has the final say as to whether a merger should be permitted or whether a monopoly situation should continue.

There are other controls. Under the Companies Acts, any company which owns more than 3 per cent of another company's ordinary share capital must declare its interest. Moreover, the Take-Over Code of the Stock Exchange requires a company with more than 29.9 per cent of another's ordinary share capital to make an offer to buy the remaining shares. This offer could result in the Director-General of Fair Trading referring the matter to the Commission.

In banking and finance the Bank of England exercises a watching brief.

ACTIVITY 5.2

Compile a small collection of press cuttings (six should suffice) about a topical merger or take-over (sometimes called an acquisition).

Listen to or watch some of the radio and TV programmes selected in Activity 2.3, to obtain information about current mergers and acquisitions (M and A, as they are known).

ACTIVITY 5.3

Pick up the list of price falls you compiled for Activity 2.1. Classify the reductions into possible causes, such as:

(a) *time* – prices of cut flowers falling after Mothers' Day or Easter;
(b) *cost of suppliers* – petrol prices may fall when the price of crude oil falls;
(c) *to increase sales and market share;*
(d) *reaction against a competitor's price cut;*
(e) *orders from an official regulator* – occasionally found in gas, water, telephones and electricity.

■ SUMMARY

1 In perfect competition there may be thousands of firms, none so large that it can by its own actions influence the price of its product.

2 Every firm is a price taker under perfect competition: it takes the market price as given and gets on with cutting its costs.

3 Marginal cost then becomes crucial in determining the level of output and the size of the firm's profits.

4 Perfect competition is rare in practice; agriculture is not a good example because there is so much government and EC intervention.

5 In the rest of industry, i.e. where firms can affect their price if they change their output, market share is important.

6 If the total market is fixed – and in the very short run it probably is – output and sales can be increased only by taking business away from competitors. This is another word for 'greater market share'.

7 Where there are considerable internal economies of scale, it is crucial for firms to maintain their output in order to continue to enjoy these economies. Hence, maintenance of market share means that these economies can be enjoyed.

8 The critical level of a market share is 25 per cent for one firm. If it exceeds 25 per cent, then the Monopolies and Mergers Commission can investigate the position.

9 Firms can choose between various strategies once they are large enough to affect their price. They can:

(a) seek maximum profit;
(b) seek a larger market share;
(c) try to be the market leader;
(d) try to lead in research and hence be assured of future profits.

10 Oligopoly exists where there are five or six main suppliers. Each is so large that if it alone changes its price then either it loses all its sales or its sales are virtually unchanged. A price rise may not be followed by its rivals, but a cut will be followed immediately, in order that each preserves its market share.

11 Oligopolists compete not by price but by non-price methods – branding, free gifts, etc.

12 UK retail banking is a leading example of oligopoly.

13 Monopoly exists where there is a single supplier.

14 A monopolist must decide whether to stabilise price or output – it cannot control both at the same time.

15 Monopolists can practise price discrimination between their customers who have differing demand curves for their products. They can also limit their profits now so as not to attract competitors into the industry who might diminish their share of future profits.

16 Sometimes a monopoly is created by a group of producers, often known as a cartel.

17 In the UK monopolies are controlled by two Acts of Parliament: the Monopolies and Mergers Act 1965 and the Fair Trading Act 1973.

18 In banking, the Bank of England must give its approval for bank mergers, as we shall see in the next chapter.

19 Finally, the principle that output rises to where marginal cost equals marginal revenue holds good for all firms – whatever their size – seeking to maximise their profits.

■ SELF-ASSESSMENT QUESTIONS

Some of the questions will enable the class to work together as a group and show you how groups do or do not function successfully. It may show natural leaders arising: if not, then the lecturer should nominate tasks or the group elect a leader. You may be involved in supervisory skills in economics!

N.B. In seeking answers to these questions, many of which can be tackled jointly by a class working together, you should never use information which may be available to you from your bank work. The latter is strictly confidential.

1 List the various estate agencies in the area where you live. From the numbers of boards outside local houses and flats, estimate the market share of each agency.

2 Does one agency tend to be 'market leader', e.g. first to open or close on Sundays?

3 During your studies, monitor these agencies for: (a) amalgamations; (b) purchases or sales by banks, building societies or insurance companies; (c) new entrants; (d) closures.

4 Which firm or industry is the largest employer in the area where you live? How large is the largest factory in your area? How much specialisation is possible, e.g. does it have its own motor transport department, staff canteen or sports and social club?

5 How large is the largest local branch of a retail bank? Does it have more than 50 employees?

6 What are the major fixed costs faced by:

(a) banks?
(b) building societies?
(c) estate agencies?

7 List as many 'one-person businesses' as you can. Why are so many builders, farmers, shopkeepers and restaurateurs one-person businesses? Are there many one-person businesses actually manufacturing goods? If not, why not?

8 Repeat Questions 1 and 2 for (a) local petrol filling stations; (b) supermarkets; (c) retail banks.

9 How many local filling stations are also becoming 'convenience stores'? What other goods do they sell?

10 Assess the amount of specialised work available in a seven-person branch of a bank and contrast it with the specialisation possible in a branch with a staff of 70.

11 'Economies of scale mean that perfect competition is impossible.' Explain.

12 If a clearing bank were to bid for a building society, do you think that the proposed bid should be investigated by the Monopolies and Mergers Commission?

13 If a foreign bank were to bid for a UK clearing bank or a building society, should the proposed bid be permitted by the government?

14 Do you think that the continued development of small personal computers and the rise of small firms, e.g. very small real-ale breweries, could indicate that the age of the large firm might be ended next century?

15 What are the economies of scale in a retail banking network of 1500 branches?

16 What is meant by (a) limit pricing; (b) dominant-firm leadership; (c) barometric-price leadership; (d) price discrimination; (e) concentration ratios?

17 What is the critical market share under the Fair Trading Act 1973 – 15, 25, 33, or 40 per cent?

18 Show how price discrimination occurs in seat prices in aircraft.

19 Give recent examples when banks have changed policies rapidly because of the need to maintain internal economies of scale.

20 Are there still cartels in banking and in building societies?

6 Prices and output – the nation

OBJECTIVES

When you have studied this chapter, you should be able to:
1 Appreciate the importance of the problem of inflation;
2 Explain what is meant by gross domestic product (GDP);
3 Describe some index numbers;
4 Know the various phases of the business cycle;
5 Appreciate the importance of the problem of unemployment;
6 Explain why inflation and unemployment often cannot be reduced together;
7 Describe some of the ways in which governments can influence their countries' economies.

■ INTRODUCTION

So far in this book, we have studied the prices of particular goods and services. Now we are going to examine the general level of all prices in the economy. If prices are rising steadily, a country is said to have *inflation*. If prices are falling, *deflation* occurs.

Your own experience will probably tell you that the trend of the prices of most goods and services is upwards. In fact, it has been so continually throughout history, with some exceptions; prices have risen every year since 1935, so that most people cannot remember the falling prices of the 1920s and early 1930s. Sometimes prices rise rapidly, as in 1975 and 1980; at the end of 1988 they were rising at about 6–7 per cent a year. Two years later, inflation had reached over 10 per cent per year, falling to 4.3 per cent in May 1992.

Although prices have been rising for over 50 years, there is a brighter side to the picture. Output, including that of services as well as goods, has also been rising for most of this time, and the actual falls in output seen widely in the inter-war period are now part of history. In general, output is on a rising trend although certain industries such as shipbuilding are still declining.

First, however, we must look briefly at a statistical concept – *index numbers*. These are a way of measuring, over a period of time, and without using pounds and pence, changes in such items as average prices and total output.

■ THE GENERAL LEVEL OF PRICES

There are two aspects to the general level of prices in a country, i.e. how the inhabitants are affected and how foreigners are affected. After all, they buy from and sell to us, so we must consider them – which we do in Chapter 12. However, for this chapter we consider what is termed the *internal purchasing power of money*.

Arithmetically, if prices in general rise then money's purchasing power falls. If prices double, we say that the purchasing power of money has halved: if £1 buys now what 50p bought ten years ago then £1 now is worth what 50p was then.

You may (or rather must) ask: How do we know exactly how much prices have risen? The answer is that it is difficult but we will go into some detail about this in the next section. Here we must state that we need a very wide-ranging measure, to cover all the various transactions involved in producing and selling goods and services. But to get a wide measure takes time and we need to measure money's purchasing power fairly frequently. Moreover, we do not want to be plagued by revisions of the figures, as frequently occurs with many economic statistics. So we have come to rely mainly on one particular set of statistics, called the General Index of Retail Prices (RPI), which is published monthly, on the second or third Friday of the month. These prices are retail; there are separate statistics for producers' input prices and their output prices, as well as estimates for the whole economy (the latter is called the *GDP deflator*).

Prices of financial and physical assets – currencies, stocks and shares and houses – are excluded from these calculations of inflation.

How the price level is measured (the RPI)

Rather like somebody shopping, the economist looks at a long list of goods and services bought by most people. Each item is recorded and compared with its price at the *base date*, January 1987.

Not all items are of equal importance to people in their spending habits. Accordingly, the government asks a group of households, spread around the country and covering most income levels except the very rich and the very poor, to record their expenditure over a period. From these records, the statisticians are able to calculate the importance (the *weighting* as it is called) of each item. The weights are then calculated to add to 1000.

The prices are collected – on a Tuesday to avoid price fluctuations at the beginning or end of a week – by a team of clerks who visit the shops and hairdressing salons, etc. They are then compared with those of January 1987 and expressed as a ratio of that date's price. Suppose that the item is a 275 ml can of light ale, costing 40p now and 31p in January 1987. The price has risen by 40/31 = 1.29.

Now we need to know the weighting of this item – suppose it is 7 (out of 1000). This figure means that most adults spend on light ale 0.7 per cent of their total spending on items included in the RPI. We then multiply the 1.29 by 7 to get 9.03, which is added to all the other price increases multiplied by their weightings. For the sake of simplicity we will take a chicken and call everything else 'other'. Table 6.1 shows how the RPI is calculated.

The index for the month in question is published after rounding to one decimal place. The last column, 1229.98, is divided by ten (122.998), and then

Table 6.1 Calculation of the RPI

Item	Price (£) January 87 (1)	(2)	Change Now (3)	Weighting (4)	Calculation (3) x (4)
Light ale	0.31	0.40	1.29	7	9.03
Chicken	1.47	1.75	1.19	11	13.09
Other	103.00	127.00	1.23	982	1207.86
RPI				1000	1229.98

rounded to 123.0. Compared to 100.0 in January 1987 prices have risen by 23 per cent, so beer drinkers are unlucky (29 per cent rise)! Perhaps the government has raised the duty (tax) on beer. The final stage in the process is to calculate the annual change by dividing this month's RPI by the figure for 12 months ago and expressing the answer as a percentage. Let us assume that the RPI was 115.3 12 months ago. Then:

$$\frac{123.0}{115.3} = 1.067$$

This is an increase of 6.7 per cent for the year – we move the decimal point two places to the right.

As we have mentioned, the index is never revised because the figures have been used in sensitive wage negotiations for many years and now they are used in capital gains tax calculations and in what is called *current cost accounting*[1]. The index's old name was *cost of living index*, giving us an idea of what it tried to measure – how much it cost a family to live.

It is also used to calculate the value of index-linked National Savings Certificates (NSCs) and social security benefits. The latter are *index-linked* because they are raised each April in line with the annual rise in the index to the preceding September. These examples of how the government uses it officially do not include all the negotiations in which it is used to support or reject various proposals, e.g. a wage claim or offer, or a proposal to raise telephone charges. Many household insurance policies link the value of the house's contents to the index. The object of index-linking is to maintain the purchasing power of these financial assets and income streams.

How governments can directly influence the RPI

To return to our can of beer – or rather the tax on it: governments can influence the index by changing taxes and subsidies on goods and services; a notorious example occurred in 1974 when the standard rate of VAT was lowered by the Labour government from 10 per cent to 8 per cent just before the second general election of that year. In 1979, just after winning the election that year, the Conservatives raised VAT from 8 per cent to 15 per cent. In April 1991 it was raised to 17.5 per cent, to compensate for a reduction in the community charge.

[1] See Karl Harper, *Introduction to Accounting*, Pitman, 1990, p. 218.

Sometimes the index is used as part of the calculations to measure real wages ('real' means ignoring changes in the value of money). If wages have risen by 9 per cent in the past year but prices generally have risen by only 5.2 per cent, then real wages (i.e. their purchasing power) have increased by 3.6 per cent (109.0/105.2 x 100 = 103.6).

Gross wages suffer a number of deductions – as a rule, income tax and national insurance contributions are the largest – before they are paid to the employee. Hence, net pay may not change at the same rate as gross pay.

The government can alter the purchasing power of wages in several ways:

(a) by taxes on goods – e.g. VAT and petrol, tobacco and alcohol duties, as we saw in Chapter 3;
(b) by subsidies – rare in industrialised countries but common in countries, such as Egypt, which subsidise petrol and food;
(c) by rationing and price controls – common in wartime;
(d) by changes in income tax, so that take-home pay changes;
(e) by changes in national insurance contributions, which bear quite heavily on those earning up to about £20,000 a year, and affect take-home pay.

The UK government has thus devised a further index to show how price rises have been offset or aggravated by changes in income tax and national insurance contributions (changes in taxes on goods and services will, of course, be reflected in the RPI). Not surprisingly, the new index is called the Tax and Price Index (TPI). It began very shortly after the Conservative Party came to power in 1979, but, as the rate of inflation soon fell faster than the taxes included, it has not received much attention.

Types of inflation – speed

For some reason, descriptions of rates of inflation are related to horses. When in low single figures, e.g. 3–5 per cent a year, it is described as *creeping*. When the inflation rate rises to (say) 25 or 40 per cent a year the adjective becomes *trotting*; when 100 per cent a year or more, inflation is known as *galloping*.

Some countries, such as West Germany and Switzerland, have for years had relatively low inflation rates. Others, such as Israel and many Latin American countries, have had galloping inflation for several years, although after 1985 Israel reduced its inflation rate to around 15 per cent.

Occasionally, there are outbreaks of *hyper-inflation*, as in Germany in 1922–3 (not the 1930s as many students state) and briefly after the Second World War. In hyper-inflation, prices change *daily*, so that wages are paid daily: it leaves bitter memories as people's savings in cash and bank accounts lose all their value. Understandably, public opinion in Germany favours very low inflation.

Types of inflation – causes

There are two main causes: one acting through supply schedules and called *cost-push* inflation, the other through demand schedules and called *demand-pull*. Since demand can pull prices up and since many prices form part of suppliers' costs, e.g. telephone calls, petrol and diesel, steel, it is very difficult to establish the prime cause. Certainly, if demand is weak (strictly elastic) then a rise in costs may have to be borne partly, if not largely, by the supplier, as we saw in Chapter 3.

Sometimes, governments can add to demand by their expenditure, as we shall see later. An external shock can on occasions cause extra inflationary pressure, as with the oil price rises of 1973 and 1979/80.

Since the early 1970s, the distinction between demand-pull and cost-push theories has become blurred, with demand-pull advocates emphasising the importance of the money supply and exchange rates. Opposed to this monetarist view of inflation are those who argue that inflation can be due to social reasons, such as the actions of trade unions in seeking and achieving excessive wage increases, or to outside influences such as a rise in import prices.

Effects of inflation

If *all* prices, including those in contracts (e.g. rents, pensions, etc.) fixed years ago, were to change simultaneously there would be few problems associated with inflation. But they don't and that is the nub of the matter.

It used to be argued that 'inflation hits the pensioner' but the state retirement pension is now increased annually in line with the RPI, while many private pensions have also been increased. Savings deposited in banks and building societies have not increased in value in line with inflation although some National Savings products have been *index-linked* to the RPI. The most well known of these are the index-linked National Savings Certificates, given the nickname 'Granny Bonds' because they were at first restricted to retirement pensioners.

Interest rates can be affected by inflation, often rising in line with prices but remaining lower than inflation. In the mid-1980s, however, interest rates did not fall as fast as the rate of inflation so they became *higher* than inflation. Economists call the interest rate adjusted for the rate of inflation the *real* rate of interest (they call everything such as output, exchange rates, etc., adjusted for inflation, 'real'!) and when it is positive (interest rates higher than inflation) the effects on the profits of businesses and home owners with substantial borrowing can be devastating. We saw these effects in 1990, when people's spending in some shops stopped more abruptly than the shops' borrowing. Savers, on the other hand, benefit from a positive real rate of interest.

So far, we have ignored the international aspects of inflation but we must mention here that if one country experiences a substantially higher rate of inflation than others, it will find it more difficult to sell its exports, and foreign goods will be cheaper in terms of its own currency. Accordingly, it will eventually have to devalue its currency against those of its major trading partners, unless the exchange rate is already floating, in which case it should move down automatically. In October 1990 the UK pegged sterling to the other EC currencies in the Exchange Rate Mechanism (ERM), so that the UK is most unlikely to be allowed by the other EC countries to use this option in future.

Because they too are in business, banks are affected by rising costs, especially salary and other personnel costs. However, their major cost (interest paid) and their major source of revenue (interest charged) are influenced by the Treasury and the Bank of England, who may be unwilling to allow the markets to push interest rates too high.

ACTIVITY 6.1

Get out the diary you were asked to keep in Chapter 1, and look at the target dates for each chapter.

We're nearing the half-way stage in the book. Are you nearly half way between the date you began studying and the date of your exam? If not, why not?

Write in the inflation rate regularly. The RPI for a month is published on the second or third Friday of the following month. There may be some figures for earlier months as well.

Is inflation below 10 per cent?

Is it below 5 per cent?

Is it rising or falling?

■ GROSS DOMESTIC PRODUCT (GDP)

This is probably the most difficult concept for students to visualise and then understand. After all, we've all seen (or think we have) a gallon of petrol or a ton of coal but you can't see a GDP in every town in the country.

GDP is the nation's *total output of goods and services*. If it is high you'll see many new cars, new motorways, clean pavements, new filling stations, new schools, new hospitals, busy shops, offices and factories. But, if you stumble on the pavement, your bicycle breaks a spoke in a pot-hole and your grandparents are on a two-year waiting list for their hip operations, the economist will say it is all a result of GDP not being as high as in other countries where these misfortunes do not occur.

The word *gross* is used to denote that it is calculated before we allow for replacing our capital assets – our *depreciation charges* as the accountants would say.

The word *domestic* is used because we are considering only that output produced in this country – some output is produced abroad by factors of production owned by UK firms (such as BP, ICI and Barclays Bank) and then the profits are remitted back to the UK. The government can influence only the domestic part of our output and has little influence over (say) ICI in countries such as the USA and Australia. Accordingly, GDP is the statistic the government watches rather than GNP (gross national product) which includes such income from abroad.

The *product* part of GDP *comprises all goods and services produced within the country*. The list is enormous and we use money as the measuring rod – the unit of account, as we shall see in Chapter 10 – rather than gallons, tons, bank accounts opened or lorries, vans and lathes built.

How GDP is measured

The way in which the calculations are made is to use the *circular flow of income* – a firm's sales are often somebody else's costs of production; your salary is part of your employer's costs and goes (rapidly) to buy goods and services from other people. So, we can *either*:

(a) add up all the wages, salaries and other *incomes* (rents, profits, etc.) of the factors of production, which we saw briefly in Chapter 1 to be labour, land, capital and enterprise, *or*
(b) add up all the *expenditure* on final sales (excluding sales to wholesalers and processors) *or*
(c) we can add up all the *net output* of every industry and service.

Income method

Here we add:

(a) income from employment (wages and salaries before tax);
(b) income from self-employment (from sole traders and partnerships);
(c) gross profits of companies and public corporations;
(d) rent from the ownership of land.

Let's take a short example of a firm importing boomerangs from Australia, varnishing them and selling them in Earls Court, a part of London where many Australians live. The 'product', for GDP, is the varnishing of the boomerang – because that's all they have done to it. We do not count the import of the weapons, only the *wages* of the labour which has gone into varnishing them and the *profit* earned by the owner of the company. We'll return to this example again.

One point must be stressed. We do not include transfer payments such as pensions, child benefit and other social security benefits. This is because they are not income for factors of production in return for their output but are given to people as of right. Similarly, interest on the national debt and dividends from shares are excluded.

We can now recap, allocating the incomes to the appropriate factor of production.

Income	Factor
Wages & salaries	
Self-employed	Labour
Rent	Land
Profits	Capital/Enterprise

Table 6.2 is a simplified presentation of the official statistics for this way of measuring GDP. The income of self-employed people is included with rent.

Profits and trading surpluses are gross, in economists' language, so that we need to deduct that part of profits which does not represent output – the increase in the value of the stocks held (due to rising prices). This use of the term 'gross profit' is different from that used in accountancy, as those readers studying *Introduction to Accounting* may have noticed.

Table 6.2 UK Gross domestic product 1991 (Income method)

	£bn	%
Income received from employers	331	66.9
Gross company trading profits	61	12.3
Gross trading surplus of nationalised industries	3	0.7
Rent, income from self-employment	103	20.8
	498	100.7
Less stock appreciation	(3)	(0.7)
Gross domestic product	495	100.0

If you ask: 'Why, when we have 'netted' profits to some extent, do we use the term *gross* domestic product?' then you have made a good point. GDP is 'gross' because it excludes depreciation – an allowance for using up our capital assets. When we make this deduction we have a figure for net domestic product, but this term is not used as frequently as gross domestic product and so students for the Banking Certificate need to go no further into it.

Expenditure method

Here we add:

(a) *consumers' expenditure* (consumption): what we individuals eat and drink and enjoy, e.g. books, holidays, examination fees(!);

(b) *government consumption*: e.g. expenditure on uniforms for the army, lighting for schools and for government offices;

(c) investment expenditure (*gross domestic fixed capital formation*) by companies (new factories for example), by individuals (new houses for example) and government (new schools and motorways). Notice that it is *new* goods, not second-hand ones, which are counted.

(d) *exports of goods and services less imports*: after all, we produce the exports for foreigners to buy and it is our production that we are measuring, so we must include exports. But total expenditure in categories (a), (b) and (c) includes imports (which we did not produce), so we exclude them here. The figures include services as well as goods;

(e) *physical increase in stocks and work in progress*: We've produced the goods, so we ought to include them even though they are in a warehouse waiting to be sold.

To return to our boomerang importers: in this case we take the value of their sales (under (a) consumers' expenditure) and subtract the cost of the imported unvarnished boomerangs (under (d) net exports).

(f) *Adjustment for taxes and subsidies*: we also have to remember that the prices of many goods and services include any taxes levied on them, such as value added tax (VAT) and tariffs. Some prices, such as bus or rail fares, may include an element of subsidy. We must therefore make an adjustment, because the price does not fully represent the money value of the item as a result of the tax or subsidy included in it. Taxes and subsidies are transfer payments, which are excluded because they do not represent output.

Figures for the UK in 1991 were as shown in Table 6.3.

Table 6.3 UK gross domestic product 1991 (expenditure method)

	£bn	%
Consumers' expenditure	368	74.3
Central government consumption expenditure	74	15.0
Local authorities' consumption expenditure	47	9.5
Gross domestic fixed capital formation	95	19.2
Physical increase in stocks (in 1991 it was a fall)	(4)	(0.8)
	580	117.2
Exports of goods and services	136	
Imports of goods and services	141	
Net imports	(5)	(1.0)
GDP at market prices	575	116.2
Less taxes (plus subsidies) on goods and services	(80)	(16.2)
	495	100.0

(handwritten annotations: 405 above 368; 617 below 580; 612 beside 575; 583 beside 495)

Output method

Here we add the net output of each industry or service – such as agriculture, mining, manufacturing, construction, banking and insurance, etc., as well as that of the government (defence, health, education, and so on). Where other industries are selling to each other, e.g. sales of coal to generate electricity, these sales and purchases need to be netted out.

Statistics for this method are usually without index numbers, so it is not possible to reconcile them with the other two methods expressing them as index numbers. The index numbers are all in real terms, i.e. excluding the effects of inflation. Table 6.4 shows data since 1989, before the recession began.

Table 6.4   UK gross domestic product 1985 = 100 (output method)

	1989	1990	1991	1985 weights
Agriculture	101.2	105.7	108.2	19
Construction	130.4	131.8	120.2	59
Other production	109.9	109.3	106.1	344
Services	117.4	119.7	117.8	578
Total GDP	115.2	116.3	113.8	1000

How the elements of GDP interact

We have seen how your expenditure will be part of someone else's salary and their employer's profits (or loss) but what happens if you don't spend all your income? The ordinary answer is: don't worry, others will be spending more than their income. The crux comes when people *in general* start to underspend: somebody has to overspend to keep the circular flow moving freely.

Overspending is always occurring, particularly by large companies investing in expensive new factories and machinery. To achieve a steady circular flow of spending/income in the system they need people who do not spend and *financial intermediaries*, such as banks, pension funds and insurance companies, to channel the funds from the underspenders to the overspenders. We shall look at these in the next chapter

Now, we ought to consider two links between categories on the expenditure side of GDP.

The accelerator

This is the first link. Imagine a fleet of ten ships, each with a life of ten years, with one ship being replaced every year. If, say, demand for the fleet's services rises by 10 per cent one year, business will increase and the fleet, including the ship due to be replaced that year, will not be sufficient to provide the service now required. Another ship will need to be built, so for that particular year two ships will be ordered. Thus a 10 per cent rise in the demand for the use of that fleet's ships has resulted in a 100 per cent rise in the owner's demand for new ships – from one to two.

Moreover, when trade declines again, there will be a complete lack of demand for new ships so that a 10 per cent fall in demand for shipping services could lead to a 100 per cent fall in new construction, with the ship being scrapped that year not needing to be replaced, because the original ten ships are able to provide the reduced service. Such a contraction in demand is very serious, because it is likely to lead to workers being made redundant.

This accelerator effect on the demand for capital goods such as ships is one reason for the very sharp booms and slumps in these types of industries.

The multiplier

The second link, the *multiplier*, is the knock-on or ripple effect of expenditure as it goes through the circular flow of income (allowing for savings, of course). Suppose that the government increases the Christmas bonus for pensioners from £10 to £20, and that there are 4m recipients. This means that £80m will be given to them and, because they are elderly and many not very wealthy, most of it will be spent (let us say £75m).

We saw in the previous section that the £80m is a *transfer payment* and not counted in GDP but the £75m of expenditure will count towards the expenditure way of calculating GDP. The shopkeepers will spend the £75m partly on wages for their assistants but are also likely to order new stocks to replace those sold to the pensioners. These new orders mean more GDP.

This second round of expenditure could total between £70m and £75m. And so the surge continues, but becoming smaller each time as some of the income generated by the initial burst of expenditure is saved, spent on imports or returned to the government in payment of taxes.

A better example of the multiplier is the Channel Tunnel. The contractors receive their fees and spend them on wages, new plant and machinery. The unfinished Tunnel will count towards GDP because there is also a category of *changes in stocks* which we saw earlier. Stocks include work-in-progress on large construction contracts such as ships, airliners, etc., and increases in them must be included in GDP. On the other hand, decreases in stocks must be *subtracted* from GDP because the result of the expenditure is not the production of a replacement item but an empty place on a shelf in a warehouse.

If we have large leakages (say 20 per cent) in the form of savings or imports the surge of expenditure may dwindle rapidly – £80m; £64m (£16m saved or spent on imports); £51.2m (£64m – £12.8m); £40.1m; £32.8m and so on. If the *marginal propensity to consume* is high – i.e. most of the extra income is spent – the tapering effect will be minimal, as in the earlier example where only £5m of the first £80m was lost.

How are the banks involved?

This question can be answered in two ways – the banks contribute *directly* to the three measures of GDP and they also contribute *indirectly* to two of the measures.

First, the banks pay salaries to their employees, and they earn profits which are added to all the other *incomes* in that method of calculating GDP. On the *expenditure* side, their purchases of capital goods such as computers and VDUs are very large. Finally, under the *output* measure, all the banks' products and services contribute to GDP.

The *indirect* methods can be grouped into payments and finance. The banks facilitate the payment of all the incomes used in the income measure of GDP – by the provision of cash, the clearing system, BACS etc. They also have a wide range of products to enable people to save rather than spend their income.

On the expenditure side, banks not only offer current accounts, cash dispensers and cheque, debit and credit cards to help consumers buy the nation's output but also a wide range of lending products, from personal loans to home loans (remember – only new homes count towards GDP), to enable purchasers to buy the output on credit. Banks also lend to business customers for the purchase of new plant and machinery and even for such large items of capital formation as the Channel Tunnel. The purchase of new plant and machinery is often financed by leasing companies, many of which are owned by banks.

ACTIVITY 6.2 •

Turn back to Table 6.3, outlining the expenditure elements of GDP. Increase consumers' expenditure by 10 per cent leaving all the other components unchanged. Recalculate GDP and the new percentage shares.

Why is it wrong to assume that all the other components will remain unchanged?

■ THE BUSINESS CYCLE

GDP does not grow or fall each year to the same extent; usually it grows but occasionally it falls, and the important question is: by how much will it grow or fall?

In general, there is a pattern or cycle to the changes, in this order: a slump of low growth or even a fall, then recovery with rising growth rates, then a boom with growth rates at their peak, followed by a recession of falling growth rates and returning to the slump conditions again. This pattern is called the business or trade cycle.

By the summer of 1992, many observers were hopeful that the UK was very likely to leave a recession, after several years of falling growth and rising unemployment. Others were more pessimistic.

Why the cycle occurs

Economists are generally agreed on why the cycle occurs, at least in theory, but they often disagree as to how the situation at any particular time has developed. Briefly, the cycle occurs because there are alternating periods of excessive or inadequate expenditure to generate income and so provide further expenditure ...

Some 70 per cent of total expenditure comprises consumer expenditure by the 45m-odd consumers, excluding the very young, sick and the very old. Surprisingly this expenditure does not change significantly; rather it is that on gross domestic fixed capital formation which can change abruptly and, especially, the levels of stocks in warehouses and of work-in-progress. Governments, too, can be fickle in their expenditure programmes. Exports and imports can vary substantially, particularly of raw materials.

How the cycle can be evened out

What is needed is some form of counter-cyclical activity, so that when growth rates are peaking they can be lowered somewhat and then, later, when output is growing less rapidly, boosted. Because private business people are concerned with profit, whether short or long term, they are unlikely to spend money when they see no profit in it for them. The only alternative source of counter-cyclical activity is the government.

Notice that we use the word 'activity' − not necessarily expenditure. The government can try to create conditions in which businesses find it profitable to continue to trade and even to expand, and increase its own expenditure. Opponents of increasing public expenditure argue frequently that all the extra expenditure may do is simply bid up the prices of factors of production already in employment, so that wages and prices rise and not the nation's total output (GDP). This argument is countered by others that maintain that the need to reduce unemployment and so stimulate growth is paramount. We shall be looking at government in greater detail in this chapter and again later in the book.

■ UNEMPLOYMENT OF FACTORS OF PRODUCTION

In everyday speech, we refer to unemployment as meaning 'unemployed people' but unemployment also means idle machinery and waste land as well as 'dole queues'. However, unwanted machinery can be cut up and urban waste land grassed over, but the unemployment of men and women, young and old, is all too frequently an intractable problem. So, we will concentrate on unemployed people.

Unemployed people

During the 1920s and 1930s the number of unemployed people in the UK never fell below 1m, a level not reached again until the early 1970s. After then, and particularly in the period 1979–82, unemployment soared to around 3m. Moreover, many observers argue that the total would have touched 4m if the statistics had not been altered and if those people on special employment measures, such as the community programme and the restart scheme, had not been excluded. From 1986 unemployment fell steadily, to around 1.6m at Easter 1990. It then began to rise.

Although almost as many people are unemployed now as were out of work at the trough of the recession in the early 1930s, the degree of hardship is less due to the much higher level of government benefits available. This is not to say that there is no poverty; there is, but generally less than there was 60 or more years ago. A further development which has helped to maintain living standards is the extent to which women have been able to become bread-winners, especially by working part-time. Between the two world wars there were not the jobs available in service industries and light manufacturing that there are now. The UK relied much more on heavy industry and coal mining.

Economists classify unemployment into several categories.

1 *Structural* unemployment occurs when an industry goes into long-term decline. Examples are textiles, shipbuilding, steel-making and coalmining. Once upon a time the West Midlands was a 'hive of industry' based on the metal trades and a booming car industry, but in the early 1980s it was almost as badly hit as the North East and North West. Manufacturing industry in the UK shed 2m jobs in the period 1979 to 1987 and this decline began again in 1991, when a further 500,000 employees lost their jobs.

2 *Technological* unemployment occurs when new methods of production cause workers to lose their jobs. Robotic engineering is an example. Another occurred in the City of London in October 1990 when a number of bank messengers had to switch to other jobs in their banks because they were no longer needed to 'walk' bills of exchange and CDs from bank to bank. In that month a new Central Moneymarkets Office was established, with transfers being recorded on a central computer and with most bills being held at the Bank of England, so that the physical movement of paper ceased.

3 *Seasonal* unemployment is particularly important in the building trades, because work is difficult in very wintry weather. It is also important in seaside resorts, for similar reasons. In these instances, the demand for labour falls when

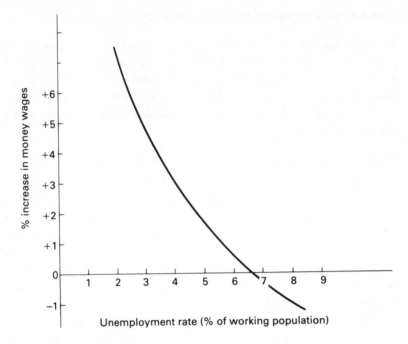

Fig. 6.1 The Phillips curve

the temperature falls.

4 *Frictional* unemployment occurs when people change jobs and spend two or three weeks searching. Unhappily, the period between jobs is now much more likely to be at least two or three months in many areas including even the once booming South East.

5 *Cyclical* unemployment is due to the business cycle but some argue that it is difficult to distinguish from structural unemployment because the downturn in the business cycle will accentuate a structural decline in important industries such as motor car manufacturing.

Unemployment v. inflation

Some economists have argued that governments have a choice: either unemployment and low inflation or less unemployment and higher rates of inflation. In the late 1950s, Professor Phillips published a curve showing the relationship between unemployment and wage inflation (annual increases in wage rates) for the period 1861 to 1957 – almost a century. This Phillips curve was somewhat like a demand curve in shape, except that it crossed the horizontal scale in the bottom right-hand of the diagram (*see* Fig. 6.1).

Notice that the vertical scale becomes negative, and that unemployment is expressed as a percentage of the total working population (at the end of 1989 it was about 6 per cent). However, by 1967, some time after the curve was published, unemployment and inflation began to rise together: this is called *stagflation*, which combines *stag*nation with *inflation*. It was then argued that workers sought increases not just in money wages but in real wages, i.e. after allowing for price rises.

For individual firms, industries and, in a competitive world, economies, it is quite possible for workers to price themselves out of jobs. Fleet Street is a leading example, where high wages and restrictive numbers of workers per machine enshrined in long-standing agreements between unions and management have forced the employers to move the printing of newspapers to new sites.

Unemployment and banking

Fortunately, most bank employees had never known unemployment until 1991. Although there had been some redundancies in banks in the City of London, nearly all those affected were able to join other banks quite rapidly. Relatively strong unions had been able to secure no-redundancy clauses in reviews of staffing levels but not in the comprehensive reductions in branch networks being undertaken in the late 1980s and early 1990s. The big retail banks are now shedding large numbers of jobs, often by voluntary early retirement and resignations, as well as by natural wastage – i.e. not replacing those that leave on their own initiative or on retiring at the normal age. But compulsory redundancies are occurring.

Until very recently, therefore, bank employees were likely to be affected only indirectly by unemployment, as it affected the business of their branches.

Government financial support for redundant workers is now much higher than it was two generations ago. Moreover, many employers, such as British Steel, British Coal, ICI and now banks, have been able to offer very generous terms for workers prepared to accept voluntary severance or early retirement. These large cash sums give good opportunities for banks to sell some of their savings products and for the former employees perhaps to set up as consultants or small businesses. So the number of business accounts could rise in branches located in areas of high unemployment.

ACTIVITY 6.3

Back to the diary again!

Begin to watch now for the unemployment figures, which are published just after the 20th of each month. They relate to a day about a fortnight earlier, i.e. in the same month. Write the total in your diary.

Obtain some graph paper, and plot both the unemployment figures and the inflation figures. You should use two colours – say, red for inflation and black for unemployment. In this way you can have the two scales – one in each colour – on the vertical axis.

Are the two lines moving in the same or opposite directions?

■ THE ROLE OF GOVERNMENT

Governments are important not only because they can tax us, but also because they control, to a greater or lesser extent, our business activities. We saw in Chapter 5 how they regulate monopolies and mergers, while earlier in this chapter we saw how they can try to iron out the business cycle.

Some governments – as in communist countries – have operated what are termed *command economies*. Here production was determined by the state or industry plan, rather than by price and profitability. Queues and rationing were commonplace. The UK economy was a command economy in the two world wars of 1914–18 and 1939–45.

Other governments – as in some SE Asian countries – operate *market economies*, with little employment legislation and great emphasis on profit-making. Yet others, such as the UK and OECD countries, operate *mixed economies*, with a balance between excessive intervention on employment conditions, wages and prices and excessive reliance on the urge to achieve profits regardless of social costs to workers and the environment.

When the UK has operated a command economy, as in the Second World War, the banks have become involved, for example in the operation of *exchange controls* (on the amount of foreign currency we are allowed to purchase). In other command economies banks are often part of the state financial system rather than profit-seeking providers of services to the community.

One of the great concerns of the 1990s will be the problems arising from the transition of the former communist countries in Europe from command economies to mixed economies.

Government policies

In mixed economies, governments avoid rationing, legislation and price/wage controls except as last resorts. They rely on other policies to achieve the goals of economic policy. These goals are fairly universal in OECD countries, comprising:

(a) price stability which is now regarded as vital, so that the other goals can be achieved for a lasting period of time;
(b) as low a level of unemployment as is compatible with (a);
(c) as high a rate of economic growth, also compatible with (a). Economic growth is not just GDP growing at a fast rate but GDP *per person* growing at a fast rate. Allowance must be made for population growth;
(d) a degree of stability in their exchange rates. Most EC countries, including the UK now, peg their exchange rates to those of other EC members, in the Exchange Rate Mechanism (ERM) for the UK, the ERM is the way of achieving price stability and is the framework of monetary policy;
(e) some financial support for the Third World.

To achieve these goals, governments have two main policies, which we shall examine more closely in Chapter 13:

(a) *Monetary policy*, affecting the supply of money and credit, the level of interest rates and exchange rates. However, in October 1990 the UK pegged sterling to the other EC currencies in the Exchange Rate Mechanism, so this option is very unlikely to be used again.
(b) *Fiscal policy*, affecting taxation, government expenditure and government borrowing. The latter can and does affect the money supply, as we shall see in Chapter 10.

Some governments (especially those of France and Japan) have been able to use a third policy, called *indicative planning* or *exhortation*. In such countries the relationship between government and business people is very close and it is easy for political and business leaders to work together with a common national aim. Regrettably, relations between business leaders and government in the UK are not as close, with business leaders often accusing the government, no matter which political party is in power, of being insensitive to their needs, particularly their financial needs.

Finally, there has been growing concern by many governments in the world about the effects of economic growth on the environment. CFCs, acid rain, the greenhouse effect, and the ozone layer are all the subjects of much research. It is likely therefore that, later in the 1990s, governments of OECD countries will include *protection of the environment* as one of their goals of economic policy. In June 1992, at the 'Earth Summit' in Rio, there were calls for:

(a) taxes on environmentally damaging emissions by industry and consumers;
(b) subsidies for environmentally friendly products, such as refrigerators using lower levels of CFCs in the Third World. For example, in the UK unleaded petrol bears a lower rate of tax than leaded petrol;
(c) protection for endangered plants and animals/insects (bio-diversity).

ACTIVITY 6.4*

Walk around your local town, looking for signs of boom or recession. Tabulate the indicators showing the way in which the economy is moving, e.g.:

Indicator	Boom	Recession
Job vacancies at Job Centre	Plentiful	Not many

■ SUMMARY

1 Inflation is rising prices, deflation is falling prices.

2 Price changes are measured by index numbers and the one in general use in the UK is the Index of Retail Prices (RPI).

3 The RPI is never revised and can be used to *index-link* financial assets, e.g. some NSCs – and income streams, e.g. state retirement pensions – thus protecting their purchasing power.

4 Governments can affect prices by changing taxes on goods and services included in the RPI.

5 Inflation can grow faster or slower. When very fast, it is called hyper-inflation and wages may be paid daily, because their purchasing power will fall overnight.

6 Inflation can be caused by too much demand in an economy, or by sharp rises in costs, e.g. oil or wages. It can also be inbuilt in the wage-bargaining and price-setting structure of an economy.

7 Inflation will hurt all those living on fixed incomes or on savings, although index-linking offers some help.

8 Inflation will cause interest rates to rise and make exports quite expensive to overseas buyers.

9 Because money is losing its value rapidly, foreigners will not want to buy a currency suffering from inflation, so the exchange rate will fall.

10 Gross domestic product is the total output of goods and services produced by a country:

(a) it is *gross* – excluding deductions for depreciation;
(b) it is *domestic* – excluding imports but including exports and ignoring output produced overseas by its firms;
(c) it is *product* – goods and services and any physical increase of goods held as stocks in warehouses.

11 GDP is measured in three ways:

(a) income received by factors of production in return for the output they produce;
(b) expenditure on that output, after allowing for changes in unsold stocks;
(c) the extra value (the net output) contributed by each industry.

12 The accelerator shows the link between changes in consumption and changes in capital investment. It can be quite severe.

13 The multiplier shows the link between additional expenditure, perhaps by the government, and the total effect in the economy as that extra spending creates a ripple effect.

14 The business cycle shows how economies go through periods of boom and recession alternately.

15 The cycle can be evened out by the government restraining demand in a boom and stimulating it in a recession.

16 In a recession, unemployment will rise.

17 Unemployment can be grouped into several types: structural, technological, seasonal, frictional and cyclical.

18 There is a complex link between inflation and unemployment, often illustrated by a 'Phillips curve'. It is hard to reduce both at the same time.

19 In the UK and other OECD economies, governments seek to:

(a) contain inflation;
(b) reduce unemployment;
(c) stabilise the growth of GDP;
(d) keep the exchange rate steady;
(e) help the Third World;

and (possibly in a few years' time) protect the environment.

20 To achieve these aims, they use:

(a) monetary policy – money, credit, interest rates and, to a lesser extent, exchange rates; and/or
(b) fiscal policy – taxes, government spending and borrowing.

■ SELF-ASSESSMENT QUESTIONS

1 In which of the three ways of measuring GDP, if any, do the following appear:

(a) your salary as a bank employee;
(b) your day-to-day expenditure;
(c) your grandparents' state retirement pensions?

2 What are the major goals of economic policy pursued by governments of OECD countries?

3 By what policies do they try to achieve these goals?

4 Are some of the goals and the policies inter-dependent, if not contradictory?

5 What is likely to be the effect on GDP of an increase in the number of nannies paid to look after young children and doing work formerly done without payment by wives?

6 Explain, in ordinary language, what are meant by the accelerator and the multiplier.

7 Should governments control the wage increases which employers may pay, in particular your annual salary increase?

8 Should governments control price increases, by requiring manufacturers to obtain permission from a 'Price Control Commission' before prices are raised?

9 Should governments have regulations to govern working conditions in factories, mines, transport, shops, warehouses and offices?

10 What are the various headings of expenditure used to calculate GDP? In what ways do banks finance this expenditure?

11 What are the various categories of income used to calculate GDP? What bank savings products can be sold to the factors of production (or their owners) receiving this income?

12 What are 'transfer payments' and why are they excluded from the calculations of GDP? What bank products can be used to facilitate these payments?

13 If all state retirement pensions are paid only to bank or building society accounts, what is the likely effect on the bank accounts of all the 20,000-odd sub-post offices?

14 Make a guess as to your salary in ten years' time. How much of the increase do you think will be due to your likely promotion, scale rises (if any), performance bonuses and how much to inflation?

15 Try to calculate your own 'marginal propensity to consume'. What percentage is it of your marginal pound of income?

16 If the bank were to pay you a windfall bonus of (say) £300, how would you divide it between spending, saving and giving cash to relatives (buying presents is spending)?

17 If you lost your job because your branch was down-graded or closed, where would you seek other employment?

18 Imagine you are 20 years older. How would you come to terms with unemployment at the age of about 40?

19 If rationing were introduced in a time of extreme crisis, would you buy extra goods on the black (unofficial or illegal) market?

20 What is the most expensive item (e.g. car, holiday) you have ever bought? Did you have any financial help in paying for it (gift/loan from parents, bank loan, HP, etc.)? In which expenditure category of GDP did it feature?

7 Banks

OBJECTIVES

When you have studied this chapter you should be able to:

1 **Define a bank;**
2 **Classify the various types of banks;**
3 **Explain the differences between banks, building societies and other financial intermediaries;**
4 **Distinguish between retail and wholesale banking operations;**
5 **Identify the various markets in which banks operate;**
6 **Outline some of the products sold on these markets.**

■ INTRODUCTION

In this chapter we look at the work of banks, not at branch level but rather as financial firms operating in their various markets. This may seem strange because you are probably working in a local branch which competes in the retail market for the business of personal and small business customers. Those of you who have just entered banking are strongly advised to read one of the books written for 'The Business of Banking' examination, e.g. the author's *Banking: The Business*, (Pitmans 1990). Even those who have passed this examination may find it useful to read one of these books again to get a fuller picture of what banking is all about.

Because we are all busy doing our daily routine work it is difficult to obtain an overall picture of how our bank is performing and changing in the competitive environment of a mixed economy. It is hoped that this chapter will help you.

■ BANKS: THE VARIOUS TYPES

First, we must answer the question: what is a bank? There are two answers.

An economist will reply that a bank is a *financial institution whose liabilities (banknotes or deposits) are generally accepted by the community as money.* In Chapter 10 we shall see how notes and bank deposits comprise most, but not all, of what are termed the *monetary aggregates*. We shall also see how building societies' deposits are increasingly regarded as money.

A non-economist would give the answer that a bank is *a financial institution authorised as a bank under the Banking Act 1987.* In other words, it's a matter for the lawyers and you will doubtless study the Act in 'Banking: the Legal Environment' and for 'Customer Services: Marketing and the Competitive Environment'.

Retail and wholesale banking

Next, we must distinguish between *retail banking* and *wholesale banking*.

Retail banking comprises accepting deposits, granting loans, providing payments systems and a host of other services or products to millions of customers, of all types and sizes – to you, me, ICI and BP! At present, retail banks 'deliver' their products through large networks of branches but in the next century the telephone, PC and fax are likely to replace much of these branch networks. TSB Bank has pioneered telephone banking and Midland has created First Direct, which is a 24-hour telephone retail banking division located in Leeds.

The other major feature of retail banking is membership of APACS, which is responsible for the clearings, and most of its specialist companies. When cheques and other paper vouchers are superseded by electronic clearings, the high technological costs of installing the equipment are likely to continue to restrict the number of retail banks. However, major store groups, using electronic scanners for stock control and totals at checkouts (EPOS) and accepting debit and credit cards (EFTPOS), may consider a move into the electronic clearings as being technologically possible. Whether they will judge such a move to be profitable is more uncertain.

Wholesale banking is very different from retail banking. It operates from one branch, or possibly two, using dealers rather than cashiers, and involves transactions for an average amount of well over £1m. The absolute minimum is £50,000! Because of the large sizes of the transactions, the total deposits of a wholesale banking branch can be enormous. Wholesale banks do not belong to APACS, but use a London clearing bank to clear their cheques for them.

Although wholesale banks – such as the London branches of Japanese and most American banks – usually avoid becoming involved in retail banking, the opposite is not true. UK retail banks are very much involved in wholesale banking. In fact, the wholesale deposits of one of the Big Four are likely to exceed those of many a small wholesale bank. UK retail banks use the sterling wholesale money markets to 'top-up' the deposits gathered from their branch networks.

The Bank of England classification

At the top of the banking tree, as it were, sits the Bank of England. It is the *central bank*, providing banking services to the government and to other banks as well as undertaking a host of other functions, such as printing bank notes. In the UK, as in most countries, the central bank is responsible for carrying out monetary policy. It does not compete with the other banks, rather it supervises them, and we shall study it in much greater detail in Chapter 13.

Most other banks in the UK are *commercial banks* of one kind or another. Classifications change from time to time but the following should be helpful. These are used by the Bank of England and are shown in the order in which they appear in the Bank's *Quarterly Bulletin*. Figures are for deposits at the end of March 1992.

1 *Retail banks*, with £383bn, comprise largely the London and Scottish clearing banks, which now include the TSB and Abbey National. Also in this category are Girobank, Yorkshire Bank and the Co-operative Bank. Only some 19 per cent of their deposits are in foreign currencies and this percentage has fallen slightly now that the Abbey National is included. If we were considering solely sterling deposits then the retail banks would be far ahead of all the other banks. Because all retail banks have branch networks, they are often known as 'high street banks'.

2 *British merchant banks* include the old established merchant banks, members of the former Accepting Houses Committee. An *acceptance* is a bill of exchange which has been endorsed by a bank, and if this bank were a member of the Accepting Houses Committee then the bill could be sold for a better price than if the bank were not so highly regarded. Barings and Lazards are two of the most famous of these merchant banks. It has been said that 'merchant banks live on their wits, clearing banks on their deposits'. This comment is borne out by the relatively small size of their deposits, £48bn, of which about 35 per cent are in foreign currencies. The Accepting Houses Committee has been replaced by a larger organisation – the British Merchant Banks' and Securities Houses Association – but the statistics still refer largely to the old Committee members.

3 *Other British banks*, with deposits of £42bn; over 80 per cent of their deposits are in sterling. Standard Chartered is in this category.

4 *American banks*, with deposits of £78bn, were formerly more important, but this total has fallen from £115bn since March 1990. Some 82 per cent of their deposits are in foreign currencies but in the 1960s they provided stiff competition for the clearing banks' sterling business with UK companies.

5 *Japanese banks*, with deposits of £213bn. About 86 per cent of their deposits are in foreign currencies, so that their sterling business is still quite small. One particular niche of the market in which they have specialised is lending to local authorities. In 1990 they began to reduce their currency deposits in the UK, possibly as a reaction to problems in their domestic markets in Japan. In two years, these currency deposits fell from £230bn to £182bn.

6 *'Other overseas banks'*, which means all overseas banks except those from the USA and Japan. They comprise banks from EC countries, from Canada, Australia, Hong Kong, South America and the Middle East, as well as many other countries. They, too, have most of their deposits in foreign currencies, out of a total of £368bn.

7 *Consortium banks* are included with 'other overseas banks' and are owned by at least two or more other banks. They are not very active, because the owning banks, one of which had to be an overseas bank, now prefer to do the business in their own name and so the deposits of consortium banks, of which 87 per cent were in foreign currencies, totalled only £15bn in 1987.

Please notice the importance of deposits in currencies other than sterling. In the late 1950s London became the world's leading centre for this type of business, which is largely in US dollars. Many branches of retail (high street) banks maintain such accounts, known as *retained currency accounts*, for important

Table 7.1 Deposits March 1992

£bn	Sterling	Foreign currencies	Total
UK retail banks	310	73	383
British merchant banks	31	17	48
Other British banks	34	8	42
American banks	14	64	78
Japanese banks	31	182	213
Other overseas banks	93	275	368
Total	513	619	1155
For comparison			
Building societies	222	7	229
National Savings Bank	11	—	11

Note: There are no official statistics for banks from the other 11 EC countries.

customers, but most of the balances are maintained in the treasury departments at the banks' head offices.

Savings banks are no longer important in the UK, now that the TSB has become a commercial bank with its shares quoted on the Stock Exchange. Savings banks differ from commercial banks in that their prime function is to receive deposits, which are then on-lent to the government; they do not lend to the private sector. The *National Savings Bank* is the major example, with two main products: the ordinary account, with two rates of interest (the first £70 of interest each year is free of income tax), and the investment account (INVAC). Balances in INVAC are subject to one month's notice of withdrawal but they receive a relatively high rate of interest which, like interest on the ordinary account, is paid gross of tax. All interest from INVAC is subject to income tax, so depositors must declare it on their tax returns. The National Savings Bank is not been regarded as a bank for the statistics of the money supply, because it does not lend money to customers, only to its owner – the government.

Other financial intermediaries

Other financial intermediaries (OFIs) comprise a whole range of financial institutions, such as building societies, insurance companies, pension funds and unit trusts. These take in money now and pay it out later, either when we ask for it or when a life insurance policy matures or when we start to draw a pension from a former employer. They are:

1 *Pension funds*, with assets approaching £370bn, are the largest.
2 *Life insurance companies* (£283bn).
3 *Building societies*, with about £229bn, mostly funded from their branch networks and which are becoming more like banks than specialist providers of home loans.
4 *Unit trusts* and *investment trusts* are much smaller: about £51bn and £24bn respectively.

5 The new *centralised mortgage institutions* are even smaller (perhaps £10bn).

6 *Finance houses* are for some purposes OFIs, although many are classed as banks.

7 *Friendly societies* are small mutual life assurance companies.

8 *Credit unions*, which are very small mutual loan clubs.

What do financial intermediaries do?

Their major function is to channel finance from ultimate lenders to ultimate borrowers and then channel it back again. You can see this occurring in your branch; elderly customers may have substantial credit balances and the young marrieds may have low credit balances, substantial home loans and personal loans as well. In effect, your branch lends the elderly customers' deposits to the young marrieds.

You may not have realised that *life insurance companies*, for instance, do much the same thing. They invest the policyholders' premiums in government securities, ordinary shares and property and then credit policyholders with part of the income in the form of bonuses, declared every year. In principle, it's like a deposit account, except that it might be costly to withdraw your savings. However, you can borrow from the insurance company on the strength of the premiums you have already paid.

Pension funds are also much the same sort of intermediaries as life insurance companies, investing their members' contributions in the same range of assets. Although they do not lend to members in the same way as life insurance companies to their policyholders, some of them are involved in a fast-growing new product called a *pension mortgage.*

Unit trusts invest in shares, and they show the rises and falls of the shares they own as changes in the prices of their units which are sold to small investors. Only a very few provide loan facilities, of up to half the value of a unit-holder's holding – and they give no publicity to such facilities – but they all buy the units back from us fairly quickly. Unlike life insurance companies, they do not usually invest in government securities or property.

Investment trusts are PLCs, quoted on the Stock Exchange, which invest in the shares of other companies in the UK and overseas.

Centralised mortgage lenders are the newest type of financial intermediary, having started in the mid-1980s. Although there are only a handful of them, they are quite large, in spite of their small total assets. The Mortgage Corporation had home loans totalling more than £3bn in early 1990, with an average mortgage advance of about £55,000. This equates it to the size of a middle-ranking building society. These new financial intermediaries borrow their funds on the Stock Exchange or the wholesale money markets and sell their mortgages through estate agents or insurance brokers. They do not have branch networks.

So, we can see that financial institutions channel funds from 'surplus units' (you and me on pay day!) to 'deficit units' (you and me the week before pay day!). Sometimes they channel the money from people to people, as building societies have done for many years, and sometimes from people to firms (the economists' definition of a firm), or firm to firm or from people and firms to the government. This process is called *financial intermediation* and thus banks and OFIs are termed *financial intermediaries*.

Occasionally, the lenders and borrowers contact each other directly (as when individual investors buy shares in BP or ICI – or lend money to a relative). This process is called *disintermediation*.

To use even more jargon, banks and OFIs have been diversifying and intermingling. The banks' profits have been susceptible to changes in interest rates, so they have begun to branch out into what are termed *non-funds-based products*. Unit trusts and insurance policies are two such examples – anything where the income is in the form of a fee or commission or service charge rather than interest. Similarly, the OFIs have noticed the high profits of banks when the margin between interest charged and interest paid is wide and they have begun to encroach on the banks' 'core business' of lending and also providing cheque facilities.

In particular, the largest *building societies* have begun to provide cheque accounts, insurance, personal loans and credit cards, now that the Building Societies Act 1986 is in force. Indeed, some societies now have their own sort code numbers just like banks. People can have their salaries paid directly to a building society account on which they can draw cheques. The Act provides a method whereby a building society can convert itself into a PLC and thus a bank, but only the Abbey National has done so. However, although regarded by the Bank of England as a bank, the Abbey National prefers to call itself 'a personal financial services group'. Another building society – the Alliance & Leicester – has bought Girobank from the Post Office, but without most of Girobank's commercial banking business. There have even been reports of some foreign banks seeking to buy a building society.

To some extent, therefore, the economist's definition of a bank, which we gave earlier, must now be extended to building societies, whose shares and deposits now feature in several of the monetary aggregates, as we shall see in Chapter 10. However, before we come to that, in the next chapter we shall examine the competition between banks and building societies.

ACTIVITY 7.1

Walk around the town where you work, and list the names of all firms offering financial services – either directly or indirectly. These will include:

(a) banks;
(b) building societies;
(c) other OFIs such as insurance companies;
(d) other firms such as insurance *brokers*, solicitors and accountants.

Total the number of names on your list and see how long it is.

Express the numerical share of the banks by dividing the number of banks by the total, to arrive at a percentage. Then add:

(a) stores which offer their own credit cards, e.g. Marks & Spencer, Texas Home Care;
(b) shops and garages which offer hire purchase finance.

■ FINANCIAL MARKETS

At one time, banks and building societies could picture their markets geographically. A branch in, say, Derby would not wish to compete in, say, Nottingham. Their own branch there could handle the business. There were exceptions, because distant customers could always use the post and cash cheques at a local branch. And, for a long time, there has been the discount market in the City of London, which handled funds from all over the country and was the only wholesale money market.

Recently, however, markets have begun to become structured according to the size of the sums involved and the nature of the products being sold. Regional branches have been established by banks to handle trust and investment business (these date back many years), international business, large corporate customers such as ICI and BP who are serviced from London generally, and more recently the medium-sized commercial firms, with annual sales exceeding, perhaps, £0.5m.

Most important of all, new wholesale money markets have developed, notably the very large inter-bank market.

Retail markets

These are the concern of the majority of bank and building society branches, i.e. the high street branches. The markets can be sub-divided into:

1 *Personal* – individuals, families and clubs and associations. Further sub-divisions include students, young marrieds and the elderly, and special products have been devised for these groups, e.g. student accounts, budget (revolving loan facility) accounts and free banking for the over-55s. But all these products are sold by every branch, and this is a characteristic of much of the personal banking market. Formalised sub-markets do exist:

(a) *High net worth individuals*, i.e. rich people, who are sold asset management products either from regional branches or from a private bank, such as Coutts, the NatWest subsidiary which provides banking services to the Royal Family. A typical asset management package includes a high interest cheque account, an instant savings account (with a 'sweep' to maintain a certain balance on the cheque account), a gold card and management of stock exchange investments.

(b) *Expatriates* are those working and living abroad for a spell but who maintain close links with the UK. These customers have special tax problems and are sold products by bank officials who fly out to the Gulf, for example – where much of the business has been located. Most of the expatriates maintain accounts at branches in the Channel Islands or the Isle of Man, to be outside the tax system of the UK.

All personal customers now have a published tariff of charges to which they can refer and they are wooed with a range of products, from current accounts to credit cards, home loans, personal loans and share dealing accounts.

2 *Commercial*, ranging from the local newsagent to firms with sales up to

£500,000 p.a. (£10,000 per week). Their charges are assessed on a different tariff because of the nature of the work the branch does for them. For instance, shopkeepers will pay in bulky credits of cash and cheques, while surveillance of their accounts will involve technical balance sheet and cash flow analysis.

Their banking products, too, are very different in detail from those of personal customers. In particular, banks have devised special loans for small businesses, although criticism has been made of the difficulties claimed by some business people that banks want excessive security from them when they are setting up and have no proven track record.

Small businesses will have a small business adviser at or close to the branch to help them. Larger firms, e.g. with a net worth of up to £25m, will probably be serviced by a specialist regional or area commercial banking branch.

Corporate banking

The very large companies, e.g. Shell, ICI and BP, will have accounts with retail bank branches, but their main banking relationships are now with the corporate banking divisions at the banks' head offices.

A bank's corporate bankers liaise closely with its treasury division so as to ensure the finest investment rates for their corporate customers. The corporate bankers will try to ensure a *relationship-based* connection, i.e. continuous, with each company, rather than a *transactions-based* connection, where the company merely shops around for the best terms from a very large number of banks.

ACTIVITY 7.2

Obtain the annual report of your bank and read it thoroughly. Cut out important references to your bank from your quality newspaper and insert the cuttings in this report. In March, get the next annual report and compare the figures and comment on your findings, referring to both reports and the cuttings from the papers.

Wholesale markets

It is here that we see those foreign currency deposits which we came across. The total of bank deposits, including deposits *between* banks, in the UK in March 1992 was well over £1 trillion. Using the now universal American usage, that is £1000bn (or £1 million million), which is a lot of money! Of this total, some £619bn is in foreign currencies, deposited and lent on the wholesale markets, where deals are done by telephone or on VDUs rather than face to face (at the counters of high street banks). Of course, they are confirmed in writing. The minimum amount is $50,000 or £50,000, and the average amounts are much larger. The transactions are unsecured, so that banks rely on the reputation and the standing of their fellow banks. But there is one exception, i.e. the discount market where loans from banks are secured.

The function of these markets is to enable the members – mainly banks, but also including large companies, building societies, local authorities and central government – to adjust their liquidity positions and their borrowing. Retail banks use them as a marginal source of deposits for funding their assets, as we shall see in the next chapter.

The London discount market

This comprises the Bank of England, the nine discount houses, together with the clearing and other banks which lend the houses money against the security of bills and other assets. The total outstanding in the market is about £16bn, of which the bulk is in sterling.

In 1988 the Bank of England invited applications from newcomers to act as discount houses, but only two firms persevered with their applications, joining the market in 1989. This lack of enthusiasm was due to the small profit margins achievable and the probability of losses on the capital value of bills etc. when interest rates rise unexpectedly.

The discount houses buy bills and other *financial instruments* – legal documents which can be bought and sold – at a discount, which means at less than their face value, and can then hold them until maturity or sell them before maturity. A bill for £100,000 to be paid in three months' time may be bought today for £97,500. When the bill is paid on maturity the house will have earned £2,500 on its outlay of £97,500: slightly over 10 per cent a year.

However, the house can borrow perhaps £92,000 from a bank by handing over the bill as security. Such borrowings are nearly always secured on the bills and other financial instruments owned by the houses. They are also either at 'call' or 'overnight' – i.e. very short term. The difference between the loan and the face value of the bill is known as the *margin*, which is a third meaning of that word! As a result of the loan, the house can then discount further bills.

In the last century, commercial bills of exchange drawn by partnerships and, later, companies were the core business of the market. In 1877 the Treasury bill was invented, by which the government could borrow from the market for three months in the same way as commercial firms did. The houses agree to buy any Treasury bills unsold at the tender held each Friday by the Bank of England. For much of this century the Treasury bill was the market's core business and commercial bills fell into disuse. But since 1976 there has been a great revival of commercial bills and a decline in Treasury bills, in spite of the Bank of England's introduction in 1989 of regular weekly issues of 182-day sterling Treasury bills, as well as the traditional 91-day and occasional 63-day ones. The Treasury bill may have been brought back to life, but most now go to banks and overseas holders, who tend to hold them until maturity, enjoying the high rates of interest available.

In recent years the principal financial instruments of the discount market have been commercial bills. In March 1992 Treasury bills discounted were less than £0.3bn, while commercial bills totalled £4.3bn. If a commercial bill has been 'accepted' (endorsed) by a bank recognised by the Bank of England it is known as a bank bill; if not, it is known as a trade bill.

Recently, however, another financial instrument has become more important because the market now holds more of them than any other asset. In March 1992, it held some £5bn of sterling certificates of deposit (CDs) which are, in essence, promissory notes issued and traded by banks and building societies. We shall examine them in greater detail in the very shortly.

The discount market is unique, not only because it is the only wholesale market in secured money, but also because it is the only wholesale money market in which the Bank of England is active. The foreign exchange market is the other financial market in which the Bank of England operates but it is not a *lending* and *borrowing* market but one of *buyers* and *sellers*.

The Bank intervenes in the discount market in its role of *lender of last resort* to the commercial banks. When short of liquid assets the banks will call in their loans to the discount market. If the houses find that other banks are unable to lend them the funds they need, then they will turn to the Bank of England, which will lend to them, usually at the prevailing market rates of interest. The Bank also signals its wishes for the future trend of interest rates, as we shall see in Chapter 13. And because there are so few Treasury bills, the Bank operates by buying and selling mostly commercial bills. The discount market may be small, but it is very important, as Table 7.2 shows.

Table 7.2 Discount market March 1992

Liabilities	£bn	Assets	£bn
Capital	0.4	Treasury bills *	0.3
Borrowing in sterling		Other bills *	4.3
from UK banks	8.6	UK bank CDs *	5.0
from other lenders	2.5	Building society CDs *	
		and time deposits	0.7
		Loans to UK banks	0.4
		Loans to other UK and	
		overseas residents	0.5
		Investments (mainly	
		with building societies)	0.2
		Other	0.1
Total sterling liabilities	11.5	Total sterling assets	11.5
Borrowing in foreign		Foreign currency	
currency	0.4	assets	0.4
	11.9		11.9

Note: Over 80 per cent (£8.9bn) of the market's sterling borrowing was either call money or overnight money.
* Financial instruments

Parallel money markets

These are all the other money markets *except* the discount market. They cover sterling and foreign currencies; the earliest – the local authority market – began in about 1955. Although they are supervised by the Bank of England, they are different from the discount market in several ways:

(a) none of the loans or deposits are secured;
(b) the Bank of England is not an active participant entering into a market only occasionally, perhaps to carry out a deal on behalf of one of its central bank customers;

(c) there is no lender of last resort.

The inter-bank market

This market's name describes its members, i.e. solely the commercial banks. What it does not tell us is that it is subdivided into the various currencies – mainly sterling and the US dollar – that the deposits and loans are unsecured, that the sums involved are very large, although this should be evident from its wholesale nature, and that there is no lender of last resort. Its interest rates – London Inter-Bank Offered Rate (LIBOR) and London Inter-Bank Bid Rate (LIBID) – are used as yardsticks of market trends much more than those in the traditional discount market.

The inter-bank market is the largest sterling money market, with about £158bn of deposits. In March 1992 sterling deposits between UK banks were over £84bn, while there were £74bn of deposits from overseas, much of which was lodged by banks not represented in the UK. For currency deposits, the totals were £78bn from UK banks and £441bn from overseas.

Certificates of deposit (CDs)

Commercial banks and building societies issue CDs for periods of from seven days to five years, acknowledging the deposit of the sum stated. They are issued in sterling or foreign currency for a minimum of £50,000 or the foreign currency equivalent.

The holder does not have the right to 'call' his deposit (demand repayment) but may sell the CD for cash in a 'secondary market'. Surprisingly to an outsider, the buyer of the CD is likely to be another bank or building society which will include it as one of its liquid or short-term assets. Accordingly, CDs can appear on both sides of a bank's or building society's balance sheet. Those which it has issued will be part of its liabilities and those of other banks or building societies which it has purchased will appear on the assets side. If it buys one of its own CDs, it will cancel it.

The CD market is the link between the discount market and the sterling inter-bank market. The discount houses buy and sell existing sterling CDs and the banks' treasuries decide whether to fund an increase in assets by selling new CDs or by bidding for inter-bank deposits. So, a change of interest rates in the very large sterling inter-bank market will be transmitted to the discount market by way of the prices of sterling CDs. However, CDs are not eligible at the Bank of England as security for borrowing by discount houses: the Bank does not deal in them.

Local authorities

Local authorities have a special market, in which they can borrow short-term funds pending the receipt of revenues, many of which are paid half-yearly. Historically, this market is older than the inter-bank market, dating from the early 1950s, when local authorities were freed from the requirements of having to borrow solely from the central government. There is a sub-market in bonds, which are loans to local authorities of up to about two years.

Inter-company market

The inter-company market is where companies lend and borrow directly among themselves, rather than using banks. This is the technique known as *disintermediation*, because the companies are short-circuiting the financial intermediaries. The market was developed by companies in the late 1970s, to overcome very tight lending controls imposed on banks by the Bank of England. The banks merely process the cheques for the loans in this market and get nothing by way of interest, because the loans are not on their books.

Sterling commercial paper market

To some extent the inter-company market has been superseded by the sterling commercial paper (SCP) market which began in spring 1986. On this market very large companies issue 'paper', similar to Treasury bills or CDs – IOUs or promissory notes in effect – which can be bought and sold. The commercial banks have taken advantage of the trend towards disintermediation because they help in launching 'paper' and 'make a market' in it (undertake to buy and sell it at the market price).

Finance house market

The finance house market dates back to the mid-1950s, when finance houses were known as hire purchase companies. Today, they finance small and medium-sized businesses as well as lending on hire-purchase agreements and on second mortgages. The largest are owned by the retail banks. Their total lending of nearly £40bn is funded by their capital and reserves, borrowing from parent banks, bills of exchange and borrowing on the finance house market.

ACTIVITY 7.3

About once a month cut out the money market section from your quality newspaper. Note any changes in the various interest rates, ready for the next chapter.

Cash and derivative markets

So far the markets we have described have all been *cash markets*, where there is a payment of money from the lender to the borrower and later back again, or from the buyer to the seller of a financial instrument, e.g. a commercial bill or CD.

LIFFE

However, since 1980 a number of markets dealing in *derivatives* – rights and obligations to futures or option contracts – have developed. The best known of these is *LIFFE* – the *London International Financial Futures and Options Exchange*, founded in 1982. In 1991 LIFFE merged with the London Traded Options Market, keeping the abbreviation LIFFE but adding 'and Options' in the middle of its name. For our subject, you need not study derivative markets in any detail, but they will be important in the Associateship examination.

■ SUMMARY

1 A bank is defined by economists as a financial institution whose liabilities (notes or deposits) are generally acceptable as money, i.e. can be used in the settlement of debts.

2 Central banks are usually bankers to the governments and banks of their countries, and implement the government's monetary policy. There is usually only one central bank in each country.

3 Commercial banks serve the whole country and there are generally quite a number. They seek profits, unlike central banks.

4 In the UK the Bank of England classifies banks into one of several categories:

   (a) retail banks;
   (b) British merchant banks;
   (c) other British banks;
   (d) American banks;
   (e) Japanese banks;
   (f) other overseas banks;

5 Apart from the National Savings Bank, the UK has no savings bank.

6 Other financial intermediaries are those whose liabilities – deposits, policies, pensions, etc. – are not accepted in settlement of debts.

7 Building societies are in a unique position – they are changing into banks for ordinary people. The Bank of England and the Treasury consider the societies' liabilities to be money in many of the 'monetary aggregates'.

8 Apart from building societies becoming banks, other financial intermediaries include:

   (a) pension funds;
   (b) life insurance companies;
   (c) investment trusts;
   (d) unit trusts;
   (e) centralised mortgage lenders
   (f) finance houses.
   (g) friendly societies;
   (h) credit unions.

9 Financial intermediaries link ultimate lenders with ultimate borrowers, taking the business on to their balance sheets. Do not confuse them with estate agents, insurance agents and mortgage brokers, who merely act as contact people, earning a fee rather than interest.

10 Retail financial markets are local, served by branch networks.

11 There are many personal sub-markets, mainly by age, but there are others: high net-worth individuals; expatriates.

12 Commercial banking attends to the needs of small and medium-sized businesses.

13 Corporate banking looks after the largest companies and can be relationship-based or transactions-based.

14 Wholesale markets are now very large. They comprise:

(a) discount market, in which the Bank of England operates;
(b) the parallel money markets:

- inter-bank;
- CD;
- local authority;
- inter-company;
- sterling commercial paper;
- finance house.

The above are all cash markets but, since 1980, markets have developed in derivatives – options, futures, etc. The best example of one of these is LIFFE.

■ SELF-ASSESSMENT QUESTIONS

1 Distinguish between a central bank and a commercial bank.

2 Place the following banks in the correct classification used by the Bank of England:

(a) Girobank;
(b) Bank of Tokyo;
(c) Deutsche Bank;
(d) Banque Nationale de Paris;
(e) Citibank;
(f) Abbey National;
(g) Hambros;
(h) National Savings Bank;
(i) Midland.

3 List the parallel sterling money markets in approximate order of size.

4 What are the financial instruments dealt with on the various wholesale money markets?

5 Why are loans and deposits not regarded as 'financial instruments'?

6 Explain, in everyday words, what is meant by financial intermediation.

7 What is different about banks and building societies as financial intermediaries?

8 Give an everyday example of disintermediation.

9 Why is a bank or building society a firm (in the economist's sense)?

10 What was the approximate figure for sterling deposits with UK retail banks in December 1991? (a) £90bn; (b) £180bn; (c) £270bn; (d) £310bn.

11 Distinguish a CD from CP.

12 Distinguish a unit trust from an investment trust.

13 Barclays Bank's total deposits are approximately how many times as large as those of the National Savings Bank? (a) two; (b) five; (c) ten; (d) fifteen.

14 Place the following in the correct sub-market for personal customers.

(a) a student with an income of £25,000 p.a. from a family trust;
(b) an engineer and family working in Singapore; home in York;
(c) a Unilever pensioner and wife living on the Wirral, pension £15,000 p.a.;
(d) an ICI pensioner and wife living in the Algarve, pension £19,000 p.a.;
(e) a chartered accountant, salary £55,000 p.a., house in Solihull worth £470,000, mortgage £120,000.

15 Describe what is meant by retail banking.

16 Describe what is meant by wholesale banking.

17 Why do wholesale banks usually avoid undertaking retail banking operations?

18 Why do most retail banks engage in wholesale banking activities?

19 Name the odd one out: NatWest; Ulster Bank; Coutts & Co.; Lombard North Central plc.

20 What are non-funds-based products?

8 Interest rates and banking competition

OBJECTIVES

When you have studied this chapter you should be able to:
1 Appreciate the significance of interest rates, particularly when compared to inflation;
2 Describe the wide range of interest rates – from minimal rates on current account credit balances to those levied on unauthorised overdrafts;
3 Identify the banks' principal competitors in the financial markets;
4 Understand how and why banks and their competitors are adapting in the face of this competition.

■ INTRODUCTION

To cut a long story short, interest rates are the price of money to lenders and borrowers. You possibly studied the arithmetic of calculating and charging interest last year in Business Calculations, so you may be relieved to know that this chapter is *descriptive* rather than mathematical.

Banks make most of their profits and losses on lending money and it is only right that we should spend some time looking at the prices of these loans. But we must also look at the actual loans themselves and, briefly, the way in which they and all the other bank products are 'delivered'. (Next year, having passed this subject, you may be studying these topics in greater detail.)

■ INTEREST RATES

An interest rate is the price of a particular sum of money and, although economists talk glibly about the *rate* of interest, there are in fact a great many. A clearing bank may pay 2 per cent p.a. on branch seven-day deposits but could charge 28 per cent p.a. on unauthorised overdrafts. The period of the loan can vary from overnight in the inter-bank market to ten years for a loan to finance a power station or a ship.

The reasons for this wide spectrum of interest rates are many. They include the period of the loan, the security (if any) offered, the nature of the borrower, the nature of the lender (HP companies charge more than banks because they cannot borrow to finance the loan as cheaply as banks) and the purpose of the loan (export projects traditionally attract a lower rate of interest than, say, loans for second homes). Even the size of the loan can affect the rate. In the past, many of the interest rates charged by clearing banks for lending money have been linked to *base rates*. For instance, a reputable business customer might be charged 2 per cent p.a. over base rate, while a borrower with a reputation for exceeding his limits might be charged 4 per cent over base.

A bank's base rate is the guideline interest rate for pricing much of its lending. Because most retails banks are oligopolists, their base rates are the same and, indeed, base rates are effectively controlled by the Bank of England, as we shall see in Chapter 13.

Larger corporate customers, however, have been able to 'persuade' the banks to switch their charging from being based on base rate, which is determined by the Bank of England, to being linked to an interest rate determined by market forces. The rate chosen instead of base rate was the *London Inter-Bank Offered Rate* (LIBOR), which is that rate charged on the loans which the banks offer on the inter-bank market. LIBOR is now fairly well known, unlike its fellow rate – London Inter-Bank Bid Rate (LIBID), which is quoted when banks bid for deposits. The spread, or difference, between the two is the banks' profit margin on this business.

On home loans, the banks now quote a home loan or mortgage rate which need not necessarily change when base rate changes. When banks first began to grant loans for house purchase, the interest rate was linked to base rate, whereas the building societies' rates were not. For instance, a bank might have charged 2.25 per cent over base, while the building society charged 12.5 per cent. If base rate were 10 per cent this translated into a home loan rate of 12.25 per cent. This made comparisons difficult since borrowers had to know the level of base rate as well as the margin over base rate. The mortgage rate is an 'administered rate', as are the rates on personal loans, budget accounts and home improvement loans.

Some banks, scenting higher profits, have opted for monthly interest rates, e.g. instead of 18 per cent a year, why not charge 1.5 per cent a month? The bank will be paid its interest monthly, which is a benefit for its cash flow, and the compound rate goes up to about 19.6 per cent: a clumsy figure to conjure with, but 1.5 per cent a month is so simple.

Charting interest rates

Economists, particularly those employed in the treasury departments of banks and building societies, plot interest rates on graphs. They don't compare the various levels of rates charged to different borrowers as we discussed in the previous section, but rather the rate of interest on a particular financial instrument or in a particular market over a period of time. Take, for instance, the sterling inter-bank rates on 28 December 1988 (we use these as they demonstrate ideally the way in which rates rise up to three months, then level off and fall). The *Financial Times* showed these to be as in Table 8.1.

The wide range on overnight money is very common, as banks balance their books. The non-arrival of funds could cause banks to pay excessively to cover the gap – and then if the funds actually arrive they may have to be placed on the market at an unprofitable rate. If you ask why banks do choose to do this (and you should ask it) the answer is that it is better to earn some interest than

Table 8.1 Inter-bank interest rates

	LIBOR	LIBID		LIBOR	LIBID
Overnight	12 3/8	2	Three months	13	12 7/8
Seven days' notice	12 3/8	12	Six months	13	12 13/16
One month	12 13/16	12 5/8	One year	12 11/16	12 9/16

earn nothing.

A typical yield curve is shown in Fig. 8.1

Obviously the further we look ahead the less we can be certain and so interest rates tend to be higher. However, if we fear a crisis soon but then look forward to better times there is likely to be a hump at the beginning of the curve, as shown by the dotted line in Fig. 8.1. This dotted line is in the shape of the yield curve at the end of the 1980s. Look again at the LIBOR and LIBID in Table 8.1 rates for six and twelve months. The twelve-month rate was the lower of the two, which is what we expect when short-term rates are raised by the government.

Nominal and real rates of interest

If you were in business and expected, first, that the price of, say, blankets would rise 10 per cent during the next year and, secondly, that the rate of interest you would have to pay would remain at 8 per cent, you could borrow £10,000 to buy blankets, sell them for £11,000, pay £800 in interest to the bank and have £200 as profit.

This example illustrates how stocks can be financed reasonably cheaply when interest rates are below the rate of inflation or, at least, below the rate at which the price of the stocks increases. But in May 1992 the annual rate of inflation in the UK was 4.3 per cent and the base rates of the London clearing banks were 10 per cent. So, our blanket-holders would have had to pay perhaps 13 per cent (3 per cent over base rate) and would have been lucky had the value of their blankets risen by 5 per cent over the year. They would have been out of pocket.

The rate of interest prevailing in the market is known as the *nominal rate*. After we deduct the annual rate of inflation we have the *real rate of interest*. Table 8.2 assumes that the nominal rate of interest is 12 per cent p.a. and shows how rises in the annual rate of inflation will cause the real rate of interest to change from positive to negative.

Should you study 'Investment' for your ACIB, you will learn that the strict way of calculating real rates of interest is by dividing – e.g. 1.12 (12%) ÷ 1.06 (6%) = 1.0566 (5.66%).

Because so much of the banks' costs comprise nominal interest paid on deposits, as we shall see in the next chapter, the real rate of interest is not so important to them as it is to their customers. But if the customers begin to borrow substantially from banks when real interest rates become negative, the banks will have to resort to the inter-bank market as their source of marginal

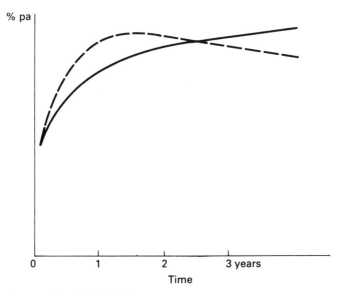

% pa

0   1   2   3 years

Time

Fig. 8.1 A typical yield curve

Table 8.2 Inflation and real interest rates

Inflation	Nominal rate of interest (% p.a.)	Real rate of interest (% p.a.)
6	12	+6
8	12	+4
10	12	+2
12	12	0
14	12	−2
16	12	−4
18	12	−6

deposits. The inter-bank rate is the marginal cost of funds to banks. In other words, the *indirect* effects of negative real interest rates can be serious for banks, so they seek to finance the loans and overdrafts requested by their customers. Likewise, when real interest rates are positive, as they have been since the beginning of the 1980s, the banks tend to be 'under-lent' and actively seek to lend. Hence their great interest in home loans in 1987 and 1988, when house price inflation was about 20%, far above the rates of interest on mortgages.

Purists will note that we have excluded the effects of taxation, which can lower the nominal rate of interest for businesses which can claim tax relief on all interest paid, although personal borrowers are restricted to interest paid on loans of up to £30,000 for house purchase. However, we all are liable to pay tax on interest received. After income tax at 25 per cent is allowed for, an interest rate of 12 per cent becomes 9 per cent, so that the real rate of interest could become negative if the inflation rate rose to 10 per cent p.a.

ACTIVITY 8.1

Plot the inflation figures you drew in Chapter 6 in red, on a new sheet of graph paper, with the months along the horizontal axis. Plot the base rate of your bank in black, on the same sheet, for the same months.

Draw a dotted black line 3 per cent above the base rate, to represent the cost of borrowing for a reputable customer. Where the dotted black line is above the red inflation line, shade the area between the two lines in black; where it is below the red inflation line, shade the area between the two lines in red.

The shadings represent the real rate of interest:

(a) negative where the shading is black;
(b) positive where the shading is red.

'True' rates of interest

On borrowing

Do you remember our example of a bank charging 1.5 per cent a month, instead of 18 per cent p.a.? We mentioned that the compound rate of interest was somewhat higher than 18 per cent, more like 19.6 per cent. This is the 'true' annualised rate of interest for that particular product.

Now let's turn to a personal loan of, say, £1000 at a flat rate of 10 per cent. Assume that is is to be repaid by 12 equal instalments. The interest, i.e. 10 per cent of £1000 = £100, is immediately added to the principal to make £1100, which is then divided by 12 to give 11 monthly instalments of £91.66 and a final one of £91.74. But the *average* amount of the loan outstanding over the year is roughly £550, being half of £1100 after allowing for the capital repayments which are made at the *end* of each month. Thus the £100 interest is actually being charged for an average loan of £550, a rate equivalent to about 18 per cent p.a.

In 1974 the Consumer Credit Act was passed. This complicated piece of legislation includes a requirement that all credit transactions for sums of £15,000 or less to personal borrowers must show an Annual Percentage Rate of charge (APR). The APR features in many advertisements and indicates the 'true' rate of interest as compared to the flat or the nominal rate. It is termed APR of charge because it also includes fees, e.g. registration fees or credit protection insurance, which are part of the financial package to sell the item on credit.

'True' rates of interest are rarely negative in real terms; they are generally well above the rate of inflation.

On deposits

As regards interest *received* by customers on their deposits with banks, there are two features of note.

First, some savings products have interest allowed monthly or quarterly, so that the rate is compounded and annualised to enable comparisons to be made. One per cent per month compounded and annualised becomes 12.7 per cent p.a. The abbreviation for *compounded annualised rate* is CAR, and it is shown for many products in the Saturday financial pages of quality newspapers.

Secondly, since 1985 the government has required banks to pay interest 'net of tax' to customers, just as building societies have done for many years. This means that if we receive interest of £10 a quarter on our staff account with the bank, we are not liable to pay income tax at the basic rate (25 per cent in the tax year 1992/93) on this income, provided it has had this basic rate of income tax deducted.

Since April 1991 customers who are not liable to pay income tax may complete a 'self-certification' form supplied by the Inland Revenue and often called a 'BRT form' in banks. When a customer presents such a form to a bank or building society, interest will be credited without any deduction of tax. Before April 1991 such people had been unable to reclaim any tax deducted at source by the bank or building society.

Customers must still declare all interest received from banks and building societies on their income tax returns, and must pay additional income tax if their marginal rate of tax exceeds the basic rate. Incidentally, many students do not realise that this BRT (Basic Rate Tax) is not a separate tax on income received but just part of income tax.

Tiered and banded rates of interest

Before about 1970 interest rates were relatively simple to remember: on deposit accounts banks paid (say) 5 per cent, whether the balance was £1 or £100,000, on savings bank accounts they paid 2.5 per cent on the first £100 and then 5 per cent – the deposit rate – on any excess. Savings bank accounts were launched in the 1930s to compete with the Post Office Savings Bank, which paid only 2.5 per cent p.a. for over 100 years.

'Tiered' rates

Today interest rates are very much harder to remember. Let's take an imaginary account which might have been launched in summer 1992. There is not just one rate of interest but five levels.

£1 – 999	2.5%
£1000 – 1999	7.1%
£5000 – 9999	7.4%
£10,000 – 24,999	7.6%
£25,000+	7.9%

As the balance on the account rises so the interest rate increases – the interest rate is often said to be *tiered*, to use the jargon. Thus, a balance of £500 earns 2.5 per cent p.a., net of tax, but if it rises to £1500 the rate of interest paid on the *whole balance* rises to 7.1 per cent net of tax.

Most banks and building society accounts have such tiered rates on their deposit and lending products – but not all!

'Banded' rates

These are different because the higher rate of interest applies only to the higher bands or slices of the balance. They work in the following way.

An account has, for example, these rates of interest:

6% p.a. on balances up to £1000
7% p.a. on balances between £1001 and £2500
8% p.a. on balances exceeding £2500.

The annual interest credited on an account with £7000 to its credit throughout the year will be:

6% on	£1000	=	£60
7% on	£1500	=	£105
8% on	£4500	=	£360
Total =	£7000		£525 which is 7.5% p.a.

If the interest had been tiered, the amount of interest at 8 per cent p.a. would have been £560. So-called banded rates are used by the Co-operative Bank and a few Midland Bank products. Their advantage to the bank or building society is that they are less expensive than tiered rates but the disadvantage is that knowledgeable customers may seek to transfer the whole balance to a rival product offering a tiered rate – i.e. of anything over 7.5 per cent p.a.

Unfortunately, not all banks keep to this terminology. For instance, NatWest pays the top rate on the complete deposit, but its leaflets refer to interest rate 'bands'. So, let the buyer beware!

■ COMPETITION BETWEEN BANKS

Interest rates

With much of their deposits purchased on the inter-bank market, banks are in no position to move out of line with one another on price. The international banks and the foreign banks have quite small market shares, so that they tend to approach the conditions of perfect competition rather than oligopoly, as discussed in Chapter 5. However, much of the business is syndicated or shared between the banks with non-funds-based fees being determined by the roles played at each management level of the syndicate of banks. In such syndications, the rate of interest is agreed between the borrower and the bank 'mandated' (or contracted) to put together the banks which will provide the bulk of the finance.

Retail banks, on the other hand, are much more likely to be in an oligopoly situation, with market shares of between 15 and 25 per cent in some cases. Some retail banks, such as the Yorkshire Bank, the Co-operative Bank and those branches of Indian and Pakistani banks serving local immigrant communities, have small market shares and therefore must act more cautiously when considering interest rate changes, although they may be able to count on the loyalty of their customers.

When the Bank of England signals clearly that interest rates must change, by varying the rate at which it acts as lender of last resort to the discount market, then the clearing banks move very rapidly, probably within an hour, moving their base rates as indicated by the central bank.

Other interest rates may move, but the banks may bide their time. Building societies usually change their interest rates less frequently than banks change their base and deposit rates and so the banks try not to change their home loan rates too frequently, especially if they have to raise them. On the other hand, the banks might prefer to lower their home loan rates immediately after a clear signal from the Bank of England that rates should fall, in order to gain an edge on the competition and increase market share.

Sometimes, interest rates seem poised for a fall but the Bank of England gives no clear indication of its intentions. Because retail banks still rely to a considerable, though diminishing, extent on interest-free current account credit balances for their funding, there is an *endowment element* in high interest rates which benefit their profits. They receive interest at a higher rate across, say, 93 per cent of their assets (excluding cash and fixed-rate assets), whereas they may pay interest on perhaps only 87 per cent of their deposits. Consequently, banks may be loath to be the first to cut their administered interest rates on deposits and so lose what remains of this endowment effect. Moreover, other banks may not follow. Instead, the banks may lower the interest rates on lending products not related to base rate or may introduce new products at the lower level of interest rates or alter the tiers in the existing products.

When deciding to change its administered rates, a clearing bank's chief executive will take into account what the Bank of England is signalling (via its intervention in the discount market), recent movements in LIBOR, the extent to which the bank is funding its assets from the inter-bank market as compared to the retail market and, finally, what its competitors are doing. If the market leader moves, other banks will follow. If LIBOR is falling and the bank is relying more on the retail market for its funds (where rates are relatively higher) it may wish to cut its deposit rates and thus its average cost of funds, and to reduce the administered rates on its loans by less than the cut in base rate.

ACTIVITY 8.2

On Saturdays, most of the quality newspapers publish tables of the principal rates of interest for depositors in the retail market.

Construct a monthly table for these rates, extending for a year from now, because these interest rates will be important for your studies for Customer Services – Marketing and the Competitive Environment. Are the rates rising or falling?

Non-price competition

Between these bursts of activity, when interest rates change, banks compete among themselves by emphasising quality of service, and generally 'packaging' their products so as to differentiate them from those of their rivals. The responses are the classic features of oligopoly:

(a) colour – Barclays blue, Lloyds green;
(b) slogans – the Action Bank, the Thoroughbred Bank;
(c) product branding – Cashpoint, Classic, Special Reserve, Orchard;
(d) location of branches is still important but the emphasis is on refurbishment

and accessibility. New branches are not likely to be opened, in view of the ability of ATMs to provide cash and meet other needs.

Telephone banking is still in its infancy, using one of the following methods of delivery:

(a) a personal computer linked to a bank mainframe computer by telephone (modem);
(b) voice communication by ordinary telephone to a 'personal banker', as with Girobank or Midland's First Direct;
(c) a TV set, suitable for Prestel, linked to the bank's computer.

Competition between banks and building societies

Banks began to compete seriously with building societies in the 1980s, with the competition taking the following forms:

1 Banks offered home loans in 1981.
2 Building societies issued CDs in 1983, to tap the wholesale money markets used by banks.
3 Banks offered better interest rates on their deposit and savings accounts.
4 Building societies sought authority from Parliament to operate current accounts. This was given by the Building Societies Act 1986, along with many other powers, including conversion to a bank.
5 In 1989 the banks responded by offering current accounts paying interest on credit balances, following the success of the interest-bearing current accounts launched in 1988 by Abbey National and Nationwide Anglia.

In July 1989 the Abbey National became a bank and in 1980 the Alliance & Leicester Building Society bought most of Girobank from the Post Office. However, Girobank's leasing business went to the Norwich Union insurance group, and much of its commercial lending to a merchant bank.

At present, there is no competition between banks and building societies for commercial customers, but this could occur by the end of the century. Banks and building societies compete fiercely in the following markets:
(a) current accounts;
(b) deposit and savings accounts, which are increasingly named savings and investment accounts;
(c) home loans, often termed 'mortgages'.

They compete less fiercely in these markets:
(a) travel facilities – travellers' cheques and foreign currency;
(b) personal loans;
(c) insurance;
(d) personal equity plans;
(e) credit cards.

At present building societies do not offer credit cards but at least one major society is about to join SWITCH, the major debit card network.

(For a more detailed discussion of this competition , see the author's *Banking: The Business*, Pitman, 1990, Chapter 16.)

Competition between banks and 'non-banks'

Surprisingly, the banks believe that the major threat is coming from 'non-banks' – not from overseas banks. These are likely to buy a UK bank or building society rather than create a new network of branches. There are two major threats from 'non-banks'.

1 In the personal market, as we have seen, building societies are now providing many of the products which banks have provided in the past. Cheque books, credit cards and personal loans are now part of the product range of major building societies, some or which are already members of APACS (Association for Payment Clearing Services Ltd).

2 In the corporate market, served from London, the threat comes from the *securitisation* of debt. Instead of large companies borrowing from their banks, they will issue short- and long-term securities which will be bought by banks, other companies and the various NBFIs described in the previous chapter, with the probable exception of building societies. To be able to service this need of companies to issue securities, such as sterling commercial paper, the banks must have the resources (i.e. factors of production – labour and capital) to help the companies issue and then 'make a market' in them.

This blurring of the distinction between banks and stockbrokers and jobbers is one of the very important changes brought about by Big Bang in October 1986, since when banks have been able to buy brokers and jobbers trading on the London Stock Exchange. There is also a fear that the Japanese securities firms, particularly Nomura Securities, may be able to take a large share of this business and use this as a base from which to expand in the UK retail banking market.

Threats in minor markets come from accountancy firms (personal taxation products), insurance brokers (insurance) and travel agents (banks such as the Midland and the Royal Bank of Scotland now own travel agents).

In competition with public sector financial institutions such as the National Savings Bank and National Savings Certificates, the banks are competing on much more of a 'level playing field' after the changes of April 1991. A savings account with a bank will be as tax effective for a non-taxpayer as an account with the National Savings Bank, provided that the customer completes the self-certification form. The competition will be on the rate of interest, terms of withdrawal and location of bank branch and post office. National Savings Certificates will continue to be tax-effective for taxpayers because they are free of all income and capital gains tax.

In the long term, banks face competition from stores – in particular Marks & Spencer. In the USA, Sears Roebuck has become a major provider of financial services and 'St Michael' could follow suit, building on its customer base of more than two million cardholders. Unlike other stores, Marks & Spencer does not accept other credit cards, so that it has a very active set of cardholders. Most other stores face competition from Access, Visa and the T and E cards (travel and entertainment – Diners Club and American Express) as they try to promote their own store cards. Store cards give cardholders the chance to preview sales, but they cannot yet provide a cash dispenser network comparable to those available to Access or Visa.

Finally, there is the possibility of telephone companies moving into banking. It would not be so strange, because we now depend on telephones to an ever-increasing extent. When people depended on the letter post, the post offices provided a banking service, which is now owned by a building society. So far, there are two areas where telephone companies are already active:

(a) selling phone cards, which are small 'cash deposits' with the company;
(b) providing telephone lines to banks and building societies and shops to process data from cheques and credit cards.

In the USA a large telephone company issued a credit card and is reported to have obtained 1 million cardholders with a day! Within six months, there were more than 5m holders of its Universal card which can be used to pay for telephone calls as well as to buy goods and services.

ACTIVITY 8.3

Visit your local Marks & Spencer store and local DIY shops, collecting leaflets about their own credit cards. Compile a table of APRs, from the lowest to the highest. Is there an APR below 25%. Is there an APR above 40%?

■ SUMMARY

1 Interest rates are one of the prices of money.

2 In real life there are many rates of interest depending on:

   (a) whether the bank or building society is lending or borrowing;
   (b) the credit-worthiness of the borrower;
   (c) the purpose of the loan;
   (d) the period of the loan;
   (e) whether the loan is secured or unsecured;
   (f) the tax laws concerning the interest payments;
   (g) the size of the loan

3　Banks publish a base rate, on which many of their lending rates are based, but they also use:

   (a) LIBOR – London Inter-Bank Offered Rate – from which loans to large corporate borrowers are calculated:
   (b) managed interest rates, such as mortgage rate or personal loan rate which need not change every time the Bank of England signals a change in base rate.

4 Nominal rates of interest are those published and forming part of the loan contract.

5 Real rates interest are nominal rates of interest *minus* the rate of inflation.

6 True rates of interest include compulsory fees and show the average annual rate on the average balance outstanding. They are in contrast to 'flat' rates of

interest, which are calculated on the original amount of the loan. The APR is the statutory true rate for loan interest.

7 Tiered rates of interest apply to the *whole* of the balance on an account rising as the balance rises.

8 Banded rates of interest apply only to the amount *within* each band and not to the whole balance.

9 Some banks calculate and charge or pay interest monthly, others quarterly, half-yearly or annually. To enable a fair comparison between competing products with these different intervals between interest calculations, these credit interest rates are also published as compounded annualised rates (CAR).

10 Important changes took place in April 1991 in the procedure for deducting income tax on interest rates paid by banks and building societies.

11 Banks do not usually compete with one another by seeking to pay the highest rate of interest. Rather, they will seek to improve a product by allowing easier access to cash or by inserting a new interest rate tier.

12 Banks compete with building societies for personal accounts but not for business accounts, because societies are not allowed to provide these.

13 In the corporate markets, large companies can now issue short-term securities – commercial paper – to a wide range of investors and not just banks.

14 In the long term, banks face possible competition from store groups, such as Marks & Spencer, Japanese banks and securities houses – and from telephone companies.

■ SELF-ASSESSMENT QUESTIONS

In this chapter we have stressed from time to time how the contents of the book line up with some of the other subjects you are studying. Accordingly, some of these questions not only relate to earlier chapters but also involve topics which you covered last year in 'The Business of Banking'.

1 Did you ask yourself, when reading the section on the London discount market: Why have there been such changes since the mid-1970s in the bills etc., dealt with in the discount market? If the answer is 'no', or 'yes' but you didn't give the reasons, don't worry because we shall examine them in Chapter 13.

2 Explain the meaning of APR and CAR.

3 'The marginal cost of funds to a commercial bank is LIBID.' Explain.

4 Watch for building societies turning themselves into public limited companies and see whether this change makes them more liable to be taken over by banks or whether it enables them to buy other financial intermediaries, such as HP companies or insurance companies.

5 What is meant by oligopoly? In what ways do clearing banks behave as oligopolists when:

(a) changing their base rates?
(b) changing their other interest rates?

6 Name five stores issuing credit cards. What competitive edge have they over Access, Visa and T and E cards? What competitive edge have these credit and T and E cards over store cards?

7 Examine how banks, building societies and insurance companies were entering the estate agency market in the late 1980s and how the agencies seemed powerless to react.

8 Compare the retail banking structure outlined in the previous chapter with that in your bank. If your bank is small, is its 'delivery system' for the products different? Or does your bank not sell these products?

9 Who are likely to be the banks' principal competitors in the 1990s?

10 Why is it old-fashioned to write about 'joint-stock banks'?

11 Watch the development of home banking (banking by telephone linked to a central computer). Why was it pioneered in the UK by the Bank of Scotland and a somewhat small building society (the Nottingham)? (Turn back to the section 'Monopoly – in practice' in Chapter 5 where you will see something akin to this, only on price rather than product.)

12 Find out more about pension mortgages (the Saturday financial pages will feature them from time to time). Watch to see if banks feature them more prominently in their range of products.

13 Who owns the major hire-purchase companies? Is this an example of vertical or horizontal integration? Are the Japanese banks moving in on any independent HP companies?

14 Look at Question 6 again, visit your local branch of Boots and then examine the prices of the goods. Why did Boots withdraw its store card in the late 1980s?

15 What shareholdings, if any, does your bank have in other financial intermediaries? Does your branch earn commission for placing business with them?

16 'A bank's costs are largely salaries and interest'. How true is this statement when technology is increasingly important?

17 How informed about your bank's activities are:

(a) your colleagues?
(b) your customers?

18 Do you find your customers initiating requests for new products or do you have to approach them first to tell them about the options open to them?

19 Which of your bank's products are most suitable for:

(a) students?
(b) young marrieds – both working?

(c) young marrieds with children – one partner working?

(d) the recently unemployed?

(e) the over-55s (the empty-resters)?

20 Examine the annual report of your bank's pension fund and find out how it invests its assets in order to be able to pay your pension in the year 2030 or thereabouts.

9 Banks and their finances

OBJECTIVES

When you have studied this chapter you should be able to:
1 State which items feature on the assets side and which on the liabilities side of bank balance sheets;
2 Appreciate the relative importance of each of these items;
3 Explain how each item generates either outgoings (on the liability side) or income (from assets);
4 State, within the limits of the information divulged by the banks, the importance of the profits (or losses) generated in the various sections of the banks' activities and by the major product groupings;
5 Use the information to understand your own bank's figures, which should be published in early March each year.

■ INTRODUCTION

Economists, you will not be surprised to learn, have not been very accurate in their balance sheet analysis of the banking system, because their totals of assets and liabilities rarely equal each other! This is not due to poor arithmetic but to the economists turning a blind eye to the banks' capital and reserves, which they have never regarded as having much importance. The Bank of England certainly *is* very interested in the banks' capital and reserves and so should you be, as students of banking and bank employees.

The banks have usually been slow to reveal the breakdown of their assets, liabilities and profits although matters have improved recently. Banks do give a geographical breakdown of their assets and liabilities as well as profits/losses. Divisional figures are also published by some banks.

Consequently, we have official data for the various types of banks described in Chapter 7, which do not add up to the same totals for assets and liabilities and which ignore capital. And for individual banks we have figures which do not correspond to those in the official statistics.

Not a very promising start to your studies, you may think. Perhaps not, but we'll try to make it as interesting and as helpful as possible.

■ LIABILITIES

The liabilities of people and firms are their obligations owed to other people, firms and to the government. They appear as credit balances in the accounts.

Banks' liabilities comprise mainly deposits from customers at home and abroad, in sterling and in foreign currencies. If deposits are in foreign currencies, they are converted into sterling at the exchange rate prevailing on the day the balance sheet is compiled. CDs issued appear here.

Other liabilities include trade creditors, e.g. bills for electricity, gas, telephone, stationery supplies, just like other companies. The money owed to the Revenue for corporation tax also features as a liability.

Another liability is the credit balance on the profit and loss account, after the dividends have been paid and after any sums have been transferred to reserves.

Deposits

Economists would like to see a breakdown of deposits by sector (personal, company, bank, other financial and government) as well as by currency and geographical area. But that's asking too much! Lloyds Bank Plc publishes an analysis of deposits by type. For 1991 the percentage breakdown was as in Table 9.1.

Table 9.1 Average UK sterling deposits of Lloyds Bank, 1991

	%
Non-interest-bearing current accounts	12
Interest-bearing current accounts	14
	26
Savings and investment accounts	30
Other branch deposits (receiving money market rates of interest)	14
Total retail funds	70
Market funds (inter-bank and CD)	30
	100

Notice how important are the deposits raised by bidding on the inter-bank market and by issuing CDs – 30% of the total. For every £1 lodged at a branch, another 43p is raised on the wholesale markets – the inter-bank and CD markets.

Secondly, notice that interest-bearing deposits comprise 88 per cent of all deposits, leaving only 12 per cent of non-interest-bearing current accounts to provide the endowment element. The total of non-interest-bearing current accounts was, on average, £575m lower in 1991 than in 1990.

Capital

Capital comprises that part of a company's liabilities which are not claimed by outsiders: by people who have sold it goods, lent it money (the depositors in the case of a bank) or the taxman. Capital is what the company owes itself and its members, i.e. the shareholders.

As we have seen, economists have ignored capital, concentrating on the deposits of banks. But since about 1960 the need for commercial banks to have an adequate cushion of capital has become apparent to the world's leading central banks and regulatory authorities. Moreover, because international banking has worldwide ramifications, these central banks are trying to co-ordinate their requirements for the capital ratios of commercial banks.

Financial analysts, when analysing the liabilities of industrial and commercial companies, refer to a concept called *gearing*, i.e. the relationship between a firm's capital (its own funds) and the moneys borrowed from banks and other outside sources. Rules of thumb are dangerous to apply but analysts look for a ratio of between 1:1 and 1:2 between 'inside' and 'outside' finance. If they were to apply the same criteria to banks the analysts would discover that banks were very highly geared, with ratios of perhaps 1:15 between capital and deposits. When profits increase, a highly geared company has a large number of fixed-interest creditors who do not have any share in the profits which are available for the shareholders. However, when times are bad and income is falling, the highly geared company has to pay its fixed-interest creditors before any dividend can be declared from the lower profits.

This extreme dependence on borrowed money makes banks highly vulnerable to loss of confidence, particularly in the wholesale markets, where each bank sets limits, just like overdraft limits, on the deals it will accept with individual banks. If a bank finds the limits accorded to it by other banks are being reduced it may have difficulty in renewing wholesale deposits as they fall due.

One of the ways in which banks seek to inspire confidence in the business and financial community (apart from their reputation) is to build up their capital base. Much of the detail of the structure of a bank's capital is outside our syllabus but all who work in banks must be aware of the outlines.

On 31 December 1991 the capital resources of Lloyds Bank Plc totalled £4.9bn, divided into the categories shown in Table 9.2.

Table 9.2 Capital resources of Lloyds Bank Plc

	£m
Issued share capital	1254
Reserves	1222
Total shareholders' equity	2476
Minority interests	498
Undated loan capital	991
Dated loan capital	955
	4920

Share capital is owed to the shareholders, but is payable only if the company goes into liquidation. In the meantime, the shareholders are entitled to dividends if the profits are sufficient to permit their payment. Share capital can be increased in several ways:

1 A *rights issue* inviting existing shareholders to buy new shares at an attractive price. When the shareholders pay for the new shares, so the company's cash

flow improves and liquid assets rise.

2 A *scrip issue* or *capitalisation of reserves* whereby sums are transferred from reserves to share capital. With a scrip issue there is no change in cash flow. The reserves fall and share capital rises by the amount transferred; the shareholders make no payment for their shares.

3 Shares can be issued to purchase another company or part of a company. If the assets acquired with the company include cash then the cash flow will change.

4 A recent development has been the opportunity for shareholders to take their dividends not as a cheque or credit transfer but in the form of further shares. Lloyds Bank, for example, introduced this in 1987. Cash flow benefits because no money is paid to the shareholders, who elect to receive shares, apart from a minimal sum to maintain the shares' status as 'trustee investments'.

Reserves are funds on call or on stand-by, representing previous years' profits not distributed to shareholders or perhaps a windfall profit from the sale of an asset. From time to time retail banks revalue their properties, and any surplus over book values can be credited to reserves. But reserves usually grow by transfers each year from the surplus on the profit and loss account.

Some banks have prided themselves on raising all their capital by ploughing back their profits into reserves. Others, in particular National Westminster in 1986 and Midland in 1987, have had substantial rights issues. Midland also sold its Scottish and Irish subsidiaries in 1987, in order to generate cash and increase reserves which can be credited with the profits made on the sales.

Minority interests are the outside shareholders of these subsidiary companies which are not wholly owned by the bank.

Loan capital comprises long-term loans, which cannot be repaid before the due date. In some cases there is no date for repayment. Such capital is closely monitored by the Bank of England, as you will discover in your studies next year.

■ ASSETS: LIQUIDITY V. PROFITABILITY

Assets are possessions or claims, such as houses, motor cars and debts due from other people. Assets are debit balances.

There is a much wider range of items on the assets side of a bank balance sheet. Assets range from cash to advances and are usually shown in a certain order in bank balance sheets. The most liquid (and least profitable) are shown first and the least liquid (most risky and hopefully most profitable) last.

Let's see how Lloyds Bank allocated its assets on 31 December 1991.

Banks face an age-old problem in that they need to have enough liquid assets to meet the day-to-day demands of their customers to repay their deposits and, at the same time, to have profitable assets in order to pay the interest on their deposits, the salary bill and the dividend to the shareholders and still be able to transfer some profit to the reserves so that the business will continue to grow. The problem is that no asset is both very liquid and very profitable.

Table 9.3 Lloyds Bank's assets (including foreign currency assets)

	£m	%
Cash and short-term funds		
Cash in hand and with central banks	504	1.0
Money at call and short notice	2908	5.7
Treasury and other bills	2480	4.8
Certificates of deposit (CDs) purchased	1328	2.6
	7220	14.1
Cheques in course of collection	852	1.7
Investments	643	1.2
Advances and other accounts	39,848	77.7
Long-term assurance business	831	1.6
Trade investments, including associated companies	226	0.4
Premises and equipment	1686	3.3
	51,306	100.0

Liquidity is defined as *the ability of an asset to be turned into cash rapidly, without cost and without loss of capital and/or interest.* You may say that cash is the most liquid asset and you are right. Those of you with a practical turn of mind will remark that cash may be liquid enough for emergencies but that it is also very expensive to hold. Not only is interest forgone but costly vaults and security systems have to be installed to prevent it being stolen. Cash is the only asset which costs the banks money!

Advances, regarded as the most profitable asset, are not only very illiquid (would you like to repay your car loan on demand?) but also the most risky, as the problems over loans to the Third World and to UK borrowers illustrate.

The Bank of England checks the liquidity of all banks and the riskiness of their assets, as we shall see later in the book.

So let's look at the assets of a bank, in order of decreasing liquidity and increasing profitability. We will use the seven headings shown in the accounts of Lloyds Bank for 31 December 1991.

ACTIVITY 9.1

Using your bank's directors' report and accounts, compare its figures carefully against those shown here. Calculate percentage shares wherever possible, so as to make comparisons easier.

Liquid assets – cash and short-term funds

These comprise at least *eight* types of asset:

1 *Cash in hand* is mainly Bank of England notes and 'coins of the realm'.
2 *Balances at the Bank of England* are traditionally regarded as cash, partly because the accounts are debited when the bank draws notes from the Bank of England. The balances at the Bank of England are of two types:

(a) *Cash ratio deposits*, which are required from all UK banks. They must deposit

0.35 per cent of their 'eligible liabilities' (broadly, sterling deposits from outside the banking sector for an initial period of up to two years) and these deposits earn no interest. Such assets are *not* liquid assets. This ratio was lowered from 0.40 per cent in January 1992.

(b) *Operational deposits*, which are held at the Bank largely by the London and Scottish clearing banks, in order to make settlements between one another and, most importantly, *to and from the government*. Again, no interest is paid but the deposits *are* liquid assets. Target balances for such deposits are agreed between the Bank of England and individual clearing banks.

3 *Call money* is lent to discount houses against the security of treasury bills, commercial bills, local authority bills and sometimes gilt-edged securities. The loans are callable (repayable) instantly and are highly liquid.

4 *Money at short notice* is also lent to the discount houses against similar security but can be at two to seven days' notice. No loss is involved but it is not as liquid as call money. However, it does yield a higher rate of interest.

5 *Treasury bills*. These have been scarce in recent years, but are still held by banks. They can be sold instantly for approximately what the banks paid for them, but there is a slight chance that the price may have moved adversely (*see* section on *Investments*).

6 *Commercial bills*. These, too, can be sold rapidly and without substantial loss. Most will be bank bills, i.e. endorsed or accepted by a bank recognised as such by the Bank of England.

7 *Local authority bills*. These may be issued by local authorities in anticipation of receipts from the community charge and the uniform business rate.

8 *Certificates of deposit*. Many of these will be sterling CDs, issued by other UK banks and building societies. They can be sold quickly to the discount market or direct to another bank or building society. Like all fixed-interest securities, they are subject to the risks described below (*see* section on *Investments*).

Cheques in course of collection

These are the cheques drawn on other banks and collected by Lloyds Bank, which will receive the proceeds in the next two days. Obviously, these items are of great practical importance to bankers (particularly if the cheques are returned unpaid, as some will be) but they are of little concern to economists because there is a contra item in 'current, deposit and other accounts' on the opposite side of the balance sheet – namely, the Lloyds cheques cross-stamped by other banks. The two flows of cheques are roughly equal and any differences are settled by drawing cheques on the banks' operational accounts at the Bank of England.

Investments and their risk

These comprise mainly gilt-edged securities issued by the government, plus some issued by local authorities. They can be quite remunerative but they also fluctuate in value considerably.

Let's take a simple arithmetical example, using a stock which pays £2.50

for every £100 worth held. In jargon this is said to have a *coupon* of 2.5 per cent. But you should notice that 2.5 per cent is a low return – we can get more than that at the Post Office from the National Savings Bank.

In fact, as we saw in the previous chapter, interest rates are much higher than 2.5%. How then can a stock with a 2.5 per cent coupon exist when interest rates are, say, 7.5 per cent? The answer lies in the price, which moves to equate the yield from the stock to the current level of interest rates. If I can obtain 7.5 per cent by buying stock on the market today, clearly I will not buy anything with a coupon of only 2.5 per cent unless the price is so low that £100 invested will yield me £7.50, i.e. the price is £33.33 per £100 of stock. For £100 I can buy £300 of stock at 33.33 and this £300 of stock will provide me with (3 x £2.50) of interest, i.e. £7.50.

So, when interest rates rise, the prices of fixed-interest securities fall and vice versa. And we learn from history that interest rates rise and fall, sometimes abruptly. Accordingly, the prices of these investments can fall and rise just as abruptly. By our definition, therefore, they are not liquid because, although there is an active market in which they can be sold, there is no guarantee that they cannot be sold at a loss. Indeed, many banks and discount houses have made losses on their fixed-interest securities when interest rates rose.

Advances and other accounts

These are the largest category of a commercial banks' assets. The loans and advances are to personal borrowers, industrial and commercial companies, other financial intermediaries, other banks and governments around the world.

For sterling lending to UK customers, Lloyds Bank has published a breakdown shown in Table 9.4 into several major categories.

Table 9.4 Lloyds Bank sterling lending 1989

	%
Mortgages	20.0
Personal loans and credit card lending	5.9
Other personal	10.9
Total personal	36.8
Small and medium-sized businesses	30.7
Large corporate, leasing, etc.	32.5
	100.0

These figures relate to average balances in 1991.

Long-term assurance business

This comprises the net tangible assets of the life assurance companies owned by Lloyds Bank and is, more importantly, a conservative valuation of the companies' surpluses on their investments, as compared to their liabilities, plus the value of the life policies in force.

Trade investments

These will vary from bank to bank but could comprise a shareholding in *3i*, a financial intermediary for lending to and investing in smaller firms. It is owned by the Bank of England and the clearing banks. Other trade investments could include shares in a hire-purchase company, in a leasing company and perhaps a stake in an estate agent. Because the balance sheet is a consolidated one, the item will not include subsidiaries – where the bank owns 51 per cent of the company's shares – nor associated companies where the bank's stake is between 10 per cent and 50 per cent.

Premises and equipment

These describe themselves. Premises are freehold, long or short leasehold, except for those overseas where different tenures apply. As we mentioned earlier, surpluses arising on revaluations are usually credited to reserves (debit the asset, credit the liability) but short leaseholds are a depreciating rather than an appreciating asset. Equipment is very illiquid, although vital if the bank is to function effectively, and should be written down rapidly, certainly before it is replaced.

Special deposits

From 1960 to 1981 the Bank of England frequently called upon banks to lodge special deposits with it, as one of its instruments of monetary control. These deposits, upon which interest was usually paid, were very illiquid and designed to squeeze banks' liquid assets. Because they have not been used since 1981, they are not discussed further.

■ CONTINGENT LIABILITIES

Contingent liabilities comprise those liabilities which *might* arise in the future and include liabilities on forward foreign exchange contracts and indemnities and bonds given on behalf of customers. In every case *there is a contra asset*: a sale or purchase of foreign exchange or a counter-indemnity from the customer. However, losses can occur on contingent liabilities, as some banks found when performance bonds were called (enforced) on contracts in the Middle East undertaken but not fulfilled by customers. Unfortunately, the contra assets (counter-indemnities) proved to be inadequate.

ACTIVITY 9.2 *

Using your money market cuttings, write in pencil in the margin of this book the typical rates of interest available on each type of liquid asset.

Compare these rates with a typical rate charged on many loans and bank advances – say 3 per cent over base rate. Which is the highest rate and why?

■ ASSET MANAGEMENT

In your studies for the Business of Banking you may have read about goldsmiths issuing receipts for gold, many of which were not presented for payment for a considerable time. The receipts were simply passed from hand to hand or paid in and drawn out again, without gold being demanded. You will remember that, eventually, the goldsmiths found that they had liabilities, i.e. notes, which exceeded their stock of gold, the balance of their assets being loans to the people to whom they had lent money in the form of notes. The goldsmiths had become bankers.

These goldsmiths were managing their assets from their premises. As the gold and the receipts/notes were paid in, so their deposits rose and enabled them to create new assets. This was elementary *asset management* of the balance sheet – a technique whereby deposits are regarded as a relatively fixed element, so that a bank must rearrange its assets to achieve the balance between liquidity and profitability which we noted earlier. It is a typical retail banking concept, with special departments managing cash, money market, advances, premises and investments. It is a structure very familiar to your middle-aged colleagues who joined the bank in the 1950s when the only form of deposit was what we now term a *retail deposit*. Please note, however, that it has little to do with the asset and management products sold to high net worth personal customers.

■ LIABILITY MANAGEMENT

This became the vogue in the later 1960s when aggressive American banks began to compete with the London clearing banks for the business of large corporate customers. Lacking branches in the high street, these banks had no retail deposit base and had to rely on the newly born wholesale markets for their deposits. Their technique was to target a potential borrowing customer, call on them and, if the loan was agreed, the bank's treasury in London would bid for the necessary deposits.

The treasurer's job was to fund the loan as profitably as possible, managing the liability. Interest rates on the loan were linked to LIBOR so that the bank made a profit on the margin between the interest rates received and paid.

Since the 1960s, most banks in the UK have resorted to an increasing extent to the wholesale markets for their deposits. Perhaps 30–40 per cent of a clearing bank's sterling deposits come from the wholesale market, in which they use the techniques of liability management pioneered by the Americans.

Even building societies are becoming dependent on the wholesale markets but they, unlike banks, have a statutory ceiling of 40 per cent of total deposits above which they cannot tap the wholesale markets. Building societies even issue CDs and are now learning the techniques of liability management. Moreover, the large multinationals such as ICI, Shell and General Motors also use the concept, so that their treasury offices resemble those of banks, borrowing and lending funds and buying and selling foreign exchange.

■ PROFIT AND LOSS ACCOUNT

The yields obtainable on the assets described earlier can be found in the financial pages of quality newspapers. For short-term assets, they appear under *money and exchanges* or *money markets*; LIBOR is termed *inter-bank*. The yields on gilts are quoted in the stock market prices under *British funds*. Base rate is displayed in branches, and the margins above it charged on advances vary from 2 per cent to 5 per cent. However, the margins above LIBOR are generally well below 2 per cent, arising from the greater standing of the companies able to arrange these market-related terms with their bankers.

The interest rates paid on their deposits are displayed in branches and are published in the personal financial pages of quality newspapers on Saturdays.

Interest received is by far the largest source of a bank's income, as shown by the following breakdown for Lloyds Bank for 1991 in Table 9.5.

Table 9.5 Lloyds Bank: income

	%	£m
Interest	81.2	7041
UK current account fees	3.7	
Other UK commissions and fees	5.6	
International commissions and fees	2.6	
Increase in value of long-term assurance business	2.9	
Estate agencies	0.8	1627
Credit cards	0.8	
Foreign exchange trading income	0.8	
Insurance broking	1.0	
Securities gains	0.6	
	100.0	8668

Other sources pale into insignificance against interest but their marginal effect can be seen if they can be increased at a time when interest income is falling. Interest paid is also the largest component of expenses (*see* Table 9.6).

Table 9.6 Lloyds Bank: expenses

	%	£m
Interest expense	58.1	4688
Staff costs	17.3	1395
Premises and equipment	6.5	521
Specific provisions for bad and doubtful debts	11.1	898
Other (e.g. stationery, advertising)	7.0	562
	100.0	8064

Banks pay particular attention to the *net* interest received because this registers the value of their 'turn' or differential between interest paid on deposits and earned on advances.

The profit and loss account is published in the form shown in Table 9.7.

Table 9.7 Lloyds Bank Profit & Loss Account 1991

	£m
Interest income	7041
Interest expense	(4638)
Net interest income	2353
Other operating income	1627
Total income *	3980
Less: Operating expenses *	(2458)
Less: Provisions for bad and doubtful debts	(918)
Operating profit	604

* These two figures, when income is divided into operating expenses, gives the *cost income ratio, viz.* $\dfrac{£2458m}{£3980m} = 0.618$

(usually expressed as a percentage, *viz.* 61.8%).

Those readers who are studying Introduction to Accounting may know that the next stage in the analysis is the preparation of the profit and loss appropriation account. Part of this is shown in Table 9.8, which is again for Lloyds Bank Plc for 1991.

Table 9.8 Lloyds Bank: Profit & Loss Appropriation Account 1991

	£m
Operating profit	604
Share of profits of associated companies	12
Profit before taxation	616
Taxation charge and exceptional item *	(167)
Profit after taxation	449

* Exceptional items relate to any activities but they are shown separately because of their size. Another name is abnormal items. Here the item is the release of provisions by a company in which Lloyds Bank holds shares.

In 1987 and 1989 most retail banks made exceptionally large provisions for lending to countries experiencing difficulties in making repayment. Brazil, Mexico, Argentina and Venezuela head the list of countries, which totals 38. The result of these exceptional items was to transform Lloyds Bank's profit before taxation in both years into a loss, which was financed by a transfer *from* reserves. Normally, there is a profit on the profit and loss appropriation account, some of which is transferred *to* reserves. Because the provisions were so large, most of this lending has provisions equivalent to 75 per cent of the debt, so further enormous provisions for problem country borrowers are unlikely. However, large provisions were made in 1990 and 1991 for domestic corporate and small business lending where the borrowers were in financial difficulties. Provisions were also made for mortgage lending.

■ SUMMARY

1 Liabilities are obligations and nearly all the obligations of a bank are owed to its depositors.

2 Retail banks are paying interest on an increasingly larger proportion of their deposits, mainly as a result of competition from building societies.

3 Retail banks also use the wholesale markets for their deposits – just under one pound in every three pounds of deposits is raised by the banks' treasuries bidding for deposits.

4 In addition, quite a large proportion of branch deposits receive interest at money market rates.

5 Capital is also a liability – owed to the bank's shareholders rather than to outsiders.

6 Capital acts as a cushion against losses and extra large expenses. It comprises:

(a) share capital raised by the shareholders and returnable to them if the bank ceases trading;
(b) reserves set aside by the bank from past years' profits;
(c) long-term loans.

7 Share capital can be increased in two main ways:

(a) asking shareholders for more cash, and issuing new shares for this cash (a rights issue);
(b) transferring balances from reserves to share capital and issuing new shares 'free' to shareholders (a scrip issue).

In both cases the extra shares on the market will depress their price.

8 Assets are the possessions of a firm or person or debts owed to the firm or person.

9 For banks, most assets are debts owed to it – loans and advances mainly – but they do own cash, bills of exchange, CDs, investments and premises and equipment.

10 Banks seek to arrange their assets to achieve a balance between:

(a) *liquidity* – needed to keep the depositors content and monitored closely by the Bank of England;
(b) *profitability* – needed to pay dividends to the shareholders and purchase new premises and equipment.

11 Liquid assets comprise:

(a) cash – notes and coin;
(b) operational balances at the Bank of England;
(c) call money;
(d) money at short notice;
(e) bills – commercial bills, Treasury bills and local authority bills;
(f) CDs issued by other banks and building societies.

12 Advances are the largest of banks' assets, the most profitable and the most risky. They comprise about 75 per cent of total assets.

13 Other assets include:

(a) investments in

- gilts;
- insurance companies;
- estate agents' chains;

(b) premises and equipment;
(c) cash ratio deposits at the Bank of England.

14 Banks use both asset management – deposits first, then arranging the assets in the correct order – and liability management. With the latter, the treasury and product development sections seek the most stable and cost-effective way of funding the assets, which are mainly loans and advances.

15 Profits come largely from interest received on advances.

16 Expenses are largely interest paid on deposits and salaries.

ACTIVITY 9.3 *

Balance sheet items for XYZ Bank Plc on 31 December 199– are set out below. Study the items and answer the questions which follow.

XYZ Bank Plc	£m
Advances (sterling)	3000
Balance of profit & loss account	50
Balance at Bank of England	14
Money market assets	1146
Deposits (sterling)	3800
Treasury bills	2
Advances (foreign currency)	3000
Paid-up share capital	200
Notes and coin	2
Capital reserves	400
Deposits (foreign currency)	3900
Gilt-edged securities	86
Investment in UK leasing company	500
Commercial bills	600

Note: There are 500 employees, of whom 200 have managerial status; all work in one office in Lombard Street, London, EC3.

On 31 December 199–, the date of the balance sheet, outstanding forward foreign exchange contracts totalled £20,000m.

(a) From the data given, compile the balance sheet of XYZ Bank Plc.
(b) From the information given, state whether the bank is a retail bank or a wholesale bank. Give reasons for your answer.

■ SELF-ASSESSMENT QUESTIONS

Note: Some of these questions (and those in the remaining chapters) relate to topics covered in earlier chapters. These 'trick' questions concern relevant matters – you should be on your guard!

1 Insert the missing words.

(a) In bookkeeping credit balance on an account is either a profit or a
....

(b) A debit balance on an account is either an expense or an ....

2 Explain why bank loans to a borrowing company appear as credit balances in the *company's* accounts.

3 Obtain a copy of your bank's annual directors' report and accounts and compile similar tables to those in this chapter. Are there any significant differences?

4 The accounts you have used will probably contain figures for the previous year. Are there any noticeable changes between the two years, for instance in the proportion of deposits on which no interest is paid?

5 Some Scottish banks still issue notes. Where do these notes appear in their balance sheets?

6 Explain the difference between liability and asset management of a balance sheet. Are building societies likely to follow banks and concentrate more upon liability management?

7 Explain, in everyday language, what is meant by (a) nominal rates of interest; (b) real rates of interest; (c) the APR; (d) CAR.

8 Why are banks so concerned about net interest received, after deducting interest paid?

9 If a bank has a rights issue, what will be the effects on:

(a) its share capital?
(b) its liquid assets?
(c) its capital reserves?

10 If a bank has a 'scrip issue', what will be the effects on:

(a) its share capital?
(b) its liquid assets?
(c) its capital reserves?

11 If GDP for the UK were to grow at a real rate of 3 per cent, after allowing for inflation, what effects might this have on life in:

(a) South East England?
(b) Northern Ireland?
(c) Liverpool and Merseyside?
(d) your own area, if not in the above districts?

12 If house prices continue to fall, relatively to the rate of inflation (RPI), would

there be a significant increase in demand to buy houses? Or do you think that the faster house prices rise, the greater is the demand for houses?

13 What is meant by the 'endowment element' in a retail bank's profits? Is it becoming smaller, and if so, why?

14 Construct a table from newspaper cuttings showing the monthly rates of interest and APRs charged by the leading credit cards and store cards.

15 Which balances at the Bank of England are liquid assets to the banks lodging them?

16 If banks are charging much the same rate to most borrowers, does this indicate that they are losing their monopoly powers and not practising price discrimination?

17 What are meant by 'contingent liabilities?

18 Banks are able to sell jointly loans and insurance products. Are there any products which could be sold jointly with bank deposits? In other words, when customers acquire a large cash sum which needs investment, what products might such 'high net worth individuals' need?

19 When might banks offer 'deposit products' to newly unemployed customers?

20 Should banks close branches which are consistently unprofitable?

10 Money

OBJECTIVES

When you have studied this chapter you should be able to:
1 **State the assets which comprise money and quasi-money;**
2 **Know that these assets are the liabilities of the banks and building societies which issue them;**
3 **Understand how the government, the banks and their customers, and people overseas can all cause changes in the money supply;**
4 **Appreciate the contentious nature of the theories of interest rates and of the effects of changes in the money supply;**

■ INTRODUCTION AND REVISION

You may be unaware that economists use 'money' in a stricter sense than we do in everyday life. 'What's the money like in her new job?' really means 'How well or badly paid is she in her new job?' Money to an economist does not mean *pay* but rather any *asset* (not a commodity) generally acceptable in settlement of a debt.

We may also have to do some revision before beginning this chapter. For instance, can you recall the *characteristics* of money? Money must be acceptable, recognisable, portable, divisible, uniform, durable, scarce and stable in value if it is to perform its functions. A cheque has most of these characteristics, with the exception of acceptability for we may not know or trust the person who signed it (*drew* it is the legal term). Moreover a cheque is a legal instrument which transfers a bank deposit or bank loan from one person to another. It's the bank deposit which is money. So many students become confused between the characteristics and the functions of money that we should stress that the characteristics, or qualities, mostly end in 'able', 'ible' or 'ity'.

Money has two *main functions*.
1 As a *medium of exchange* it enables specialisation to occur, so that the average costs of producing goods and services fall dramatically. Without specialisation, a country's output of goods and services would be very small, and its standard of living very low.
2 As a *liquid store of value* it enables savings and capital investment to be undertaken by different groups of people. As a result, an economy can build factories, roads, hospitals, schools, etc. and so enjoy a better standard of living. For instance, the Channel Tunnel is being financed by many of the world's leading banks, and by the shareholders, but the actual construction is being undertaken by a consortium.

Money has two *minor functions*.

3 As a *unit of account*, facilitating profit and loss accounts, stock-taking, budgeting, forecasting and cost and management accounting. Its use enables modern managers to apply techniques to combine factors of production in the most efficient way.

4 As a *standard of deferred payments*, so that money values can be used in long-term contracts for the borrowing of money and the use of factors of production, e.g. loans and rent.

The various qualities of money all enable the assets we use as money to perform these four functions *more effectively* and so give us greater output and a higher standard of living.

■ MONEY: A DEFINITION

Money comprises all assets which are generally acceptable in payment of debts. In whichever way we define the money supply – and there are a number of *monetary aggregates* – the largest component comprises the deposits of banks and building societies. Notes and coin are the 'small change' of money.

One of the problems of discussing money is that there is a wide range of assets which can perform some but not all of the functions of money. The test is to take the two major functions, i.e. medium of exchange and liquid store of value, and decide if the asset in question is:

1 generally accepted as a medium of exchange;
2 a liquid store of value (remember, we defined *liquid* in the previous chapter).

Building society shares and deposits are regarded by many people as stores of value and they are quite liquid but they are now becoming generally accepted as a medium of exchange, resulting from the building societies' provision of cheque-book facilities to some of their share accounts and deposits.

Quasi-money

This is also called *near money* and comprises those financial assets which fulfil some but not all of the four functions of money. Building society shares and deposits used to be the prime example of quasi-money but they are coming to be regarded as part of the money supply. In March 1992 they comprised nearly 36 per cent of the major broad monetary aggregate.

The major quasi-money assets are published by the Bank of England in a list of *Liquid Assets outside M4*. There are over 30, including UK residents' foreign currency and sterling deposits at banks outside the UK, the overseas sector's deposits at UK banks, all National Savings products, sterling CP and, surprisingly, gilts maturing in under five years and unused sterling bank credit facilities.

Narrow and broad money

These terms are used increasingly today. *Narrow money* refers to those assets which act as a medium of exchange. Notes and coin are, obviously, narrow money because we spend them rather than save them. But not all bank and building society deposits are intended to be spent − or exchanged. Some represent savings rather than purchasing power.

Broad money includes narrow money plus those assets which are also used as a liquid store of value. Please remember that broad money covers both functions. It includes all types of bank and building society deposits, as well as notes and coins, as we shall see in the next section.

■ MEASURING THE MONEY SUPPLY

Money supply measurements are constantly changing, although they usually follow some general rules. In general, they exclude money, i.e. notes, coins, bank and building society deposits held by:

(a) banks and building societies;
(b) people and firms resident outside the UK, e.g. a Japanese car manufacturer located near Tokyo;
(c) the UK government, local authorities and public corporations (nationalised industries.

Hence, *by definition,* the money supply will fall when taxpayers pay taxes to the government and rise when the government spends that tax income. Likewise, money supply falls when people pay their poll taxes to the local council and rises when teachers are paid their salaries by the local authorities which employ them.

By definition, money spent on imports by the UK is money moving into the hands of overseas residents (the foreign suppliers). Moreover, if these overseas residents sell their sterling to UK banks in exchange for their own currencies then, *by definition,* the UK banks' holdings of this sterling do not feature in the statistics of the UK's money supply.

As we stated earlier, changes occur quite frequently in these definitions and, following the conversion of the Abbey National Building Society into a bank in the summer of 1989, a number of these *monetary* aggregates ceased to be published. You should, of course, be asking: Why? The answer is that the enormous size of the Abbey National meant that any measures which comprised solely bank deposits were swamped by some £30bn of Abbey National deposits when the society became a bank. But readers should be pleased, because the changes are simplifying the measures considerably!

Formerly, there were seven official monetary aggregates. Now there are only three: M0, M2, and M4. M1 and M3 are no longer published and M5 has followed them. M4c replaced M3c and it too is no longer published.

M0 is a very important measure of narrow money and M4 measures broad money. Their definitions will not change in the near future but M2's definition has been altered slightly to bring it more into line as a narrower and smaller version of M4.

The 'wide monetary base' M0

First, M0 includes notes and coins in circulation outside the Bank of England, i.e. it includes those in the banks' tills and cash dispensers. Secondly, it includes part, and only a small part, of the banks' deposits with the Banking Department of the Bank of England – their operational deposits.

In March 1992 the composition of M0 was:

Notes and coin in circulation outside the Bank of England	£18.2bn
Banks' operational deposits with the Bank of England	£ 0.2bn
	£18.4bn

M0 was (at June 1992) the sole 'monetary target' of the government and we shall discuss its role more fully in Chapter 13.

M0 is unusual in that it comprises the banks' operational deposits at the Bank of England, together with their holdings of notes and coin. These two items are, in fact, assets of banks rather than their liabilities. However, the notes and the operational deposits *are liabilities* of the Bank of England. In your studies for the Associateship you must study this difference in greater detail and also why M0 is given the name 'the wide monetary base'.

Most non-technical observers, however, regard M0 as the smallest measure of narrow or spending money.

Transactions balances M2

This is an attempt to sweep the 'store of value' money balances away from M4 by excluding large wholesale balances. M2 comprises cash with the non-bank public and sterling non-interest-bearing sight deposits with UK banks but then includes sterling *retail* interest-bearing bank deposits and building society *retail* deposits.

Retail deposits are defined as balances of less than £100,000 and with a maturity of less than one month. Deposits in the ordinary account of the National Savings Bank are now excluded. Sight deposits are, simply, those repayable on demand – i.e. with immediate access.

Although supposed to be a measure of narrow money, M2 is quite large, totalling £280bn in March 1992.

Broad money M4

M4 was introduced in 1987 and has never been targeted by the government. However, like any monetary aggregate, it is closely watched by the Bank of England and the Treasury.

Other measures

At present there are none. However, the Bank of England publishes its Liquid Assets outside M4, which is just a straight list with no 'netting' to avoid double counting. The total is over £500bn.

Broad money M4 (June 1990)	£bn	%
Notes and coin outside the banks	15.4	3.4
Deposits in sterling with banks by the UK private sector (including CDs)	283.0	62.1
Deposits in sterling with building societies by the UK private sector (including CDs)	157.1	34.5
	455.5	100.0

For details of any further changes, students should read *Banking World* each month. Teachers should not only read *Banking World* but also the *Financial Review* published at the beginning of each term by the Banking Information Service.

ACTIVITY 10.1 *

Look up the definition of money in a good dictionary. Does it include deposits at banks and building societies? If not, why not?

■ THE DEMAND FOR MONEY

This section of the syllabus is one which you should have little difficulty in grasping, because we all like more money in our purses, wallets and bank accounts!

Transactions demand

Really, this is common sense: we need to have some money in order to buy things. Because our income comes to us weekly or monthly (or half-yearly if it's in the form of dividends on shares) it is 'lumpy', whereas hardly a day goes by without our spending some money. Our bank statements will show that the number of debit entries invariably far exceeds the number of credit entries. So, we need some day-to-day working balances to pay for the goods and services we know that we shall be buying before the next receipt of income.

Transactions demand for money does not vary greatly, because it depends on our income and our spending habits. These habits reflect whether we use cash, cheques or credit cards when we spend our salaries.

Precautionary demand

During the next year or so we suspect that some nasty events will occur: the car may break down or the pipes burst in our house but we don't know exactly when or where. Accordingly, we have a reserve of money which we try not to touch unless we really have to. Some of you may say that you don't do this because your credit card enables you to draw cash to pay the plumber or the garage. This may be true, and also shows how habits are changing, but many people still keep money for that 'rainy day'.

Precautionary demand, like transactions demand, does not change significantly, being determined by income and habit.

Speculative demand

In the last chapter we saw how the price of fixed-interest investments rose and fell in the opposite way to changes in the rate of interest. Economists argue that one way of avoiding the loss in value of these investments is to sell them when interest rates are low and about to rise, i.e. prices are high and about to fall, and buy again at the lower price.

In other words, we are speculating with our money on the chances of a rise in interest rates. The rich investor may sell gilts and deposit the sale proceeds in a high-interest bank account. The bank clerk may transfer some of his or her staff account to a building society account or even a high-interest cheque account.

Speculative demand, unlike the other two demands for money, *does* vary greatly, according to expectations of changes in interest rates. If interest rates are thought to be about to rise, people move into interest-bearing money. They move out of fixed-interest rate securities, whose prices are thought to be about to fall.

It is this speculative demand or *liquidity preference* which causes total demand for money to change – because the other two demands do not change very much.

Not all economists agree with this analysis: some argue that the demand for money is really a 'demand for money to borrow' as we shall see in the short section on interest rate theories.

■ SUPPLY OF MONEY: HOW MONEY IS CREATED

Because money is a liability of the banking system – almost its sole liability, as we saw in the last chapter – one way of watching how money is created is to see how the contra items of the liabilities (the assets which are the counterpart of the increase in bank deposits) are created. Here we shall look at this process in outline; we go into it in more detail in Chapter 13. In brief, the banks' assets, and hence their liabilities, which approximate to their deposits, increase when people borrow from them. And the chief borrowers are you and me (and ICI!), the government and foreigners. Let us look at each in turn.

Private sector borrowing from the banks

This is when customers draw upon their loan accounts or increase their overdrafts to finance their spending. Most of the receipts from this expenditure will be paid into credit balances at various banks and the totals of these credit balances, which form part of the money supply, will rise accordingly. In the words of the old adage: 'Every loan creates a deposit.' The truth of this can be seen when a customer draws down the loan and his or her current account is credited with the proceeds.

Now, one bank cannot 'go it alone' and create new loans and deposits on its own because its customers will spend most of the loans with traders who bank with competitor banks. The result will be a tide of cheques presented by these banks at the clearing house, and the lending bank will see its operational deposit at the Bank of England being rapidly depleted to pay the other banks.

Fortunately, the causes of a rise in bank lending are not at the whim of a particular general manager who wants to increase his or her lending but result from a widespread perception that the economic and business outlook is sufficiently promising for increased lending to be permitted by the Bank of England. If the Bank wanted to check the rise in lending, it could signal its intention for interest rates to rise (*see* Chapter 13) and the rise in interest rates, which are the price of loans, should cause the demand for loans to contract.

But we must stress that it is the banking *system* which creates deposits by its increased lending rather than one bank 'going it alone'.

Government borrowing from the banks

If the government borrows money from a bank, whether by issuing a liquid Treasury bill or an illiquid gilt-edged security, it will spend the money (just as the private sector did) and the expenditure will flow to the banking system in the form of increased deposits. We have seen how one bank had about 14 per cent of its assets in liquid form: this core of liquid assets acts as a base on which banks in general can increase their lending.

Let us assume that the banking system's liquidity ratio was at the minimum level of 28 per cent in use from 1963 to 1971 and that the government issued extra Treasury bills to borrow money which it would spend on, say, aid to farmers. The banks would pay for the extra Treasury bills from their operational balances at the Bank of England, thus not affecting their deposits from the private sector. Money supply at this stage is unchanged. When the farmers' bank accounts were credited with the government aid, bank deposits would rise by the amount of this expenditure and liquid assets would rise by the increase in operational balances at the Bank of England. So, in the end, the money supply would rise by the increase in the farmers' bank deposits.

Now, if the increase in liquid assets was sufficient to raise the banks' liquidity ratios from 28 per cent (the minimum) to say 30%, some banks might feel confident enough to begin to increase their lending and to see a run-down in liquid assets as loans were paid over to banks which were not increasing their lending so rapidly. This lending causes a second-round increase in bank deposits, and thus in the money supply, in addition to the first-round effect described in the previous paragraph.

We must stress here that the government is outside the banking system so that payments to it reduce bank deposits (and liquid assets) until the government spends the money again. This it usually does, but see also Chapter 13.

Notice too that this section is headed 'government borrowing *from the banks*'. If the government borrows from you and me to pay the farmers more aid, all that happens is that our bank deposits fall when we lend the money and those of the farmers rise eventually. Money supply is unchanged.

External transactions

Since the end of exchange control in 1979 these have become not only massive but also very complicated. However, the sort of transaction which could increase sterling bank deposits of the UK private sector, i.e. the money supply, is a foreigner borrowing sterling in Paris (on the Euro-sterling market there) which is then lent to a UK resident who pays it into an account with a bank in London. Bank deposits and the money supply have both risen by the amount of the deposit. A surplus on the current account of the balance of payments will have an expansionary effect on the total of bank deposits as exporters acquire sterling with the foreign exchange they earn.

■ HOW MONEY IS NOT CREATED

This is called *disintermediation* and occurs when borrowers and lenders go direct to each other. If I lend you the money to buy this book, my bank account falls by the price of the book, yours rises (temporarily) and then the bookseller's rises. Money supply is unaffected but the sales of the book have risen.

Governments don't like disintermediation because economic activity can increase outside the control of the Bank of England. If the government wants to curtail this increase, which it may consider to be inflationary, it will have to go outside the banking system and use legislation.

■ INTEREST RATE THEORY

We saw, in Chapter 8, the wide spectrum of interest rates, some changing hourly on money and stock markets and others (the administered rates) changing far less frequently. Now we move into the realm of theory to see the ways in which economists argue that interest rates are determined.

Interest rates are one of the prices of money – strictly the price of borrowing it. Exchange rates are the other price of money – the price of buying it on the foreign exchange market. Later we shall see how interest rates and exchange rates are very closely connected.

'Real' theories

Here *real* means *non-monetary* and the interest rate acts as the price which clears the market for savings and capital investment. Savings are sometimes regarded as the supply of *loanable funds* and investment as the demand for these loanable funds to finance new construction, machinery and equipment. Such theories are often called 'loanable funds' theories.

Monetary theories

It was the great economist Keynes who drew people's attention to the three types of demand for money which we saw earlier in this chapter. He went on to argue that it is the liquidity preference of financial investors which determines the price of money (the rate of interest) and that it is the speculative demand for money which fluctuates considerably, unlike the transactions and precautionary demands. Supply is fixed by the authorities, i.e. the Bank of England and the Treasury, and does not depend on a flow of savings.

Neo-classical theories

Subsequent theorists have combined these two elements – the real and the monetary – into what are called IS-LM curves. These are diagrams very much like the scissors diagram of Chapter 2 but with different meanings. The IS curve shows the equilibrium rate of interest for the *real* market of capital investment (I) and savings (S) at various levels of output, while the LM curve shows the rate of interest which brings about equilibrium for the liquidity preference of financial investors (L) and the supply of money (M), also at various levels of output. We won't show the curves, because deriving them is quite complicated and you'll be relieved to know that you don't even need to study them for the Associateship examinations!

■ THE ROLE OF MONEY

Since the early 1960s the debate has become very heated between economists of opposing views about the effect of changes in the money stock on the rest of the economy. Immediately after the Second World War, most economists were convinced that the money supply was not very important.

At that time it was felt that the *Quantity Theory of Money*, outlined earlier this century by Irving Fisher, had been proved to be not an equation but merely an identity, valid for whatever numbers were inserted into it. The equation was:

$$MV = PT$$

where M was money supply;

       V was velocity of circulation, i.e. the number of times the money stock changed hands each year;

       P was the price level;

       T was the total of transactions (approximating to GDP in some cases) in real terms.

The equation, when expressed in words, reads that *the amount of money in an economy multiplied by the number of times it changed hands is equal to the real output of the economy times the price level.*

Opponents argued that M might change but V would probably move in the opposite direction: if M rose people wouldn't need the extra supply of M and so V would fall as people didn't bother to spend the extra M. So nothing would happen to P or T. Others argued that there was nothing in the equation which showed whether P or T would change in response to a rise in the left-hand side.

Monetarism

Headed by Professor Milton Friedman, the monetarists have argued in the second-half of this century that money does matter. First, they say that V remains constant – the technical phrase is that there is a stable demand function for money – so that changes in M *will* affect the right-hand side of the equation. Secondly, they say that an increase in M will affect T until the economy is fully employed, when P will begin to rise. In effect, therefore, there is a grave danger that increases in M will cause P to rise, because bottlenecks in production prevent T from rising immediately.

In short, the monetarists argue that the relationship between M and T (and P) is direct, because there is a wide range of goods and services on which the increase in M can be spent. To control P, the government should control M.

Keynesianism

Keynesians argue that the relationship between M and T is not direct but *indirect*. An increase in M will affect the rate of interest first, causing it to fall. This fall will stimulate capital investment which will have *multiplier effects* on GDP, i.e. T, as people are employed on construction work etc., spend their new incomes in the shops, which increase the shops' orders ... etc.

There is no stable demand for money, because demand for it depends largely on speculative motives, i.e. how people expect interest rates to change. Because costs, especially wages, are rigid, attempts to reduce inflation by reducing the money supply will fail. The government should seek to restrain the growth of wages and not the growth of the monetary aggregates.

ACTIVITY 10.2 •

Your branch has a French trainee banker attached for a week. She has asked you why UK retail banks have so many products for their customers, i.e. far more than French banks.

Outline your reply to her question.

ACTIVITY 10.3

Budget day is getting nearer – perhaps only weeks or days away. It's usually a Tuesday in March.

Find out the date and make a diary note to buy a copy of the *Financial Times* on the following day: it will give complete details of the Chancellor's speech and his proposals, together with a full commentary.

This will last you a whole year, so it's money well spent. By the time you sit Customer Services – Marketing and the Competitive Environment, the proposals will have become law (perhaps with some minor amendments) and may feature in your examination for that subject.

■ SUMMARY

1 Money is any asset generally acceptable in payment of debts.

2 Money has two *major functions*, as:

(a) a *medium of exchange*, facilitating specialisation;

(b) a *liquid store of value*, enabling saving (which is not spending) to be done by separate groups from those investing (spending extra).

Both functions result in extra output.

3 It has two *minor functions*, as:

(a) a *unit of account*, for accountancy and management;

(b) a *standard of deferred payments*, for financial and property contracts.

Again, both functions yield benefits to the community.

4 Its *qualities* – scarcity and stability, profitability, uniformity, durability, recognisability, acceptability, and divisibility – enable assets to function effectively as money. These *assets* are:

(a) bank notes and coin;

(b) bank deposits;

(c) building society deposits.

5 *Narrow money* comprises those assets used primarily as a medium of exchange.

6 *Broad money* comprises narrow money and those assets used primarily as a liquid store of value.

7 *Quasi money* is a term used to describe those assets which function mainly as a liquid store of value.

8 *Money supply* statistics generally exclude money holdings of:

(a) banks and building societies;

(b) government;

(c) overseas residents.

9 At present there are three principal *monetary aggregates:*

(a) M0: notes and coin in use, plus banks' operational balances at the Bank of England.

(b) M2: comprises mainly non-interest-bearing deposits and those interest-bearing bank and building society deposits which are considered to be retail – less than £100,000 and able to be encashed within one month. Notes and coin are, of course, included.

(c) M4: which is the principal measure of broad money. It comprises notes and coin plus all UK private sector sterling deposits of banks and building societies.

10 The *demand for money* comprises:

(a) transactions demand – for day-to-day spending;

(b) precautionary demand – for emergencies and the future;

both of which are stable, and

(c) speculative demand – to escape losses on fixed-interest securities when interest rates rise – which is very unstable.

11 Another theory says that the demand for money is for money to borrow.

12 The *supply of money* comes from:

(a) bank and building society lending (every loan creates a deposit);

(b) government borrowing from banks in order to finance its expenditure;

(c) a surplus on the current account of the balance of payments, as exporters seek sterling in exchange for their foreign currency.

13 *Interest rate theories* are of three groups:

(a) *Real* – loanable funds, where the rate of interest is the price equating the demand for money to borrow for new projects, etc. with the supply of loanable funds.

(b) *Monetary* – Keynesian, where the demand for money is largely the speculative demand from financiers, seeking to avoid losses when interest rates rise, and the supply of money is fixed by the government.

(c) The neo-classicists, seeking to combine the above theories into a complicated equilibrium of both the real and the monetary markets.

14 The impact of *monetary changes* on the economy is just as disputed. The *monetarists* argue that the relationship between M and P and/or T is *direct*, arising from actual expenditure. *Keynesians* argue that the relationship is *indirect*, with changes in the quantity of money affecting first the rate of interest. In turn the new rate of interest affects spending on new projects etc.

■ SELF-ASSESSMENT QUESTIONS

1 Why don't banks pay interest on all their deposit liabilities?

2 List the components of M0. How many of them, if any, earn interest for their holders?

3 Why do building societies pay interest on all their shares and deposits?

4 What are the capital goods industries and why do they experience severe recessions?

5 What is meant by the term 'barometric price leadership? Why is the Cheltenham and Gloucester Building Society's Gold Account a good example of it?

6 'It is essentially the status of the lender rather than the method of borrowing which determines the impact of government borrowing on the money supply.' Explain.

7 Read the April issue of *Banking World* to learn which monetary aggregates (if any) the government is targeting.

8 What are the principal types of financial intermediaries in the UK?

9 Why did M4 become an increasingly important monetary aggregate after an Act passed in 1986?

10 Why aren't cheques considered to be money?

11 What are the unique features of the discount market compared to the other wholesale money markets?

12 Name the two opposing theories concerning interest rates.

13 Why aren't insurance *brokers* and estate agents considered by economists to be financial intermediaries?

14 If these two groups are not financial intermediaries then why are so many financial intermediaries seeking to expand into the groups' areas of business?

15 In what sense are banks a unique type of financial intermediary? Do building societies perform a similar role?

16 What are the qualities needed by assets if they are to be used as money?

17 What is meant by the term 'disintermediation'? Why are the inter-company market and the sterling commercial paper market examples of disintermediation?

18 Why are there so many rates of interest in a country such as the UK?

19 What are the two major functions of money?

20 To what extent, if any, are some of the banks' deposit liabilities considered to be quasi-money rather than full money?

11 International trade and the balance of payments

OBJECTIVES

When you have studied this chapter, you should be able to:

1 Understand why international trade occurs;
2 Appreciate how important it can be in our daily lives and for our banks;
3 Be aware of some of the problems involved, how governments tackle these problems and how the banks may be involved;
4 Understand how nations account for their international transactions (the balance of payments);
5 Place transactions in the correct section of a balance of payments;
6 Be aware of how the various sections of a balance of payments finance one another, so that there is an overall bookkeeping balance;
7 Demonstrate how governments try to correct surpluses and deficits within the total balance of payments and how banks may be involved.

■ INTRODUCTION

To appreciate the importance of international trade in our everyday lives we should perhaps walk down our local high street, or just look at the goods in our living rooms. In the greengrocers, there may be French apples and Egyptian potatoes, as well as bananas, oranges and lemons from tropical and semi-tropical countries. At home, the chances are that the TV, hi-fi/video, Walkman and camera are all imported.

Away from the High Street, great changes have been taking place. The UK is now a net exporter not only of crude oil (thanks to the North Sea) but also of cereals (thanks to the high prices of the European Community's Common Agricultural Policy). In the North-East of England, some of the old coal staithes (wharves) are now used to load grain, following the decline of our coal exports.

We asked a bank manager how much of his business was based on international trade. He thought for a while and replied: about 30 per cent. The question that should now spring to your minds is: What sort of branch did he manage? His branch was in a large suburb of Greater London, with little manufacturing industry.

■ WHY TRADE?

The short answer may be: because we all specialise in one way or another and

142

the division of labour is worldwide. However, such a bald statement will not earn many marks from an examiner or even from our supervisor at work. We must be more constructive and try to show how it can be beneficial for a country to produce *less* of one commodity in return for producing *more* of another.

Economists love to make assumptions and international trade theory abounds with them. Some assumptions are open or declared, others are hidden. We shall state the open ones first, spend some time outlining the theory and then return to the hidden assumptions.

The *open assumptions* are: two countries, two commodities, complete mobility of factors of production and no transport costs.

The theory of comparative advantage
Stage 1

We begin by showing the output of the two commodities in each country produced by a fixed combination of factors of production, with no trade taking place. (*See* Table 11.1.)

Table 11.1

	Redland	Blueland	Total output
Motor cars	300	400	700
Wheat	500	100	600

It should be seen that, using the same combination of factors of production, Redland is more efficient at wheat growing and that Blueland is more efficient at making cars.

Let them each specialise, with Redland transferring the factors of production from motor cars to wheat so that it now produces 1000 tonnes of wheat and no cars; Blueland switches factors in the reverse direction, ceasing to produce wheat and increasing motor car production to 800. As a result, there are an extra 400 tonnes of wheat and another 100 motor cars for the inhabitants of both countries to enjoy. (*See* Table 11.2.)

Table 11.2

	Redland	Blueland	Total output	Extra output
Motor cars		800	800	100
Tonnes of wheat	1000		1000	400

Each country specialises in producing the product in which it has the greater advantage, i.e. is more efficient.

Stage 2

The interesting feature of the theory occurs when one country is more efficient at producing *both* commodities than the other. Is it really worthwhile specialising? Let's try another example. This time our table (Table 11.3) will show the production as output *per unit of factor of production* combined in a fixed way (a 'bundle' of factors). In other words, we are featuring *productivity* rather

Table 11.3

Per factor bundle	Redland	Blueland
Motor cars	50	20
Wheat (tonnes)	40	30

than total output. Redland produces more of both commodities per 'bundle'.

If we transfer three 'factor bundles' in Redland from wheat to motor cars then motor car will rise by 3 x 50 = 150 cars, and wheat output will fall by 3 x 40 = 120 bushels.

We can then obtain these 120 tonnes of wheat by transferring four 'factor bundles' in Blueland from car production to wheat. Each bundle – and there are four of them – produces 30 bushels of wheat or 20 cars, so we get our 120 tonnes of wheat (4 x 30) by sacrificing the output of 80 (4 x 20) cars in Blueland. But we have an extra 150 cars from Redland, so that total output is an extra 70 (150–80) cars. *Each country specialises in the production of the good in which it has the greater comparative advantage.*

Redland specialises in car production, at which it is more than twice as efficient as Blueland, which specialises in wheat, where it is at a smaller disadvantage than Redland, which is only one third more efficient than Blueland. In our example, the countries do not specialise *entirely*, which makes it much more like the real world.

The problem is then to find buyers for the 70 cars, or to use the surplus factors to produce something else instead of the 70 cars. But what happens if those factors cannot produce anything else? This is answered in the next paragraph.

Hidden assumptions

We have now discovered one of the hidden assumptions, i.e. that *all factors of production are fully employed* and are likely to be fully employed. When there is not full employment the opportunity cost of producing wheat is not the cars forgone, but zero. With over 2.7m people unemployed in the UK in May 1992, we know only too well that this assumption is not valid.

Other hidden assumptions include the *possibility for all the extra output to be sold profitably either at home or in the other country*. There may not be the markets for profitable sales, so goods are sold for less than total cost, i.e. at a loss. When such surplus output is exported and sold at a loss, 'dumping' is said to occur.

Another hidden assumption is that *prices (including exchange rates) are very flexible*, so that they adjust rapidly to the new levels of output. But we know that prices are often slow to change, partly because of the slopes of the demand and supply curves, but also because of price agreements, including fixed exchange rates under the European Monetary System and during the 'Bretton Woods era' from 1948 to the early 1970s. These are discussed in the next chapter.

Next, the assumption of *complete factor mobility* within a country is unreal. Not only is it difficult to switch rapidly to producing an entirely different product but the cost schedules are unlikely to be rigid and cost curves more likely to be quite steep so that the ratio of one car to four bushels of wheat quickly changes to complicate the examples even further. In economists' jargon, there are no constant returns to scale.

Moreover, the supply and demand curves for cars and other manufactured goods are frequently more elastic than those for wheat and other foods and raw materials. This means that (say) a 5 per cent change in the output of cars will be accompanied by a less than 5 per cent change in their price, whereas a 5 per cent change in the output of food will result in a price change of more than 5 per cent.

Finally, the assumption that there are *no transport costs* is unreal. For instance, although the UK can manufacture cement more cheaply than Nigeria, the cost of shipping it (the 'freight') is very high. So, the UK does not export much cement to Nigeria.

ACTIVITY 11.1

Find out how many of your friends drive (a) British-built cars; (b) foreign-built cars. Take care – many Fords, for example, are built overseas, while some Nissans are built in Sunderland!

■ SOME PROBLEMS OF INTERNATIONAL TRADE

Theory may teach us that international specialisation leads to increased output but the practical constraints often result in this specialisation not being implemented to its fullest extent.

Unemployment caused by 'unfair competition' from overseas is seen as a very real problem by domestic manufacturers and their governments. Wages in many developing or Third World countries are much lower than in the industrialised West and so 'cheap' imports such as textiles, shoes and other manufactured goods from the Third World cause great concern to established manufacturers in the industrialised countries. We are all too aware how the UK motor manufacturing industry has declined in the face of competition from Japan. There are benefits from buying these cheaper articles, as we have seen, but the costs involved in contracting our existing industries may outweigh, in the eyes of the government, the gains from international trade.

We have mentioned how manufactured goods may have price elastic demand and supply curves, so that changes in output tend to be greater than price changes. This means that there may be problems of over- and under-capacity in the leading industrial nations. For food and raw materials, supply and demand tend to be price inelastic so that price changes are more violent than output changes – and output can fluctuate quite significantly with good and bad harvests as well as labour and technical problems in the mines.

Then there are tariffs (taxes on imports), which can be imposed to raise revenue for governments, or to protect domestic industry or in retaliation for a country failing to curtail exports. They act in much the same way as an additional transport cost and are a source of concern to all parties involved – exporters seeking to have them lowered by importing countries, and domestic competitors fearing their reduction by their own government and seeking to maintain them or even raise them.

Next are the problems of differing standards. To give some instances: different voltages are used in different countries for domestic electrical goods, some countries still drive on the left, while differing amounts of lead are permitted by countries in goods such as petrol and toys.

Immigration controls, i.e. on the import of labour, one of the three factors of production, are sometimes very important. Another problem with labour is that many immigrants have difficulty in learning a new language.

Exchange rates can be manipulated by governments – down to help exports and up, to keep down the price of imports for their political supporters.

Finally, there is national security. No large country welcomes the thought of being totally dependent on foreign countries for the supply of armaments, computers and other essential equipment.

More barriers imposed by government

Apart from tariffs, there are other ways in which governments can impede the free flow of goods.

1 *Quotas*, which set a limit on the number or total value of the articles of the relevant commodity imported during a specific month, quarter or year. Because the quantity is restricted, the importer or exporting manufacturer can raise the price in order to contract the demand, shifting the supply curve upwards, as we saw in Chapter 3.

2 *Quality legislation* can be devised to deter imports, e.g. by requiring motor vehicle engines to emit very low quantities of exhaust, so that countries which do not have such rigid requirements for their home markets will find it expensive to make the necessary alterations to their exports. The UK imposes stringent restrictions on the import of liquid and UHT milk.

3 *Voluntary export restraints* (VERs), whereby the exporting country voluntarily agrees to restrict its exports of a particular commodity to a particular country for a limited time. The attraction for the exporter is mainly this limited time, because it means that the VER will be reviewed in a very short time, unlike a tariff which is likely to be imposed indefinitely. There is another attraction: the restriction on the quantity will enable the price to be raised.

4 *Import deposits*, which require importers to lodge a very large deposit in domestic currency with a bank before an import licence is granted. The deposit can be as high as 150 per cent of the invoice value.

5 *Exchange controls.* These are restrictions on the amount of money (in domestic and foreign currency) which may be taken in or out of a country and they are imposed not only on individual travellers but on all companies, partnerships and bodies seeking to remit funds into or out of a country. They usually extend not only to payments and receipts for goods but also for services and the remittance of interest, profits and dividends. Even if such *current transactions* are

exempt from exchange control, there may be restrictions on the movement of capital, e.g. for the purchase/sale of shares and land. The UK abolished nearly all exchange controls in 1979 and the Exchange Control Act of 1947 was repealed in May 1987. Most EC countries have abolished exchange controls, and Greece and Portugal should have done so by the end of 1993.

Commercial banks were intricately involved in administering exchange control in the UK, as agents for the Bank of England. Even now, our bankers must be aware of other countries' exchange control regulations because, while it may be easy to remit funds from the UK to a country to buy an asset, it may be very difficult to bring the sale proceeds back to this country.

How these problems are overcome

At the end of the Second World War, many countries signed the General Agreement on Tariffs and Trade (GATT) which regulates trade in manufactured goods between the countries concerned. In 1987 talks began in Uruguay to extend the GATT's provisions to trade in agricultural goods (such as wheat, palm oil, coffee, cocoa, sugar and tea) and services (such as banking and insurance). The 'Uruguay round' includes negotiations on quotas and quality legislation. In its title, GATT recognises the existence or the inevitability of tariffs but it has achieved a series of negotiated reductions in tariff levels since 1945. Also at the end of the Second World War, the International Monetary Fund was set up to provide exchange rate stability. You will study the IMF in slightly more detail for the Associateship examinations but you should be aware here that it seeks to eliminate exchange controls and artificially high or low exchange rates.

The next development is confined mainly to Europe. It is, of course, the European Community which comprises Germany, France, Italy, the Netherlands, Belgium, Luxembourg, the UK, Ireland, Denmark, Greece, Spain and Portugal. Austria, Finland and Sweden have applied to join, and they are likely to become full members by the end of the century, long before countries such as Czechoslovakia, Hungary and Poland have joined.

The Community aims at political and economic integration of its member countries and, to this end, it has established a common external tariff which is levied on imports from outside the Community. Tariffs on trade *between* the members are being eliminated. By 31 December 1992, the Community plans to eliminate all non-tariff barriers to trade between its 12 member states – such as restrictions on employment, the movement of capital and people and setting up businesses across the boundaries of its members. This is the Single Market, of which we hear so much.

The influence of the Community extends to 66 countries in Africa, the Caribbean and the Pacific (the ACP countries), most of which were colonies when the Community was established in 1958. These ACP countries have certain privileges in their trade with the Community.

By the end of the century, most EC countries plan to have a single currency, as well a making substantial progress towards political union. The UK, however, has serious doubts about these plans.

Where do the banks fit in?

Because nearly every country in the world has its own currency, international trade usually involves the exchange via banks of one currency for another, since the exporter can do little with the importer's currency except sell it for his or her own. The exporting firm *sells* foreign currency to its bank, which *buys* it. With imports, the roles are reversed, with the banks *selling* the foreign currency to the importer.

However, after about 1975, the amount of trade conducted under barter arrangements (counter-trade is another word for it) increased and many large banks now have specialised barter and counter-trade sections to act as go-betweens and handle the documents.

Also, because the parties are usually far apart, so that the paperwork and the actual goods do not arrive together at the destination, the banks and traders have devised special products to facilitate international trade. These include documentary credits, bills of exchange, the negotiation of bills and cheques denominated in foreign currency and the collection of such bills and cheques. *Negotiation* means that the payee (the exporter) is credited with the proceeds forthwith, subject to being debited if the cheque/bill is dishonoured; *cheques for collection* are not credited to the payees' accounts until the collecting bank is satisfied that they have been paid by the bank on which they are drawn. Obviously, the charges for negotiations are higher than for collections.

International tourism is becoming increasingly important and products such as foreign currency tills (bureaux de change), travellers' cheques and Eurocheques have been created to help tourists.

The banks benefit from these products in that not all are balance-sheet based, i.e. they do not involve assets, which require funding from deposits and which are based upon part of a bank's capital. They all generate fees and commissions (non-funds-based income) featuring only in the profit and loss account, as we saw in Chapter 9. Nevertheless, although they do not use scarce deposits or capital resources, they do require the use of skilled and expensive personnel and premises.

Some of the banks' products for international trade do involve their balance sheets – for instance, loans.

(For a more detailed account of international trade products, see the author's *Banking: The Business*, Pitman, 1990 pp. 175–180.)

■ THE BALANCE OF PAYMENTS

Most countries publish statistics showing their *balance of international payments*. However, a word of warning is necessary because the statistics are more like a profit and loss or trading account than a balance sheet. You will remember from your studies of accounts that a balance sheet resembles a photograph taken on one special day whereas a trading or profit and loss account records the flows of transactions over a year or a quarter. A balance of payments records all transactions between one country and the rest of the world over a year or a quarter.

What does it comprise?

In short, every transaction between that country and the rest of the world is included, under one of several main classifications.

Visibles

Merchandise (visible) trade is very closely controlled by each country's customs authorities and so the visible trade statistics are often the most readily available section of a country's balance of payments. Another word of caution: the balance of payments is also a balance of payments *and receipts*. So, we need two columns: one for receipts (from exports) and a second for payments (for imports).

Unfortunately, the customs officers are only really interested in the values of goods as they cross borders, not in how much it will cost Ford to ship a consignment of cars to (say) Norway or in how much has been paid in insurance premiums. However, economists are interested in these payments partly because the freight and insurance charges increase the cars' cost to the Norwegian buyers and hence the total value of cars sold to Norway. More important, however, is the need to know how much we are paying foreigners for freight, insurance, etc., and how much they are paying us for these items.

When we come to look at the figures for our visible imports, however, we find that the customs statistics *include* the freight, insurance and handling charges. In short, exports are shown *free on board* (fob) and imports are shown including *cost, insurance and freight* (cif). Accordingly, the imports are adjusted to a fob basis. This allows us to obtain a more accurate figure for insurance and transport by excluding them from the figures for *all* merchandise trade.

Free on board includes the cost of manufacturing and transporting the item to the port, e.g. fob Bristol. But cif Bristol, for an import, includes manufacturing, transporting (the 'freight') and insuring the item for the voyage to Bristol.

As we have just seen, both exports and imports are shown fob. We use the two sets of figures to reach *the balance of visible trade*, which can be either a surplus or a deficit. Rarely is it zero.

Invisibles

These comprise current – day-to-day – commercial transactions, apart from merchandise trade. There are three main categories: services, IPD and transfers.

1 *Services*, such as insurance, shipping, airlines, and road and rail haulage, are part of what are termed *invisible trade*. They also include banking, authors' royalties, fees from TV programmes transmitted overseas and, especially, receipts from foreign tourists.

2 *Interest, profits and dividends (IPD)* are another very important section of invisible transactions. This item is traditionally very much in the UK's favour but for some countries, heavily in debt to foreign banks, governments and private investors, the net figure for IPD can be a substantial payment.

Moreover, if much of the debt is expressed in US dollars and subject to variable interest rates, a rise in US interest rates can cause the net payment to rise. 3 *Transfers* include official payments and receipts for forces stationed overseas, embassies abroad, famine relief and, for the UK since 1973, to and from the European Commission in respect of the EC budget. For the UK, the total is invariably a deficit. Transfers also include private transfers to and from relatives and friends abroad. These, too, are a net deficit for the UK although much smaller than that for official transfers. *Emigrant workers' remittances* are very important private transfers for some countries, e.g. Italy, Egypt and Lesotho, whose workers emigrate to other countries to find work.

Current account

All the visibles and invisible receipts and payments are totalled to reach the *current account of the balance of payments*. The balance on this account – surplus or deficit; large or small – indicates the financial position of the country concerned on day-to-day transactions.

The current account does not include items of a capital nature, which are shown in a separate section of the balance of payments. Let us compile a balance of payments on current account of an imaginary country, Gardenia (*see* Table 11.4).

Table 11.4 Current account of the balance of payments

	$m
Exports fob	+3500
Imports fob	−4000
Visible balance	−500
Insurance, banking, shipping (net)	−100
Tourism (net)	+600
Services (net)	+500
Interest, profits, dividends (net)	−200
Emigrants' remittances and other transfers	+100
Current account	−100

Gardenia has a visible deficit of $500m, an invisible surplus of $400m, giving it a deficit on current account of $100m. Why, you may (or should) ask, do we use dollars, rather than the Gardenia slug, as the unit of account? Well, if we used a little known currency such as the Gardenia slug, we would have difficulty in comparing Gardenia with other countries, so the IMF compiles balance-of-payments data in dollars as an international unit of account, facilitating comparisons.

You may wonder why the Gardenian current account is in deficit when we are talking about a *balance* of payments. Can there be a deficit? The answer is that there can be – indeed there is likely to be – a surplus or deficit on the current account but that it will be offset exactly by the rest of the balance of payments. The debits and credits should be exactly equal and, moreover, there is even a section for 'unrecorded items' for that part of the changes in assets and liabilities which cannot be explained by reference to other transactions. This is the 'balancing item'.

External assets and liabilities

These are transactions which are not connected with goods, services and income from investments and which, for the UK, used to be known as the *capital account*. The items – the external assets and liabilities – which comprised the capital account are quite wide-ranging but we can indicate three major categories:

(a) *direct investment* in the form of houses, shops, factories, warehouses etc.;
(b) *portfolio investment*, comprising stocks and shares;
(c) *loans*: most are bank loans, but loans made by companies to other companies are also included.

When UK residents buy an asset abroad from an overseas resident they can pay for it in one or more of three ways:

1 In cash: in which case the UK's gold and foreign exchange reserves will fall by the amount of the purchase price.
2 They can borrow some of the purchase price: in which case the reserves fall by the amount of the deposit paid and the remainder of the asset is financed by the increase in liabilities when the buyers actually borrow the money. Any income from the asset will be used to pay interest on the loan. The income and the loan interest appear in the invisibles section of the current account: the loan drawdown and repayments are part of the capital account. However, the interest payments and capital repayments are added together to obtain the figure for *debt service*.
3 They can, if they are companies, issue shares to overseas residents in exchange for the assets, in which case the UK's assets rise when the new asset is acquired, while the UK's liabilities rise as a result of the shares issued to buy the asset.

Table 11.5

	$m	
Current account	−100	
Capital account	+200	
Overall balance	+100	
Change in official reserves	−100	− = increase in a real account
	NIL	

When we add the current account balance to the capital account we should obtain a figure which is equal to, but opposite in sign to, any change in the country's stock of foreign money (more correctly, its official holdings of gold and foreign exchange).

Let us return to Gardenia which, because it is so pleasant, attracts considerable foreign investment. Table 11.5 shows the rest of the imaginary balance of payments.

The signs are a little confusing at this stage but, because a cash balance is a real account, adding an item (debit) to a real account means that the balance of the real account increases ('credit the current account – debit cash' was how we recited it as bank clerks to record the entries when current account customers deposited cash).[1]

How does it balance?

The abrupt answer is: every debit has a credit, so it must balance. In practice, the surpluses and deficits in the various sections finance and offset each other. If there is a surplus on the current account, there should be a corresponding deficit on the capital account or a rise in the official reserves. A capital account deficit means that a country is investing abroad: which is fine until other countries become tired of selling their assets to the investors from the country with a current-account surplus.

Let's look at things slightly differently. If there is a surplus on the current account, funds are flowing into the country as more goods and services flow out than flow in, on balance. These flows of funds could be gold and foreign exchange or they could be shares, loan certificates and deeds to properties, i.e. portfolio and direct investments. In other words, a current account surplus leads to an increase in external assets.

When there is a deficit on the current account, there will be a decrease in assets, which are sold to finance the excess of imports of goods and services. Gold, foreign exchange, share certificates and deeds leave the country.

In the early 1990s, only Japan has a large surplus on its current account and is investing abroad: the USA has a very large current account deficit and is borrowing heavily; following re-unification, Germany has a large deficit, although it has a surplus on visible trade. Following the development of North Sea oil the UK had substantial surpluses on its current account and made significant investments abroad but in 1986 the surplus became a deficit. We now have problems restraining imports and expanding exports. We may have problems later when we have run down our assets to finance these deficits, or when the economy begins to expand again.

Why do problems arise?

Briefly, the problems occur because it is difficult to achieve and manage change. For example, if the visible trade balance is in substantial deficit and the invisibles and the capital account are unable to provide sufficient surpluses, the strain is taken on the official reserves of gold and foreign exchange. These are limited and so, eventually, the balance of trade must be restored to

[1] Readers seeking further explanation should see Karl Harper, *Introduction to Accounting*, Pitman 1990 pp. 20–21.

equilibrium. Export receipts must be increased and/or import payments decreased.

Because total revenue equals price times quantity, policy makers must increase export sales without dropping prices too far in order that total revenue is raised as much as possible. Similarly, import volumes must be lowered, without prices rising so much that total import payments rise. It may be very difficult to increase export volumes – factories, farms and mines may be producing at full capacity already – while import cutbacks may be politically disastrous if consumers are unwilling to accept substantial reductions in imports of essential goods. Also, many countries depend on imports of spares and machinery to keep their farms, factories, mines and road vehicles operating.

Another type of problem occurs when the country faces a high level of *debt service* which, as we have seen, comprises the repayment on capital account of loans received in the past together with the payment on current account of interest charged on these loans. In such cases, any surplus on visible trade and on the remainder of the current account and the limited official reserves are unable to finance the debt service and the country has to ask its lenders for the debt to be 'rescheduled' (postponed). This, in essence, is what is called the *world debt problem*.

ACTIVITY 11.2

Towards the end of each month, the UK's merchandise export and import figures are published, together with a rough estimate of net invisibles, thus providing an estimate for the current account.

Write each monthly current account estimate in your diary. Is it falling, stationary or rising?

Multiply this monthly figure by 12 to give a very crude annual estimate. Is this annual figure below £10bn? Is it below £5bn?

How can a current account deficit be financed?

There are various ways, most of which can be used at the same time.

1 The country can *run down its reserves*.

2 The country can *sell* some of its *overseas assets*: factories, shares and houses which its citizens own in other countries.

3 The country can *borrow* from:

(a) the *IMF*, under one of its many facilities, but the more a country borrows from the Fund under nearly all its facilities, the greater the conditions the IMF imposes on it;
(b) *commercial banks*, although since 1982 this source of finance has become much less common;
(c) *foreign governments*, in the form of export credits or loans;
(d) its *suppliers*, in the form of extended trade credit (Nigeria financed much of its deficits in this way);
(e) *foreign central banks*, as the UK did in the 1960s.

Such borrowing increases the country's liabilities, i.e. its obligations. This increase in liabilities, when added to the country's assets, will mean that its *net* assets – after allowing for liabilities – will fall.

4 The country can *sell* some of its *domestic assets*, as the UK has been doing since the mid-1980s. Not only can shares in privatised industries be sold to foreign investors, but also whole companies. For instance, Nestlés, the Swiss chocolate manufacturers, bought Rowntrees in 1988. Also, in the run-up to 1992, foreign banks are buying UK banks, as mentioned later in this chapter. Sales of domestic assets to foreigners, as with sales of foreign assets, result in a flow of money *into* the country selling the assets.

How can a current account deficit be corrected?

Correcting a deficit is more difficult than financing it because it involves a change of policy by the government.

1 *Foreign exchange receipts must be increased.* If export demand is price elastic, then a small fall in the price of exports should result in a large increase in the quantities sold, so that total revenue is greater at the new price. However, there must be sufficient spare capacity for the exporters to increase the quantity sold quite rapidly; if not, supplies will have to be switched from the home market and that could cause domestic prices to rise. It should also be remembered that invisible exports should also be increased.

Export promotion schemes, exhortation, and export finance facilities will all help but the general, across-the-board way to increase foreign exchange revenues is to devalue the currency. However, a 10 per cent fall in export prices means (arithmetically) an 11.1 per cent rise in import prices (100 to 90 is a 10 per cent fall from 100 but 100 to 111.1 (100/90 x 100) is an 11.1 per cent rise). And this brings us to the next way of correcting a deficit.

2 *Foreign exchange payments must be reduced.* This is far more easily achieved administratively than is an increase in export receipts. Import licences, tariffs, quotas, import deposits and exchange controls can all be imposed overnight, provided the civil service can operate them and smuggling and evasion are not possible. There are quite a number of international agreements which prevent their widespread use, the GATT being perhaps the best known.

3 So, we are left with *devaluation of the exchange rate*, but this can have severe inflationary effects, particularly if the export drive diverts goods away from the home market. If the demand for imports is price elastic, the total import payments will be greater at the lower domestic price (the earlier one), thus achieving a saving in foreign exchange. In view of the inflationary effect of a lower exchange rate, largely as a result of rising import prices in other domestic currency, devaluation is invariably accompanied by *anti-inflationary policies*, such as higher interest rates and credit controls.

Economists have a rule of thumb for estimating the effectiveness of a devaluation. If the average of the price elasticities of demand for imports and exports is greater than 1 then the devaluation will be successful. Let's examine this a little more closely:

If export demand is price elastic then it could be	1.20
If import demand is price elastic then it could be	1.10
The average is then	1.15

However, if import demand is very price inelastic (say 0.7) then it may outweigh the 1.2 export elasticity to give an average of 0.95. And if both demands are price inelastic then by definition a devaluation will not increase net foreign exchange receipts.

■ THE UK'S RECENT EXPERIENCE

Traditionally, the UK always runs a deficit on its visible trade balance, with a surplus on its invisibles which may or may not offset this deficit: thus the current account has varied between a deficit and a surplus. However, North Sea oil coming on stream in the late 1970s, when oil prices were historically high, caused the trade balance to become a substantial surplus for the three years 1980–82, averaging £2.3bn a year with a peak of £3.45bn in 1981. Since then, oil prices have fallen and by 1986 the visible trade deficit was £9.5bn. In 1989 it was a large £24.6bn, largely because imports rose faster than exports, as can be seen in Table 11.6. By 1991, it had fallen to £10.1bn.

Worse still, the traditional surplus on invisibles had fallen substantially by the end of 1990, partly as a result of larger net transfers to European Community institutions but also because the UK had borrowed so heavily to finance its current account deficits since 1987. This meant that net IPD began to fall.

Table 11.6 UK current account (£bn)

	1987	1988	1989	1990	1991
Exports fob	79.2	80.4	92.4	102.0	103.7
Imports fob	90.8	102.0	117.0	120.6	113.8
Visible balance	−11.6	−21.6	−24.6	−18.6	−10.1
Services (net)	6.7	4.6	4.7	4.9	5.5
IPD (net)	4.1	5.0	4.1	3.2	1.6
Transfers (net)	−3.4	−3.5	−4.6	−4.9	−1.3
Invisible balance	7.4	6.1	4.2	3.2	5.7
Current account	−4.2	−15.5	−20.4	−15.4	−4.4

In 1987 the presentation of the capital account was changed substantially. It is now called *transactions in UK external assets and liabilities* and includes changes in our official reserves, which are assets of course. The *balancing item* is frequently a large and growing unrecorded surplus (see Table 11.7).

The points to stress about this table are:
(a) see and understand how the pieces of the jigsaw fit together;
(b) have some idea of how large the items are: e.g. exports, imports, borrowing from overseas and loans to overseas are very large;

Table 11.7 Transactions in external assets and liabilities (£bn)

	1987	1988	1989	1990	1991
Outward investment (assets)					
Direct	−19.2	−20.8	−21.5	−8.9	−9.8
Portfolio	−7.2	−8.6	−31.3	−12.2	−29.1
UK loans to overseas					
borrowers	−50.4	−19.5	−27.0	−39.5	+32.7
Other lending					
overseas, etc.	−5.2	−3.7	−8.8	−12.1	−10.3
Change in official					
reserves	−12.0	−2.8	5.4	−0.1	−2.7
Total	−79.6	−55.4	−83.2	−79.8	−19.2
Inward investment (liabilities)					
Direct	8.5	10.2	17.2	19.0	12.0
Portfolio	19.2	14.4	13.2	5.0	19.5
Bank borrowing from					
overseas	52.6	34.2	43.9	47.4	−23.7
Other borrowing from					
overseas	5.1	6.3	21.8	16.1	20.2
Total	85.4	65.1	96.1	87.5	28.0
Net transactions	5.8	9.7	12.9	13.7	8.8
Balancing item	−1.6	5.8	7.5	1.7	−4.4
Current account balance	−4.2	−15.5	−20.4	−15.4	−4.4

(c) do not remember the exact numbers, just the signs. A minus indicates an outflow of funds or an increase in an asset: a plus denotes an inflow of funds or an increase in a liability. In any case, most of the numbers will surely change at the next revision, but most of the signs will not.

ACTIVITY 11.3 *

Demonstrate the immediate effect on the UK's balance of payments when the UK:

1 sells exports for

(a) cash;
(b) a loan from one of its banks to the importer;
(c) a loan from a bank located overseas to the exporter;

2 sells shareholdings in foreign currencies.

■ WHERE DO THE BANKS FIT IN?

In short, they fit nearly everywhere, because the balance of payments is concerned with finance and not just goods. Banks will be concerned with:
1 *facilitating all the payments and receipts* – via SWIFT, letters of credit, collections, travellers' cheques, Eurocheques and credit cards, to name but a few products;
2 *earning foreign exchange* in the invisibles section of the current account, from

dividends from overseas subsidiaries, commissions on letters of credit, fees from company dividend payments and the net interest received (after deducting interest paid) on overseas loans;

3 *making capital investments*, e.g. when Deutsche Bank bought the UK merchant bank of Morgan Grenfell in 1989 and National Australia Bank bought Yorkshire Bank in 1990.

The problem for most bank employees in the UK is that in the provinces and London suburbs the foreign desk is not highly regarded in the promotion ladder and most ambitious people avoid it. However, in the City of London, foreign business provides an attractive and rewarding career for able and ambitious bankers.

■ SUMMARY

1 International trade brings us the benefits of worldwide specialisation. The theory of international trade is that countries will specialise in the production of those goods and services in which:

(a) they have the greatest *comparative* advantage, or
(b) least comparative disadvantage.

2 There are a number of assumptions:

(a) full employment of all factors of production;
(b) ability to sell all extra output;
(c) flexible prices and exchange rates;
(d) complete mobility of factors of production;
(e) no transport costs.

3 Problems arise with international trade not only because these assumptions are not always true but because:

(a) governments impose tariffs, quotas and a whole range of other *non-tariff barriers*;
(b) demand for manufactured goods is often more price elastic than demand for raw materials;
(c) governments have differing safety standards;
(d) governments impose immigration controls;
(e) governments are concerned about national security;
(f) governments impose exchange controls;
(g) immigrants often have language difficulties in their new countries.

4 Governments are working to eliminate many of the barriers through the GATT, IMF and regional groupings. The European Community is the leading example of 12 countries working towards a single market in 1992 and then economic and monetary union. Political union, too, is likely later.

5 Banks are concerned with international trade because currency must be exchanged, and finance provided between manufacture and delivery of the goods.

6 The *balance of payments* measures all international trade and financial flows between one country and the rest of the world.

7 Because every debit has a corresponding credit, the overall balance of payments must balance but various sections often have substantial deficits or surpluses. The various sections are:

(a) visible (merchandise) trade = exports fob minus imports fob;
(b) invisibles, comprising:

- services;
- interest, profits, dividends (IPD);
- transfers.

Together these form the *current account*.

8 The next two items, added together, should equal the current account balance numerically, but with an opposite sign:

(1) Net transactions in assets/liabilities overseas comprising;

- Direct investment – buildings etc;
- Portfolio investment – financial stocks and ordinary shares;
- Loans to/from overseas;

(2) The balancing item.

9 *Debt service* comprises interest paid overseas on the current account plus repayments of loan capital in the assets section.

10 Debt service is a great problem for developing countries faced with poor export receipts and increasing payments of interest as world interest rates rise.

11 A country can *finance* a current account deficit by:

(a) selling assets – including foreign exchange;
(b) increasing liabilities – by borrowing abroad.

In both cases *net assets fall*.

12 Problems arise when governments try to change a country's economic policy in order to correct a deficit on the current account.

13 A country can *correct* a current account deficit by:

(a) *devaluing* or *depreciating* its currency; and by
(b) *deflationary measures* to contain the inflationary effects of the fall in the exchange rate.

For a devaluation to be successful, i.e. increase net export receipts, the price elasticities of demand for exports and imports must average more than one.

14 In the 1980s the UK's current account changed dramatically from a substantial surplus to an enormous deficit. The reasons were the fall in the oil price, excessive demand at home and a stability in invisibles made worse by government transfers, mainly to the EC.

■ SELF-ASSESSMENT QUESTIONS

1 How, if at all, does the principle of comparative costs help to explain the growth of vineyards in the south of England or of tourism in Bradford?

2 Which of the following imports are likely to be affected by VERs? Footwear from Taiwan; Golden Delicious apples from France; Turkish T-shirts; Polish coal; light aircraft from Brazil.

3 If I buy and drink a bottle of German beer in Munich, where does this purchase appear in the German balance of payments? If I buy another bottle of German-brewed beer, but this time in Manchester, where does that transaction feature in the UK's balance of payments?

4 If the German beer is brewed under licence by a UK brewer in Nottingham, how much profit/licence fee is remitted back to Germany? Where does this item appear in the UK's balance of payments?

5 If a Japanese securities house buys shares in Rolls-Royce Plc from a UK resident, where does this transaction appear in the UK's balance of payments? In which section will any dividend payments be recorded in the UK's data and what will be the sign? What bank products are involved in (a) issuing the shares and (b) paying the dividends to overseas investors?

6 The Wimbledon tennis tournament attracts a great deal of media coverage. In which sections of the UK balance of payments do the following transactions occur and which bank products could be used to facilitate the financial side:

(a) *turnstile* receipts of £75,000 from overseas visitors?
(b) TV royalty fees of £190,000 to broadcast live from the centre court to overseas TV stations?

7 What measures can a country's government take to correct (not finance) a deficit on the current account of its balance of payments? How are the banks likely to be affected by and involved with these measures?

8 If the GATT negotiations in the Uruguay round succeed in removing some of the barriers to world trade in services, how would this help the business of the world's leading commercial banks?

9 If the UK runs a substantial deficit on its current account, how can this deficit be financed? What role might the UK banks play in this finance?

10 How can a country, such as India, which has no or few foreign investments to sell, finance a deficit on its current account? What roles, if any, might be played in such finance, by:

(a) Indian banks?
(b) leading commercial banks of the industrialised countries?

11 Show, by using shifts in the supply and demand curves for Iraqi goods, the effects of the UN embargo on trade with Iraq imposed in 1990.

12 If a country sells overseas assets to finance a current account deficit, how do these sales affect:

(a) the current account?

(b) the official reserves?

13 When investors in the USA, Germany, and Japan buy shares in UK companies, how can these capital transactions be financed, if the USA and Germany have current account deficits and Japan has a current account surplus?

14 If there were only two countries in the world, of equal size, and one had a deficit on the current account of its balance of payments, what can you deduce about the balance of payments of the other country? If the country with a current account deficit tried to correct it, would it be able to do so, bearing in mind that all the corrections would affect the other country?

15 If the world consisted of 150 countries of equal size, would this make the correction of current account deficits and surpluses easier or more difficult?

16 Assuming only three countries in the world, complete the following table which summarises their balances of payments:

$m	Blueland	Redland	Greenland
Current account	−200	?	?
Capital account	?	−300	?
Official reserves	unchanged	fall of 50	increase of ?

17 How helpful is it to a bank for its main country of operations to have a surplus on the current account of the balance of payments?

(Clue: have the world's most aggressive commercial banks come from countries with weak or strong current accounts?)

18 What are the likely consequences for the UK's current and capital accounts if the oil price were to:

(a) double
(b) fall by a half?

19 What factors caused the UK's current account to record a record deficit of over £20bn in 1989?

20 Choosing the correct statistics from the following figures, compile the balance of payments of an imaginary country.

	Rbn
Net capital inflow	47
GDP	740
Imports of goods	−370
Budget deficit	47
Net IPD	−23
Fall in official reserves	3
Total company profits	70
Loans outstanding to foreign banks	230
Exports of goods	250
Net tourist receipts	15
Other invisible exports	78

12 Foreign exchange and related markets

OBJECTIVES

When you have studied this chapter, you should be able to:

1 Explain how exchange rates are quoted;
2 Understand the major factors determining exchange rates;
3 Appreciate the close relationship between exchange rates and interest rates;
4 Know that currencies are *bought* and *sold* on the foreign exchange market and that they are *deposited* and *lent* on the Euro-currency markets;
5 Know how active banks are in these two markets;
6 Know that Euro-currencies have nothing to do with the European Community;
7 Appreciate that the UK has grave doubts about the creation of a single European currency by the end of this century.

■ INTRODUCTION

In the previous chapter we mentioned exchange rates, which are the prices at which we buy and sell foreign currencies. If I want to buy US dollars for my visit to the 1994 World Cup, I would normally pay for them in sterling but I could pay for them in a third currency. The foreign exchange market is one where money buys other money. Since money is the *commodity* or stock-in-trade of banks we find that banks play a very active role in the market, particularly when compared to their passive or supporting role in international trade.

Today, most banks have merged their foreign exchange dealing rooms with their wholesale deposit-taking operations (both sterling and foreign currency) into a single treasury. Although the two markets – foreign exchange and inter-bank deposit – are closely linked, we must remember that one buys and sells and the other accepts deposits and lends.

Exchange rates and interest rates are inter-linked. Both are prices of money – exchange rates are the price of money to buy and interest rates are the price of money to borrow.

We look briefly at the Third World debt problem, which has arisen out of commercial bank lending to Third World countries on the inter-bank and longer-term Euro-currency markets.

Finally, we look at proposals to abolish national currencies within the EC.

■ HOW EXCHANGE RATES ARE QUOTED

One of the problems for beginners is that there is no universal way in which exchange rates are quoted. Mostly, they show how much of a foreign currency we get for one pound sterling, e.g. $1.50, DM3 or 250 yen. It's much the same as greengrocers who sell oranges at nine for £1 and lemons at eight for £1. When prices rise, they sell oranges at eight for £1 (12.5p each compared with 11.1p) and lemons at seven for £1. So, when the dollar rises, the rate against sterling may become $1.40 or even $1.30. Sterling is then said to fall.

However, some currencies are quoted the other way round, i.e. as with goods (oranges 12.5p each, rupees 17p each). And some countries, such as Zimbabwe and South Africa, quote all exchange rates in this way.

Since 1970 three major currencies have emerged: the US dollar, the Deutschemark (of Germany) and the Japanese yen. Others, such as the pound sterling and even the Swiss franc, have become of more limited significance. Consequently, in this book we try to give examples in these three major currencies, as well as sterling. Another point to be remembered is that the US dollar is no longer the sole benchmark or *numeraire* against which all other currencies are quoted. We also use artificial currency baskets, comprising a number of the most important currencies.

The forward market, where currencies are bought and sold for delivery in (say) three months' time, has not grown in recent years as fast as the spot market, which is for deals for delivery today or up to two days' time. For the purposes of the subject 'Economics and the Banks' Role in the Economy', the forward market is unimportant, but it will be more important for Banking Operations – UK Lending and International Business – and even more so for the Associateship examinations.

■ WHO BUYS AND SELLS FOREIGN EXCHANGE?

As we would expect, banks – mainly the commercial ones – but also the central banks play a major role in the markets. The latter, often upon the instructions of their governments, may intervene to buy and sell their own currencies (i.e. sell and buy foreign exchange) in order to influence the exchange rate.

But there are other players – for instance, the largest multinational companies maintain foreign exchange dealing rooms and deposit-taking operations just like those of the banks. Here they buy and sell the currencies of the many countries in which they operate and, like the banks, try to use their holdings of currencies to achieve as great a profit as possible. Oil companies such as Shell, BP, Exxon (Esso), Mobil, Texaco, Socal (Chevron) and Gulf (which are the majors or 'seven sisters') operate in most countries and so have a need to buy and sell currencies for everyday business purposes. Along with other multinationals such as General Motors, Ford and ICI, they all have treasuries which resemble those of banks. Indeed, BP once considered establishing a banking operation.

Although most banks do not have branches in as many countries as the largest multinationals, they do have 'correspondent banking relations' with other banks in nearly every country. Their customers will want to make payments, e.g. Italian immigrants in Australia may want to send money to their relatives in Naples. So, just like the multinationals, the banks will be buying and selling their holdings of foreign currencies in order to maximise the return on these assets, i.e. the balances on their *nostro* – our – accounts in foreign currencies with their correspondent banks abroad. Likewise, the correspondent banks will maintain sterling accounts in London, which the UK banks call *vostro* – your – accounts, and these correspondent banks will use these accounts to buy and sell sterling.

Finally, in a number of centres around the world there are foreign exchange brokers who place buying and selling banks in touch with each other, for a commission. Such brokers do not deal directly with the customers of the banks.

The market operates by the brokers (and the banks) quoting both a buying and selling price: when the 'spread' between the two prices or rates is wide the implication is that the dealer is reluctant to deal; when the spread narrows (i.e. the margins between the buying and selling rates are smaller or finer) the bank signals that it is willing to deal. Convention obliges a bank to deal at the rate it quotes but it need not deal for the amount requested. Most deals are done by telephone or fax and many banks tape-record all telephone conversations, in order to minimise errors in processing the deals and in sending the foreign exchange by a SWIFT message to where the buyer wants. Errors can be costly, because they may result in accounts normally in credit becoming inadvertently overdrawn and running up debit interest.

You and I don't deal in foreign exchange, for when we go abroad we usually buy notes and coin or travellers' cheques. Separate markets exist for buying and selling these products and they are of limited economic importance. However, if we cash a Eurocheque overseas this will be negotiated through our UK bank's nostro account. In the notes and coin/travellers' cheque retail market on the streets of London, the UK banks face competition from a growing number of independent bureaux de change, and these may need to be regulated more closely in order to ensure that foreign tourists are not overcharged for their purchases of sterling.

Why is foreign exchange bought and sold?

There are many reasons: people need it to buy foreign goods and services; they have received it in payment for exports; they need it to buy a home overseas or because they are emigrating; to buy shares in overseas companies; to send to relatives abroad; to provide aid for victims of famine or disease; to pay interest to foreign investors; last but not least, to invest overseas for a short period because interest rates are very attractive in that particular country. Banks, and multinationals, will also seek that divergence of exchange rates between centres or over a short (15-minute) period of time which enables them to buy and sell again at a profit (a process known as *arbitrage*).

Of these reasons, trade in goods underlies less than 10 per cent of foreign exchange deals, so some economists believe. The vast majority of deals are connected with other financial transactions rather than with visible trade.

■ WHY DO EXCHANGE RATES VARY?

The obvious answer is because they are not fixed. But this answer attracts few marks in an exam! A more precise answer is: because supply and demand are always changing, and the movements do not offset each other.

Better still: because supply and demand change in response to many different factors, such as the growth of exports compared with imports and the ability and desire to invest in other countries – but also because dealers move their foreign exchange from centre to centre with a view to achieving the highest return on their balances. The phrase 'with a view to' is used deliberately because dealers must make a judgement as to whether they expect the existing pattern of exchange rates and interest rates to continue, so that any extra interest is sufficient to offset the dealing costs.

Let us take some practical examples.

Trade flows

A US exporter sells 500 tractors to Spain. The exporter will be paid in pesetas and so will sell them and buy US dollars to pay, amongst other things, its wages. If more and more US exporters around the world achieve similar successes, their purchases of US dollars (sales of their export proceeds) could move the dollar upwards against most other currencies. So, we must examine the factors which determine whether US exporters can export more:

1 their *products*: are they better than the competition?
2 their *prices*: are their costs too high back home at the factory?
3 their *selling ability*: can their local dealers clinch the deals in the local markets?
4 their *credit facilities*: are their interest charges too high compared with the competition's?
5 their *after-sales service*: are spares easily obtainable at a reasonable price?

If all these factors are acting against all US exporters, then the dollar will tend to fall; if all are favourable, it will tend to rise. If some factors are favourable and some against then it is not obvious which way the dollar will move; the rate may be swayed by the other factors outlined below.

Balance of payments data

Over the years, a balance of payments reveals the ability of a country to attract sufficient foreign exchange – on either current and capital accounts – for it to pay its way in the world. Obviously, a balance of payments includes trade and short-term capital movements, but the regular publication of statistics does focus dealers' attention on a surplus or deficit on current account. In the late 1980s the American deficit and the Japanese surplus were both highlighted in this way. By 1990 the UK's current account deficit was being scrutinised by dealers, but by 1991 it was much lower.

Interest rate differentials

As we have just seen, financial flows are now much more important than trade flows in determining the exchange rates of currencies. Traders and investors with surplus funds will seek to invest them in countries where interest rates are highest, subject to there being little chance of the exchange rate falling and creating a large capital loss. For instance, it's pointless to invest in a country where bank deposits earn interest at a rate of 150 per cent p.a. if the exchange rate is likely to fall by 200 per cent p.a. This might be the case in a country with galloping inflation of around 200 per cent a year.

Suppose a multinational company has 420m yen in Tokyo, surplus to needs. However, in three months' time it must make a dividend payment of $30m to its US stockholders. What will it do with this money in the meantime? When will it sell the yen for dollars?

First, we must know the interest rates obtainable on three months' deposits in New York, Tokyo and other leading centres. Assume that these are (for domestic currency deposits):

Tokyo	3.6 per cent p.a.	London	9.5 per cent p.a.
New York	5.9 per cent p.a.	Frankfurt	9.7 per cent p.a.

On the face of it, it would pay to move the funds to New York and earn 5.9 per cent p.a. on them rather than a meagre 3.6 per cent p.a. in Tokyo. But this ignores the possibility that the exchange rate in three months' time might have been so much more favourable that the profit would have outweighed the 2.3 per cent p.a. interest rate differential (5.9 per cent less 3.6 per cent) between the two centres.

The yen stood at 140 to the dollar at the time; if it had risen to 130 three months later the 420m yen (by then having risen to 423.78m yen as a result of the interest received) would have sold for $32.59m. The dividend could be paid, with $2.59m to spare. If the yen fell (the $ rose) to, say, 150, the 423.78m yen would have sold for only $28.25m, leaving a gap of $1.75m to be financed. If the yen were sold now for 140, they would have fetched $30m, which would have increased to $30.44m if interest rates in New York remained unchanged for the next three months .

Current interest rates are therefore vital, as are current and expected exchange rates. Here we should note that for short periods of up to three months interest receipts can be fixed by making deposits for fixed terms at fixed rates of interest. However, for longer periods, investment decisions also involve taking a view on future interest rates because money can be deposited for longer periods only at floating rates of interest.

Inflation

We saw earlier that there is a link between inflation and nominal rates of interest, and this link extends to exchange rates.

If inflation rises, a government may increase interest rates to curtail the excess domestic demand. This increase in interest rates often attracts foreign investors, who buy the currency, for short-term investment, and thus increase the exchange rate. But in our previous example of triple-digit (200 per cent) inflation, inflation can deter investors.

On the other hand, a low rate of inflation may make a currency attractive to foreign investors, in spite of low rates of interest. Before German re-unification in 1990, the DM was a very attractive currency for this reason.

Economic growth

Steady growth of GDP makes a currency attractive, but sudden bursts and slow-downs – such as occur in the UK – can deter investors. They fear being caught when the growth rate begins to fall and the decline in exports begins to cause the exchange rate to fall.

Government policy

This could involve high interest rates, high inflation or even a high exchange rate – the latter makes imports cheaper. However, while dealers will read the policy statements of governments, they are not compelled to believe them. Often, dealers' opinions of a government's policy are more important to the foreign exchange markets than the official statements of what that policy is supposed to mean.

A major change in a government's economic policy could affect tariffs, inflation, domestic interest rates, the budget surplus or deficit, exchange control if it exists, the attitude to foreign inward investment and the country's exchange rate policy. Such changes are likely to occur after a general or presidential election in a democracy or a 'coup' in a dictatorship. However, they can occur in mid-term, as when President Nixon caused the US dollar to break from its fixed link with gold in the summer of 1971. In dictatorships, even unsuccessful coups could depress the rate of exchange.

The price of oil

This is another factor affecting expectations in foreign exchange markets. Oil is the most important single commodity traded internationally and is vital to nearly every country. Those industrial countries blessed with oil, such as the UK, tend to see their currencies appreciate when the oil price rises, while the opposite is true for importers such as Japan. In the first weeks of the Kuwait crisis in 1990, sterling rose slightly.

Expectations and confidence

In discussing some of these underlying causes – the *fundamentals* as they are known – we have mentioned 'expectations'. Dealers not only see the fundamental data on their screens – visible trade, current account, growth rate, budget deficit, interest rates for example – but they also interpret these and other statistics (e.g. wage rates, unemployment) as well as the economic policy of the government concerned.

This interpretation is termed *judgemental* and it can be extremely important when confidence in a currency is replaced by concern and then fear. There can then be a 'run' on that currency.

If enough dealers believe that a currency will fall during the next three months they will delay their purchases of it until later, thereby decreasing the demand for it now and accentuating its decline. These decisions to delay purchases are known as *lags*, while the decisions to bring forward sales are known as *leads*. They tend to bring about the very changes which they expect.

Purchasing power parity

This is a theory which states that the exchange rate between two currencies will tend to equal the ratio between the internal purchasing powers of the two currencies. If a bundle of goods and services in country A costs A$1500 and in country B the same bundle costs B$2000 then the rate for the A$ will tend to be A$1 = B$1.333. But not all goods and services are traded between nations and there are now tremendous surges of short- and long-term capital which can swamp the exchange rate. However, the inflation rate in a country is frequently a factor influencing its interest rates and thus exchange rates, so domestic price levels are still important.

■ FIXED AND FLOATING RATES

For many years, first under the gold standard and, later, during the years of the Bretton Woods system after the end of the Second World War, the greater part of international trade and finance was conducted under fixed exchange rates. Under the gold standard, countries pegged their currencies to the price of gold, which could be freely exported and imported. If the exchange rate rose above or below the 'gold points' (the fixed gold price plus or minus the cost of shipping and insurance) it was cheaper to buy and sell gold at the fixed prices and then move it by ship rather than buy and sell foreign exchange.

At a conference held in 1944 at Bretton Woods in the USA, the International Monetary Fund (IMF) was established, with the purpose of ensuring stable spot exchange rates and to provide limited and temporary finance to enable member countries to overcome a temporary deficit on the current account of their balance of payments.

During the period 1948–71, only the USA maintained the link with gold, at $35 an ounce until President Nixon altered it in August 1971. By 1980 the price of gold had touched $800 an ounce, in a flurry of speculation, but it subsequently fell back to between $350 and $450 in the early 1990s. Meanwhile, most countries linked their currencies to the US dollar (or to sterling which in turn was linked to the dollar) and the dollar was linked to gold, so currencies were relatively stable.

The USA's break in 1971 with the $35 gold price (which had lasted since 1933) almost coincided with boom conditions for industrialised economies in 1972. The strains of adjustment within fixed exchange rates proved considerable and by 1973 most countries in the industrialised West had moved to floating exchange rates, with the exception of the European Community.

The current system, which has prevailed since then, is called *managed flexibility*, which means that central banks intervene in the foreign exchange market from time to time to bid up their currencies' exchange rates but not regularly and not to honour any obligation to the IMF. In the early 1980s exchange rate changes became much more substantial, with swings of 40 per cent or even 50 per cent being seen over a period of two or three years. This applied particularly to the US dollar/yen rate.

To reduce these excessive fluctuations, a decision was taken in September 1985 to ease the US dollar downwards and to co-ordinate economic policies. Known as the Plaza accord, because it was taken in the Plaza Hotel, Washington, it was between seven countries, known as the Group of Seven (G.7): USA, Germany, Japan, UK, France, Canada and Italy.

The decision was reaffirmed early in 1987, in what is known as the Louvre accord. However, although the names of the decisions are well known, the details of central rates, bands or margins of permitted fluctuation and the rules of intervention are not. Some observers believe the bands are 10 per cent either way, while others argue that they could be as wide as 15 per cent either way.

Advantages and disadvantages

The era of fixed rates is regarded with affection because dealers knew that variations would be minimal; however, *central banks needed considerable reserves of gold and foreign exchange* to be able to buy their own currencies at fixed rates.

Moreover, the need to defend the exchange rate meant that *a government's freedom of action in economic policy was restricted*. Not only could it not do anything which might affect sentiment, expectations and thus the demand for its currency, but it could not easily change the exchange rate as part of a package of economic policy measures.

Finally, while central banks bought and sold their currencies mainly in the spot market, intervention in the forward market was far more risky and many speculators made large profits in forward deals; the losses were borne by central banks.

Floating rates give freedom of action to governments, but they lead to uncertainty because dealers do not know how far down or up a currency will float. They also permit inflation, with internal prices rising as the exchange rate falls.

ACTIVITY 12.1

Back to the diary again! Start to record the £/DM rate over a period of, say, one month. Is it fairly close to DM2.95?

Over-valued and under-valued exchange rates

If trade flows, capital movements, interest rate differentials and relative inflation rates are all judged by observers as likely to depress a currency, so that it falls against other currencies, it is said to be 'over-valued'.

Another example occurs where these factors are tending to depress a currency which is pegged to the US dollar or to a currency basket (*see* next section). The strain is then taken not in the exchange rate but in the official reserves as people clamour to sell foreign exchange on a black market where the rate is much more favourable than the official rate. An over-valued currency means that imports cost less in domestic currency than they would if the rate were at a level where supply and demand for that currency were in balance.

When all the factors are tending to raise a currency's exchange rate over a period of time, the currency is said to be under-valued. The yen was under-valued in the mid-1980s. At any one time, some currencies will be over-valued and others under-valued, unless economic policies are very closely co-ordinated.

Spot and forward deals

Most economics books are concerned with *spot exchange rates* for deals where the currencies are exchanged within the next two working days. But there are also *forward exchange rates* where the deals are clinched now but with delivery (exchange) of the currencies up to a year later. You will study forward deals in greater detail if you go on to take the Associateship examinations.

Although forward deals 'look forward', as it were, they are not, as some people might think, predictions of the spot rate in that number of months' time.

Forward rates are spot rates adjusted by the difference in interest rates in the currencies concerned. Indeed, an eager treasury of a bank can quote a forward rate for a little known currency – such as the Finnish markka – by doing the necessary calculations between interest rates in London and Helsinki for (say) six months' inter-bank loans. Fortunately, you do not have to do such calculations for the Banking Certificate!

■ CURRENCY BASKETS

In 1967 the *Special Drawing Right (SDR)* was created by the IMF. It is an artificial currency, comprising fixed amounts of the world's leading currencies. Originally, there were sixteen currencies in the SDR, but these proved too unwieldy and there are now five, i.e. US$, DM, yen, French franc and sterling, with their proportions changing every five years; the next change is due in January 1996. Members of the IMF were given SDRs in limited quantities in the early 1970s and again in the early 1980s. Nevertheless, the use of SDRs is very restricted and they are little used in world trade. However, we should note that countries can peg their currencies to the SDR and that the occasional issue of SDRs can top up the reserves of small countries in the Third World. Moreover, some innovative banks offer deposits denominated in SDRs.

The SDR is an example of a currency *basket* or *cocktail* – an artificial combination of actual currencies – but it tends to be dominated by the US dollar, which comprises over 40 per cent of it.

Currency baskets are also used to measure the purchasing power of currencies against a wide range of other currencies, duly weighted, and index numbers are quoted for currencies against these baskets. Such baskets are known as *effective exchange rates*. In the Foreign Exchange section of the *Financial Times*, such an index is the *Sterling Index*, measuring sterling against a basket of leading currencies weighted according to their importance for the UK's export and import trade. The base for the index is the average for 1985. The index is calculated by the Bank of England nine times every day between 8.30 a.m. and 4.30 p.m.

The ECU

The European Community has its own currency basket – the *European Currency Unit (ECU)* – comprising the currencies of its twelve member countries. The DM plays a significant role in the ECU, which some observers have likened to a DM currency *bloc*. Although sterling features in the basket of currencies in the ECU, the UK did not join the exchange rate mechanism (ERM) of the Community's *European Monetary System (EMS)* until October 1990. The exchange rate mechanism, whereby currencies are pegged to central rates against the ECU, and thus to one another by bilateral central rates, is at the heart of the EMS.

One ECU is worth about 70p – two cans of soft drink.

■ THE EUROPEAN MONETARY SYSTEM (EMS)

Described as 'a zone of increasing monetary stability', the EMS was founded in 1972 and revised in 1979. It comprises the ECU, which is its currency basket and a possible European currency, and the exchange rate mechanism (ERM).

The ERM permits only narrow fluctuations between participating currencies of plus or minus 2.25 per cent away from a central rate expressed in ECUs. However, sterling, the Portuguese escudo and the Spanish peseta have a 6 per cent margin on either side of their central rates. At present Greece does not take part in the ERM.

Economic and Monetary Union (EMU)

In the summer of 1989, the EC heads of government agreed to work towards EMU, which will involve:

(a) even narrower fluctuations permitted in exchange rates, then interlocking exchange rates and, finally, a single European currency. This will be the ECU, which will cease to be a basket and become a currency in its own right, fulfilling all the functions of money and with all money's characteristics;
(b) linking the various EC central banks into a 'European Central Bank';
(c) co-ordinating government monetary policies. Little is said about fiscal policy.

In December 1991 the heads of government of all EC countries signed the Maastricht Treaty outlining proposals for EMU. By 1 January 1994 a new European central bank may have been created, with the existing central banks represented on its board. The bank and the board members will be 'independent of institutions'. By the end of 1996 there will be a review of the working of these new arrangements, in order to prepare for the decision to move to a single currency – the ECU – 'within a reasonable time'.

However, in June 1992, the Danish voters rejected these proposals, which will now be discussed again.

■ EXCHANGE RATE POLICY

Countries outside the European Community now have a choice, whether to float their exchange rates, peg them to the US dollar, to the SDR, or to another currency basket of their own choice. Former French colonies often peg their currencies to the French franc. No currencies are now pegged to sterling. Some countries choose to peg to an undisclosed basket of currencies, stated often to be composed of the currencies of their leading trading partners.

If a country manages – i.e. floats – its currency, it may then have a choice of exchange rate at which to aim. This has occurred in the UK, and in the USA and Japan, since 1973, when the period of 'managed flexibility' began. However, this choice is no longer available to the UK now that it is in the ERM.

ACTIVITY 12.2

Newspaper cutting yet again! Cut out the important decisions on moves towards EMU.

■ FOREIGN EXCHANGE RISK

Foreign exchange business necessarily involves assets (the balances in foreign currency held with other banks at home and abroad) and consequently a bank needs a capital base to support these assets as well as deposits to fund them. However, like all business, foreign exchange business also involves risk and therefore it is closely scrutinised by banking supervisory authorities – in the UK the Bank of England.

Just like multinational companies, international banks can be affected by exchange rate changes. Short-term changes in currencies may cause windfall profits or losses in the profit and loss account (*transaction effects*). Longer-term fluctuations may result in substantial valuation changes when assets and liabilities denominated in foreign currencies are converted into sterling for inclusion in the balance sheet at the end of the bank's financial year. These *translation effects* may need provisions to be made out of the profit and loss account in order that the assets and liabilities appear at the more recent sterling valuation, if sterling has fallen since the previous balance sheet was compiled.

Exchange rates also affect our lives as citizens, because an over-valued rate can depress demand for exports and attract imports. On the other hand, a country with an under-valued currency will find exports booming and imports stagnating.

ACTIVITY 12.3

If you've been abroad twice or more to the same country, try to remember the exchange rates you received for your pounds.

Did the rate move against sterling, so that you got less foreign currency for every pound on your second or third visit? Or was the movement favourable?

What about local prices overseas? Were domestic prices unchanged or were there very large price increases between your visits? If so, was there a large fall in the sterling exchange rate for that currency?

■ FOREIGN CURRENCY DEPOSITS

In the late 1950s a market developed in London for deposits denominated not in sterling but in US dollars. The depositors were attracted to London because of the flexibility of the Bank of England's regulations, with no restrictions on the maximum rate of interest which could be paid, on the minimum period of an interest-bearing deposit and with no minimum liquidity ratio. A further advantage for London was that some of the funds came from behind the Iron Curtain and the owners were wary of depositing the money in New York. These dollars were known as *Euro-dollars*, and a similar market developed in Paris, for *Euro-sterling*.

The major feature of a Euro-currency is that it is deposited and lent *outside its country of origin*. The *Euro-markets* are now very extensive indeed, with many sub-markets. We noticed one in Chapter 7: the London inter-bank market. Other sub-markets cover most of the currencies of OECD countries, with maturities extending from overnight money to five-year bonds or longer.

Banking Certificate students do not need to study these markets in detail but they are important for Associateship students, especially for those studying for the international banking options. All students, however, must be aware that *Euro-currencies have nothing to do with the European Community.*

The debt problem

One of the attractions of London, compared to New York, for Euro-dollars was the absence of rigid controls, and Euro-currency markets have always been swift to seek new bases where supervision was expected to be lax. As well as London, Paris, Zurich and Frankfurt, important 'off-shore centres' have developed in the Bahamas and the Cayman Islands, for example, while Hong Kong and Singapore are flourishing centres for Asian dollars.

The major problem has not been the collapse of a bank, although some have had to be rescued, but rather the excessive lending which was made to Third World countries until 1982, particularly to Latin America. The banks of the Western industrialised countries 'recycled' the balance-of-payments surpluses on current account of the oil exporters, especially those in the Middle East, to Third World countries to finance their balance-of-payments deficits on current account. The oil exporters' surpluses were known as *petro-dollars* and were deposited with Western banks because the local banks were not large enough to receive the money. The operation made sense at the time, but since 1982 the borrowers have been unable to meet the interest and capital repayments because of high interest rates on their borrowings after 1980, and because of the severe contraction in their export markets as the world moved into the second-worst recession this century.

By 1987 the banks had lent Brazil, for instance, over $100bn, and then Brazil refused to pay the interest. Mexico, Argentina and Venezuela are also large borrowers which have 're-scheduled' their debts to commercial banks. Re-scheduling is a polite word for postponing. Other borrowers which are or have been talking to their lending banks include Poland, Romania, Nigeria and the Philippines.

We noticed in Chapter 9 that all of the UK's Big Four banks made substantial provisions for these bad and doubtful debts in 1987 and 1989. The provisions show us all how important are these Euro-currency operations, even if we do not come across them in our work in branch banking.

■ SUMMARY

1 In the UK, exchange rates are quoted as 'so much currency' to £1, e.g. US$1.70 or DM2.95.

2 Individuals buy foreign notes and coin on a separate market, but banks and multinational companies buy their foreign exchange on a worldwide market linked by telephone, telex and fax.

3 Most foreign exchange deals are not concerned with exports or imports of goods but are finance-based – taking advantage of interest-rate differences or paying for stocks and shares.

4 Supply and demand determine the exchange rates between two currencies. The supply of one currency is the demand for other currencies.

5 Underlying supply and demand are many influences:

(a) Trade flows – goods and services. Exports from country A lead to more of country A's currency being demanded.
(b) Comparative interest rates – higher interest rates available in one country usually lead to greater demand for that currency.
(c) Balance of payments data.
(d) Inflation, which affects trade flows and interest rates.
(e) Government policy.
(f) The oil price.
(g) Judgemental factors – confidence in the currency.

6 Many currencies are now floating, although 11 of the 12 currencies of the EC are linked to one another.

7 Fixed rates inspire confidence and certainty, but they require central banks to keep large reserves of foreign exchange in order to buy a currency and so maintain its exchange rates. They also restrict the freedom of action of governments, who must try to maintain the fixed rate.

8 Floating rates lead to uncertainty and can allow inflation to persist.

9 Currency baskets – a group of currencies linked together in a fixed proportion to form an artificial currency – are designed to even out currency fluctuations.

10 The SDR is the currency basket of the IMF, and the ECU is the device of the EC – a currency basket used as a unit of account.

11 In the foreign exchange market, currencies are *bought and sold*.

12 In the Euro-currency market, currencies are *borrowed and lent* outside their country of origin.

13 Developing countries over-borrowed in the Euro-currency market and now many have great difficulty in making the payments of interest and capital to the banks of industrialised countries.

14 This 'debt crisis' has caused most of the West's banks to make provisions against these loans and so incur losses for the years when these provisions were made.

■ SELF-ASSESSMENT QUESTIONS

1 You're on a trip to Zimbabwe, and you've bought Z$200 at Z$4 to the £ from your bank in London. However, on going to pay the hotel bill in Harare you find that the rate of sterling is quoted at 2.5. There's been no revaluation, so why are the rates seemingly so different?

2 If sterling falls significantly in the foreign exchange market, why is it likely that UK interest rates will rise?

3 Your branch is in an English cathedral city, visited by many foreign tourists, and with a thriving industrial estate with several major exporting companies.

(a) What sort of bank products would your branch sell to these two markets?
(b) What would be the effect of a substantial fall in sterling against all major currencies on these two markets and on local shopkeepers and ordinary people?

4 Bearing in mind that oil is priced in US dollars and that we still import heavy crude from the Gulf and export our lighter crude, what effects would be caused to your bank's operating costs (i.e. the general level of prices in the UK) by a substantial fall in the exchange rate of sterling against the US dollar?

5 One of the major exporting companies in Question 3 has been taken over by a US multinational, paying cash to the UK shareholders. What are the effects on the UK's balance of payments? What are likely to be the effects on the company's UK bankers?

6 For what reasons is sterling likely to depreciate against the world's leading currencies?

7 What are the ways in which a country can *correct* a deficit on the current account of its balance of payments?

8 What are the ways in which a country can *finance* a deficit on the current account of its balance of payments?

9 If sterling were to rise substantially against the world's major currencies, what effects would this have on:

(a) exports of UK manufactured goods?
(b) profits remitted from overseas subsidiaries and branches to their UK parent companies?

10 Oil is priced in US dollars. If sterling were to rise against the US dollar, what effect would this have on the sterling price of North Sea oil?

11 Why do branches have to 'book a rate' with their foreign exchange dealers before accepting a large order from a customer? Would it be necessary to 'book a rate' if the exchange rate were fixed?

12 Can the UK devalue sterling against other currencies?

13 Do many customers of your branch have deposits denominated in foreign currencies?

14 Estimate how much of your monthly pay goes on imported goods or goods manufactured in the UK under licence from a foreign company. Include savings for your annual overseas holiday.

15 Re-read the section on interest rates and then re-work the example with a recent yen/US$ rate.

16 Find out from your bank's annual report and accounts what percentages of its profits/income and/or deposits/advances are denominated in foreign currencies or derived from international banking rather than domestic banking.

17 Explain what are meant by *nostro* and *vostro* accounts. How can a bank sell international banking products if it has no nostro accounts?

18 Explain what is meant by 'purchasing power parity'.

19 Why are interest rates so important in determining foreign exchange rates?

20 When is the new European central bank planned to be established?

13 Government

OBJECTIVES

When you have studied this chapter, you should be able to:
1 Distinguish between fiscal policy and monetary policy and know where they interact;
2 Understand what is meant by the PSBR/PSDR and the vital significance of the source of the borrowings/repayments;
3 Describe the wide range of the Bank of England's operations and, in particular, how they affect the commercial banks;
4 Distinguish between monetary policy and the prudential regulation of banks;
5 Explain how monetary policy is implemented;
6 State 'the monetary counterparts' (to changes in M4);
7 Know in outline the prudential controls imposed on banks by the Bank of England.

■ INTRODUCTION

We came across government intervention in the economy in Chapter 6, in respect to evening out the business cycle, and also in Chapter 5, when we looked at monopolies and mergers. Here we examine economic policy in greater detail. First we examine fiscal policy and then we look at the role of the Bank of England in some detail. It is responsible not only for managing the government's borrowing, which is part of fiscal policy, but also for implementing monetary policy. Next we study monetary policy in depth. Finally, we study in broad outline the prudential controls imposed on banks by the Bank of England.

■ FISCAL POLICY

In Chapter 6 we saw that fiscal policy is one method which a government can use in attempting to stabilise the rate of economic growth. It involves the use of government expenditure, taxation and borrowing not just to carry out the functions of defence, education, transport and health but to affect the whole economy. The questions asked when expenditure plans and the budget are prepared are not 'How do we finance this expenditure?' but 'How much expenditure should be undertaken in order to keep economic growth and inflation within their targets?' and 'How should this expenditure be financed so as to help to achieve the targets?'

The latter question subdivides into:

1 'If we are to change taxation, then which taxes and which tax rates should be altered?'
2 'If we are to increase borrowing, then should we raise our finance from banks, from the rest of the domestic private sector or from overseas?'

In nearly every year, except for the years 1987–90, the government spends more than it receives in taxation and other income such as NHS charges. This *budget deficit* has been financed by borrowing from banks, from people and financial institutions and from overseas, and the accumulated debt arising from this borrowing is known as the *national debt.*

Economists are interested not just in activities of central government, i.e. the ministries in Whitehall, but also in activities in other parts of what is known as the *public sector*, i.e. local authorities and the remaining nationalised industries. Local authorities and the public corporations which run the nationalised industries receive grants and can borrow from the central government, and the local authorities levy taxes. In 1990 the local authorities' domestic rates were replaced by a *community charge* levied on people rather than land and buildings. The ensuing political storm has resulted in recent proposals to abolish it for 1993. The charge does not directly concern the banks, because they and other businesses will continue to pay rates in the form of the uniform business rate.

However, fiscal policy does involve the banks because:

1 they pay taxes on their profits, and the uniform business rate on their branches and other buildings, thus reducing their cash flow;
2 their customers pay taxes, thus reducing their cash flow;
3 the manner in which taxes are paid, largely by customers, and the dates of the payments can be important because banks provide the payment mechanisms. If payments are all made on particular days, e.g. early January, then these can cause shortages of liquid assets as banks' operational balances at the Bank of England are run down to pay the government;
4 the government spends money, and these payments to banks' customers will increase the banks' operational balances at the Bank of England and hence their total liquid assets;
5 as we shall see later in the chapter, fiscal policy can affect monetary policy, especially the level of interest rates (because the government is such an important borrower and operator), and the banks are directly affected by monetary policy.

Public sector borrowing requirement (PSBR) and its funding

In general, a shortfall in a person's or a firm's income can be financed by either:

(a) increasing liabilities, i.e. borrowing;
(b) running down assets, i.e. selling assets or drawing upon cash balances.

These options are available to governments.

In fact, the UK government has been selling a large proportion of its assets, by privatising some of the nationalised industries. This is unusual; governments normally finance their excess of expenditure over tax and other income by borrowing. The *PSBR* is a term devised to monitor this borrowing, and it *includes not only the central government's borrowing but also that of local authorities and the remaining nationalised industries.* The figure is *net* of borrowing between the three components of the public sector, because local authorities and nationalised industries do borrow from the central government. The PSBR is a total and not a source of money, as some students wrongly believe.

The PSBR's importance for banks is not so much why the borrowing is occurring as who is providing the finance. If the government *funds the PSBR* (finances it) by borrowing from *the non-bank private sector*, rather than the banks, bank deposits fall as the government receives the borrowed funds and then rise again as it spends them. First, bank deposits fall along with the banks' operational balances at the Bank of England, but the government's expenditure subsequently restores both to their former levels. The effect on bank deposits and, thus, on the money supply, is nil and this applies whether the borrowing is in the form of sales of gilt-edged securities or of National Savings securities to the non-bank private sector.

However, if the government borrows from the banks by issuing Treasury bills, the effects are very different. The first-round effects are purely on the banks' assets, as they lose operational balances and receive Treasury bills in their place. But when the government spends the money which it has borrowed, bankers' operational balances at the Bank of England rise, as do the bank deposits of the private sector. Bankers' operational balances are restored to their former level but Treasury bills *and bank deposits* are higher. The EC may forbid this government borrowing from banks after 1 January 1994.

Public sector debt repayment (PSDR) 1987–91

After the middle of 1987 the PSBR – the borrowing requirement – became negative, i.e. the public sector was repaying debt, not creating it. This net repayment peaked in the 1988/9 financial year, at £14bn and disappeared in 1991/2. The repayments occurred because of the large increases in tax revenues arising from the growth of output and incomes, the restraint of government expenditure and the rapid progress of the privatisation of nationalised industries. This repayment has been termed the *public sector debt repayment* (PSDR) and it had important implications for monetary policy, interest rates and the banks.

First, it meant that gilt-edged stocks became rarer, so that their prices reflected a scarcity premium, i.e. interest rates on such stocks did not rise as rapidly as interest rates in the money markets. Also, the government did not have to borrow via National Savings and hence did not need to pay attractive rates of interest on NSCs etc.

Secondly, an annual inflow to the government of £12bn or more meant a weekly net inflow of about £250m, which would cause continuing shortages of sterling liquidity in the discount market unless the Bank of England took steps to sterilise or offset it by buying gilts. This it promised to do, as part of a policy of *unfunding* the PSDR (the opposite of funding the PSBR).

The PSBR 1991–

In 1991–2, the government ceased to repay debt, with a PSBR of £14bn. For 1992–3 it will be at least £28bn. Gilts are sold by auction to help fund this sum, and National Savings have been improved by, among other changes, the new bonus bonds for children and guaranteed income bonds. This reappearance of the PSBR was stated to reflect the fall in tax receipts and the rise in social security payments associated with a recession. It was not intended to use fiscal policy to bring the economy out of recession by means of an even larger PSBR.

Medium term financial strategy (MTFS)

This was first announced by the government in 1980 and comprised a rolling target for the PSBR and various monetary aggregates for up to three years ahead. While the authorities would probably argue that the single target of M0 which has existed since 1987 is in keeping with the spirit of the MTFS, there is no doubt that their thinking moved towards monitoring other targets, especially the exchange rate. In fact, the ERM is far more important now.

Because a PSBR – the essential feature of fiscal policy – can cause an increase in the money supply which, with interest rates, is an essential part of monetary policy, the MTFS still links fiscal and monetary policy.

The monetary counterparts

These are the 'contra' entries to an increase in the money supply, M4.

They form an identity, i.e. a relationship which is always true, unlike an equation – which should be learnt very carefully if you go on to the Associateship examination. However, for the Banking Certificate you should merely be aware of the nature of the various 'contra' or 'counterpart' items.

We must always remember that, by definition, the money supply excludes money held by banks and building societies; the public sector; and overseas residents.

We saw earlier that if the PSBR is financed wholly by sales of debt to the non-bank private sector then there is no change in the money supply. However, it is pure chance if this happens and, in any case, we have to take into account the bank deposits created by bank lending.

Accordingly, we begin with these three statistics – PSBR, debt sales and bank lending – and then take into account the overseas sector. The latter can lend sterling to UK residents, who deposit it in UK banks, or bank advances in sterling to UK residents can be switched into foreign currency and deposited in banks abroad. A surplus on the current account can lead to a rise in the money supply; a deficit to a fall. Finally, we take into consideration the fact that some of the increase in the PSBR and in bank lending may have as its 'contra' an increase in the banks' non-deposit liabilities, i.e. capital and reserves, and not in bank deposits.

The expansionary influences are:

(a) PSBR;*
(b) extra bank and building society lending in sterling to the UK private sector.

These are neutralised if they are accompanied by:

(c) funding – government debt sales to the private sector;*
(d) an increase in non-deposit liabilities of banks;
(e) any changes in external transactions which mean UK private sector bank deposits have fallen.

The contractionary influence for the period 1987 to 1991 is the PSDR*, which will be neutralised by the unfunding of the repayment, i.e. government debt purchases* from the non-bank sector – which is the opposite of point (c) above.

Relationship between fiscal policy and monetary policy*

This relationship is seen in the influences above marked with an asterisk – the PSBR or the PSDR, government debt sales or purchases and also in the MTFS. A PSBR will increase the money supply, unless neutralised by sales of gilts or National Savings products to the private sector. Such a programme of debt sales may require high interest rates to attract buyers. So, the economy could see monetary expansion unless there are such debt sales, accompanied by higher rates of interest. Thus, fiscal policy, by itself, can affect both the amount of money and its price – interest rates.

A PSDR has the opposite effect, unless it is neutralised by a purchase of existing debt – gilts and National Savings encashments – from the private sector.

ACTIVITY 13.1

Collect press cuttings arguing that interest rates should be (a) lowered, (b) raised; and arguing that taxes should be (a) lowered, (b) raised.

■ THE BANK OF ENGLAND

The Bank of England is the UK's central bank and stands at the head of the banking system. It was founded nearly 300 years ago, as a joint-stock bank at a time when joint-stock companies were granted royal charters. In 1946 it was at the top of the Labour Government's list of private companies to be nationalised, having become a central bank by historical development.

Students should be aware that it is usual to refer to the Bank of England as 'the Bank'. For instance, a recent examination question was worded thus:

When the Bank of England was founded in 1694, its royal charter imposed on it the duty of promoting 'the public good and benefit of our people'. Show how the Bank attempts to achieve these aims nearly 300 years later, in 1989.

Like other nationalised industries, the Bank is not a government department and its employees are not civil servants. *The Bank's role is to work within the framework of government, to contribute to the policy-making process and to implement that policy when agreed.* This work is undertaken at a series of meetings at various levels between officials of the Bank and the Treasury, culminating with meetings between the Chancellor of the Exchequer and the Governor. Almost certainly the personalities of the Chancellor and the Governor must have some effect on the relations between the Bank and the Treasury. One former Chancellor described his relationship with the Governor as 'creative tension'.

The Treasury is more powerful than the Bank of England, a relationship which has existed since the First World War, following a disagreement between the Governor and the Chancellor. The Chancellor, who was responsible to Parliament and to the Prime Minister, won. Since the early 1950s, it is understood that the Bank of England has not changed interest rates without the prior agreement of the Treasury – indeed, in November 1988 the Chancellor is reported to have stated that he had instructed the Bank of England to raise base rates!

The status of the Bank of England compared to that of the Treasury was brought into the political arena in the autumn of 1989 by Mr Lawson who, after his resignation as Chancellor, revealed that he had suggested greater independence for the Bank in a paper he had sent to the Prime Minister in the summer of 1988.

As Europe moves towards economic and monetary union (EMU) we are hearing more of the likely status of the Bank of England if or when it joins a European Central Bank, which is likely to have its central office in Frankfurt. This new bank will be 'independent of instructions'.

The Bank's functions

These are many and may be grouped into operational and advisory. However, as the monetary and financial markets become more complex and as innovative new products are launched, some of the Bank's functions become more difficult for it to perform. For instance, one monetary target (M1) became distorted when banks began to pay interest on current account and ceased to be published after the Abbey National became a bank, and such changes make the implementation of monetary policy not an easy task. Moreover, rapidly changing markets and new financial instruments increase the difficulties for the Bank in ensuring that firms in these markets act prudently rather than recklessly.

Operational functions

1 *It is responsible for the note issue,* all of which is now fiduciary – not backed by gold. In early 1992, the fiduciary issue averaged over £15bn worth of notes. Coin is the responsibility of the Royal Mint. The notes are printed by the Bank of England, as are Treasury bills.

2 *It provides banking facilities for the central government and for banks.* The Bank maintains the accounts of the Exchequer, the National Loans Fund, the National Debt Commissioners and the Paymaster General, together with accounts connected with dividends and tax collection. Local authorities and public corporations

maintain some accounts at the Bank of England but the majority of their banking is provided by retail banks.

Bankers' deposits are quite large, often running at 200 times the size of the central government's balances. The majority of £1.5bn of bankers' deposits – the typical total in early 1992 – comprised *cash ratio deposits*, which are levied on all banks, as we saw in Chapter 7. Operational balances are much smaller, and are required from retail banks for settlement of their transactions at the various clearings. Each bank maintains its operational balance at a target level agreed with the Bank of England. At the end of 1991, cash ratio deposits were £1.6bn and operational balances £0.2bn.

Banking services for other customers are minimal; the Bank's customers are its staff and old-established concerns such as the Equitable Life Assurance Society, founded in 1762. However, the Bank is acting as clearing agent for the Woolwich Equitable Building Society's cheque account.

3 *It issues gilt-edged securities* to help finance the PSBR. Gilt-edged securities are medium- and long-term borrowings by the government which are bought and sold on the Stock Exchange.

By 1990, no such securities had been issued for several years and the Bank had, in fact, been *buying* securities back from the public. However, in 1992 the government's financial position is the more normal deficit and hence the Bank is issuing gilt-edged securities again. In fact, it began to issue these in January 1991. In 1992–3, it will have to sell well over £30bn of gilts, mainly to fund the PSBR but also to replace existing stocks as they mature.

4 *It acts as registrar of the national debt*, maintaining the lists of stockholders and paying the interest on the due dates. This work involves processing large volumes of dividends and hence is very labour- and capital-intensive. The registration services have moved to Gloucester, as part of a cost-cutting drive.

The Bank also maintains an automated transfer and settlement system for gilt-edged stocks (the CGO – central gilts office) and has introduced a comparable system for the discount market (the CMO – central moneymarkets office). The latter includes commercial bills and sterling CDs.

5 *It executes monetary policy.*

The Bank of England does not *decide* monetary policy, although it will advise the Treasury. The subject of monetary policy is discussed in detail in the next section.

6 *It operates in the discount market*, partly to help finance the government and partly to execute monetary policy.

The Bank issues sterling Treasury bills, usually for 91 and 182 days but sometimes for only 63 days, to provide short-term finance for the government and to ensure the smooth functioning of the discount market. It is in the discount market that the Bank provides day-to-day support for the banking system whenever the latter is short of funds. The Bank buys, at rates of interest of its choice, commercial bills from discount houses which are thus able to repay the short-term loans 'called' by the banks.

In 1992, monetary policy is largely interest-rate policy, to keep sterling within its ERM bands, and the Bank of England alters interest rates by making a substantial change in the rate at which it provides this day-to-day support to the discount market. If the market is flush with funds, an increase in interest rates is announced by the Bank offering assistance to the discount houses by their drawing upon existing loan facilities but at a significantly higher rate of interest.

These transactions are publicised on the dealers' screens, in the financial press and, eventually, in a statistical abstract issued with the Bank of England Quarterly Bulletin each November.

7 *It operates in the foreign exchange market,* intervening from time to time to influence the exchange rate, and manages the official holdings of gold and foreign exchange reserves.

The Bank often supports the exchange rate for sterling by buying it, in exchange for the sale of some of the UK's foreign exchange reserves. Usually, the Bank will not enter the market in its own name, preferring to ask a UK commercial bank to act on its behalf, so as to preserve anonymity. Occasionally, another central bank will intervene on behalf of the Bank or the Bank may buy and sell in its own name. If the Bank sells sterling, it will buy foreign exchange, so that the UK's official reserves rise.

Since 1985 the Bank of England, along with other central banks, has intervened in the foreign exchange market to smooth out fluctuations in the rates for other world currencies – in particular, the yen and the US dollar. Now that the UK is in the ERM, the Bank is responsible for ensuring that sterling keeps within its 6 per cent band either side of DM2.95. This band is to fall to 2.25% before the end of 1993.

The Bank manages, on behalf of the Treasury, the UK's holdings of gold and foreign currencies – the 'official reserves' – which are maintained in the Exchange Equalisation Account.

8 *It supervises the banking system.*

Banks are regulated under the provisions of the Banking Act 1987, but the Bank of England also regulates the various sterling and foreign currency money markets described in Chapter 7, as well as the foreign exchange and bullion markets. The latter deal in gold and silver. In addition, it supervises the gilt-edged market.

9 *It oversees the financial system,* in particular the securities (stock exchange) and commodity markets. The Bank also keeps an overview on LIFFE. Its primary concern is to maintain 'orderly markets' rather than a series of sharp movements in prices and the numbers of dealing firms in each market.

Advisory functions

10 *It is a link between the government and the City,* but it does not act as a speaker for the City. This role was illustrated in the memoirs of Mr Denis Healey, Chancellor of the Exchequer from 1974 to 1979, who wrote: 'I upset [the Governor] by insisting on making my own personal contacts with the financial institutions in the City; the Bank traditionally regards itself as the only authorised channel of contact between the City and the Treasury.' (Denis Healey, *The Time of My Life,* Michael Joseph, 1989, p. 375.)

11 *It collects a great deal of statistics*, which help to provide a background for its discussions with the government to formulate policy. In particular, it publishes the statistics for the various measures of the money supply and for bank and building society lending.

12 *It analyses the UK economy*, and its forecasts also provide a scenario for its discussions with the government. The Bank of England Quarterly Bulletin is a forum where the Bank can express its opinions and concerns, subtly rather than forcibly. Other opportunities are provided by speeches given by the Governor and other full-time directors.

13 *It has assumed an industrial liaison role*, arising from the tribulations of UK industry in the early 1980s. Its branches, in Birmingham, Bristol, Leeds, Manchester and Newcastle, are very active in discussions with business people to assess such matters as cash flow, profitability and export competitiveness.

It played a particularly important role in the early 1980s in putting together 'rescue packages' for distressed firms under pressure from a high exchange rate, high interest rates and high inflation.

In 1990 the Bank's name was mentioned in reports of discussions over the problems of such companies as Eurotunnel, Polly Peck and Laura Ashley.

14 *It maintains relations with overseas central banks and international institutions* such as the IMF, the World Bank and the Bank for International Settlements (BIS). The BIS is a unique bank, being a sort of central bank for central banks, and monitors the Euro-currency markets throughout the world. Surprisingly, because it is located in Switzerland, a non-member of the EC, the BIS also undertakes work for the EC.

The Bank now plays an important role in discussions with other central banks in the European Community and with finance ministers.

An alternative classification of functions

There are various ways of grouping the Bank's many functions and the following one is currently used by the Bank: Operations, Markets, Supervision and Analysis, Forecasting and Advice.

Operations cover:

(a) *banking*, including being the government's banker, the size of the note issue and membership of the various clearings;

(b) *registration*, including the operations at Gloucester, the CGO and the new CMO;

(c) *printing* the notes and the Treasury bills.

Markets include the

(a) gilt-edged market;
(b) discount market;
(c) foreign exchange market;
(d) bullion market.

Supervision, comprising:

(a) banks under the 1987 Act;

(b) wholesale markets;

(c) gilt-edged market.

Analysis, forecasting and advice:

(a) international;

(b) domestic;

(c) collecting statistics;

(d) finance and industry;

(e) other financial markets.

The Bank of England affects commercial banks directly when it carries out its prudential regulation of them. They are affected indirectly by its operations in the discount and foreign exchange markets. In the discount market, it affects their deposits and liquid assets, as well as the levels of interest rates. In the foreign exchange market, the Bank's operations affect the commercial banks' liquid assets, but, more importantly, they affect the exchange rate of sterling. This affects the profitability of their international business.

The Bank is managed by a court, comprising the Governor, Deputy Governor and sixteen directors. Of the latter, four are full-time and twelve part-time; all are appointed by the prime minister for four years. The Governor and the Deputy Governor, however, are appointed by the prime minister for five years.

ACTIVITY 13.2

For a change, let's move over to TV. How many times do you see the following people 'on the box'?

Chancellor of the Exchequer
Governor of the Bank of England
President of the Deutsche Bundesbank.

What are their names? Can you recognise their faces?

■ MONETARY POLICY

This seeks to ensure through the prices and quantity of money that the government can achieve the *economic aims* which we studied in Chapter 6. The authorities – the Treasury and the Bank of England – cannot influence GDP or unemployment directly by monetary policy so they seek to control what are known as *intermediate targets*, such as the money supply and bank advances, and (from 1973 to 1990) exchange rates. In order to reach these targets, the authorities use various *instruments* such as interest rates and open market operations. In the past, these instruments have included *portfolio constraints* such as special deposits, levied on banks, as well as ceilings on bank advances and guidance to banks on priority categories for their lending. At present, all these portfolio constraints have been discarded.

Intermediate targets

In the period 1979–90 there were a considerable number of these targets. M3 (broad money) was a target from 1979 to March 1987, under its old name of sterling M3. Since then, there has been a single target, M0, which became a target in 1984, when it replaced M1. M0 contains no interest-bearing current accounts at all and comprises mainly notes and coin in circulation, together with the banks' operational balances with the Bank of England. The authorities considered that the growth of interest-bearing sight deposits, or current accounts as the public calls them, was affecting the reliability of the statistics. Customers were leaving large sums in these accounts, not to buy goods and services, but to buy and sell stock exchange investments. M0 has the advantage of not being used as a liquid store of value.

It is understood that the authorities are watching the aggregates outlined in Chapter 10, but they are committed to a published target on only one, M0. For the financial year April 1992 to March 1993 the target is an increase of between 0 and 4 per cent. A new target for M0 may be announced in the 1993 budget and, of course, other indicators may be chosen to be targeted.

The most important development in the 1980s was the gradual rise in importance of the exchange rate as a hidden, unpublished intermediate target. The authorities could have established targets for sterling against the US dollar, the DM and the yen, as well as perhaps a figure for the sterling index. In the summer of 1987, the authorities were unofficially pegging sterling to between DM2.95 and DM3.00 to £1, possibly in preparation for the UK's full membership of the European Monetary System. *However, now that the UK has joined the ERM and undertaken the obligations of such membership, it is not able to change the exchange rate as an intermediate target of monetary policy or even as an instrument.*

The ERM is now the framework of the UK's monetary policy, largely replacing the MTFS. It provides a very important target for 1992 and 1993 – joining the 2.25% exchange rate band by the end of 1993.

Another possible target for the government is the growth of *money GDP*, that is the growth in the output of goods and services as measured by current prices and before allowing for the rise in prices across the whole economy. If money GDP grows too fast, this could be because *real* GDP is growing too fast, as the economy peaks, or because prices are rising much faster than real GDP. Or, it could be a combination of these two causes.

Instruments of monetary policy

There are various ways in which the authorities seek to achieve their intermediate targets. The Conservative government's reliance since the early 1980s on interest rates as its main policy instrument caused jibes that it had a 'one club' economic policy. The suggestion was that this reliance on one policy instrument was about as useless as a golfer playing with only one club, instead of the usual 14.

Interest rates

Until 1971 the bank rate of the Bank of England was a major instrument of monetary policy. It was the minimum rate at which the Bank would act as lender of last resort to the discount market, and was penal in that it was above market rates and the loans were usually for no less than one week. Every Thursday morning the Bank announced the bank rate for the following week, but in times of crisis it could be raised at any time.

In 1971 it was superseded by the *minimum lending rate* (MLR), which was calculated weekly by a formula to give a rate slightly higher than the average rate at the Treasury bill tender for the previous Friday. MLR was abandoned in 1981, although it was re-introduced for one day in January 1985, when sterling was under pressure, and again in October 1990 for a very different reason. Since the mid-1980s interest rates have been used with a view to curtailing the growth of domestic credit as well as to the needs of managing the exchange rate.

Since 1981 the Bank of England has operated a much more flexible interest rate policy in the discount market. Every morning it publishes its estimates of whether or not the discount market will need help from it in meeting its net payments to the government. The estimates are revised several times during each day and the Bank provides any help needed by buying bills in one or more of four bands. The first band comprises bills with 1–14 days to maturity, the next 15–33 days, then 34–63 and the fourth is 64–91 days. (91 days are approximately three months.)

The rate at which these purchases are made is the best signal of the Bank's wishes for the future course of interest rates. A series of rises, such as occurred in summer 1988, will cause the banks to raise their base rates. By the end of 1989 they were 15 per cent – twice the 7.5 per cent seen in the second half of May 1988.

MLR was used again in October 1990, when the UK applied to join the ERM, timing the announcement for 4 p.m. on Friday, 5 October. Earlier that day the Bank had provided £1283m of assistance to the discount market at 14.75 per cent and 14.875 per cent. It then reactivated MLR, stating that it would be 14 per cent on 8 October; the banks lowered their base rates to 14 per cent on 8 October, following the intervening weekend. By June 1992, base rates were 10 per cent, and further changes depend largely on German interest rates and sterling's rate in the ERM against the DM.

Open market operations

Open market operations occur when a central bank buys and sells securities in the open market, so as to affect the liabilities and assets in the balance sheets of the commercial banks.

Traditionally these took place in the gilt-edged market or in Treasury bills in the discount market. However, as we saw in Chapter 7, the major assets of the discount market include commercial bills and it is in commercial bills that the Bank of England now conducts most of its open market operations.

The Bank has several ways in which it operates in the discount market:

1 It can buy the bills outright from the houses, specifying the bands of maturities and the interest rates, as we have just seen.

2 It can use a *sale and repurchase agreement*, under which it buys the bills but under which the houses also agree to the Bank selling the bills back to them at a later date, often when the Bank expects there to be a surplus of funds. This surplus could arise from the government paying substantial amounts in interest on a gilt-edged stock or in Milk Marketing Board payments to farmers.

3 It can also lend directly to houses, against the security of bills, but usually for no longer than seven days. However, such loans are not strictly open market operations.

In the gilt-edged market the Bank's primary concern in its open market operations is to ensure the steady *funding* of the PSBR – whether it be positive or negative (i.e. a PSDR) – from the non-bank private sector, i.e. the NBFIs in the main.

Portfolio constraints

Reserve requirements play a very minor role as an instrument of monetary policy today, certainly when compared to the 12.5 per cent reserve asset ratio of 1971–81. Banks above a certain, small size are required to place 0.35 per cent of their eligible liabilities as non-operational non-interest-bearing deposits with the Bank of England. Because these cash ratio deposits are non-operational, they do not appear in the statistics for M0. *Eligible liabilities* are, broadly, a bank's sterling deposits from non-banks with an original maturity of two years or less.

Special deposits have not been used since 1981. Like all portfolio constraints, they do not apply to building societies and cannot apply to banks located outside the UK. The latter weakness is important because there are no exchange controls to stop money entering the UK.

Lending ceilings also did not apply to building societies and have the disadvantage of freezing market shares and stifling competition.

Qualitative controls

Under these, the Bank of England issued guidelines to banks as to which categories of borrower should be given priority, e.g. exporters and builders. Personal loans had to be granted on the same terms as HP contracts, as mentioned in the next section on the history of monetary policy.

Brief history of monetary policy

To counter the recession in the 1930s, interest rates were kept very low and this policy was maintained during the Second World War (a 3.5 per cent war, Keynes called it, in contrast to the 5 per cent of the First World War). When interest rates rose in the 1950s, banks faced losses on their fixed-interest gilt-edged securities. During this period great attention was paid to a 30 per cent liquidity ratio for London clearing banks, which was reduced in 1963 to 28 per cent. Special deposits were first called from the clearing banks in 1960 and extended to all banks in 1971. The 1950s and 1960s were the era of qualitative controls, with Bank of England guidelines on lending by banks and with minimum deposit payments, e.g. 25 per cent of purchase price – and maximum terms, e.g. 36 months' credit – for hire purchase (HP). Personal loans from banks were subject to similar controls to those published in statutory instruments for HP companies.

In 1971 a document called 'Competition and Credit Control' introduced a 12.5 per cent reserve asset ratio for all banks, so clearing banks were not handicapped by a 28 per cent ratio in competing with non-clearers not subject to this ratio, which had affected their profitability. The clearing banks agreed not to link their interest rates to bank rate (which was replaced by MLR) and to publish their own base rates. Unfortunately, the 1971 changes did not distinguish clearly between monetary and prudential controls and the Bank of England failed to monitor the secondary banks and their excessive lending to property companies (and neither did the Department of Trade and Industry). A wit remarked that there was 'too much competition and not enough credit control'. The economy boomed, oil prices rose dramatically, as did interest rates. To restrain bank lending, punitive supplementary special deposits, nicknamed the *corset*, were introduced on interest-bearing bank deposits.

In 1981, the 1971 provisions were dropped and a second new era began with very few portfolio constraints. It relied on the price of money – interest rates and exchange rates.

It should be noted that the practice of *over-funding the PSBR* ceased in the autumn of 1985. Under this practice, the government borrowed from the non-bank private sector more than it needed to finance the PSBR. This created great pressure on the banks' liquid assets when the borrowings were paid to the government, which had no intention of recycling the money back to the private sector by spending it. The Bank of England acted as 'lender of last resort' by buying vast quantities of commercial bills from the discount market. These bills, held by the Bank, were christened the 'bill mountain'.

Questions on these events will *not* be asked in the examination for this subject, but they have helped to influence the thinking of today's decision-makers. If the political complexion of the government should change, there may be a demand for the re-introduction of some of the old techniques.

However, questions are quite likely on the levels of interest rates at the beginning of the 1990s and on any changes in monetary policy since then. *Banking World*, which members of the CIB receive free of charge each month, provides an excellent chronicle of monetary policy as well as of all banking matters.

■ PRUDENTIAL REGULATION

This is now completely separate from monetary policy and is designed to ensure that banks are not only financially viable, i.e. solvent, but are seen to be so by their customers. It ensures that banks act prudently rather than recklessly. One cause of the increased emphasis given to prudential regulation

ACTIVITY 13.3

Back to your *Financial Times* with all the budget details, please! Write, in pencil, on the right-hand side, the Chancellor's forecasts and targets for:

Inflation	..... %
PSBR	£..... bn
Current account of balance of payments	£..... bn
M0	..... %
Real GDP	..... %
Money GDP	..... %
Unemployment (change in total)	..... ('000)
Other indicators:	
.....	.....
.....	.....
.....	.....

after 1973 was the secondary banking crisis, which came to a head early in 1974, when the Bank of England had to enlist financial support from the clearing banks to prop up failing secondary banks, of which perhaps the most notorious was London and County Securities. These secondary banks had lent too much of their deposits to ailing commercial property companies and, when interest rates virtually doubled in under a year, banks in the inter-bank market marked down their limits on these secondary banks, which could not repay their inter-bank deposits as they fell due for repayment. The authorities resolved not to let a similar crisis occur again.

A second cause of the interest in prudential regulation was the UK's entry into the European Community, because the Community required a more formal approach to bank regulation. Accordingly the Banking Act was passed in 1979 and divided banks into two: *recognised banks* and a more restricted category of *licensed deposit takers*. The Act was repealed in 1987.

Banking Act 1987

This came into operation on 1 October 1987 and replaced the 1979 Act. Just like its predecessor, it was born out of a crisis, i.e. the failure in 1984 of Johnson Matthey Bankers, which was attributed to the two-tier system created by the 1979 Act. The Act is not a charter outlining the powers and duties of banks, but provides the statutory basis for the Bank of England's existing supervision of banks and continues the existing deposit protection scheme.

Its most important provision is that the business of every *authorised bank* must be conducted in a prudent manner. Each authorised bank must:

1 have adequate capital and liquidity;
2 make adequate provision for depreciation and doubtful debts;
3 maintain adequate accounting and control systems.

The Bank of England judges the adequacy of these criteria for each bank, not in relation to rigid ratios but with regard to each bank's individual circumstances.

The Bank of England approaches the first two criteria by looking at the contra items in each bank's balance sheet. Thus, when assessing capital adequacy and the adequacy of provision for depreciation and doubtful debts, which are found on the liabilities side of the bank's balance sheet, it closely examines the bank's assets and the degrees of risk attached to these assets. When assessing the liquidity of a bank's assets the Bank scrutinises the composition of that bank's liabilities and, in particular, the relative shares of wholesale and retail deposits and the currencies in which these deposits are denominated.

New banks, before they are authorised by the Bank of England, must have paid-up capital and reserves of at least £1m and, if they are to include the word 'bank' in their name, this total must be not less than £5m. There is now a right of appeal if the Bank refuses authorisation. A tribunal will be appointed for each appeal, with a right of appeal to the High Court on a point of law. In addition, people in control of banks must be 'fit and proper persons'.

The Act has also established a *Board of Banking Supervision* to oversee the banking supervisory operations of the Bank of England. It comprises three members from the Bank, i.e. the Governor, Deputy Governor and the executive director responsible for banking supervision, and six independent members.

Other legislation

In common with all financial institutions, banks are subject to the provisions of the *Financial Services Act 1986*. It affects them, not in their core banking business which is controlled by the Banking Act 1987, but mainly in connection with the way they sell their non-funds-based products such as life insurance policies and unit trusts. Each bank and building society has had to decide whether to deliver only its own products or to drop its own products and sell those of other institutions and thus rely solely on commissions rather than management fees and profit. Most banks have opted to deliver only their own products, although some trustee branches are selling a wider range, but NatWest has decided to be the odd one out and consequently had to sell its unit trust operation (it never had a life insurance subsidiary). Most building societies have now chosen to follow the banks and deliver the products of one connected supplier.

The *Consumer Credit Act 1974* is largely outside the scope of this book, and parts of it will be studied in 'Banking: the Legal Environment'.

Other protection

This includes the *Deposit Protection Fund*, which guarantees 75 per cent of each customer's protected sterling deposits with a bank, up to a maximum protected deposit of £20,000. Every bank contributes to the Fund. Foreign currency deposits are unprotected.

Personal customers in dispute with a retail bank may ask the *Banking Ombudsman* to resolve it. The Ombudsman, who is a lawyer appointed by a council of the 19 banks in the scheme, is empowered to make a binding award of up to £100,000 in each case.

In 1992 the banks and building societies, together with the clearing organisation APACS, implemented a code of banking practice, as recommended in 1989 by the report of the Jack Committee.

Finally, the government can refer proposed mergers between banks to the *Monopolies and Mergers Commission*, which can also investigate other market situations. It investigated the 'duopoly' between the rival Barclaycard and Access credit card networks some years ago but they were later the subject of a further report published in 1989. The proposed offer by Lloyds Bank to buy Midland Bank was referred to it in 1992 but the offer was quickly withdrawn. Hence there will be no report on this proposed bid.

Building societies

These are mutual societies, not limited companies. They are regulated by the Building Societies Commission, under the Building Societies Act 1986.

Each society can pursue only those activities permitted by its rules *and by the Act.*

There is a deposit protection scheme, with a 90 per cent ceiling on the maximum protected deposit of £20,000, compared with the 75 per cent limit for banks. There is also a building society Ombudsman.

■ SUMMARY

1 Fiscal policy concerns the government's spending, taxes and borrowing. When these activities occur, the banks provide the payment mechanisms and their liquid assets rise when the government spends and fall when the government borrows from outside the banking system.

2 The PSBR – public sector borrowing requirement – measures the government's shortfall in tax receipts. It is the net borrowing needed by central government, local government and nationalised industries to equate receipts with expenditure.

If the PSBR is provided from outside the banking system – from the general public and financial intermediaries other than banks and building societies – then the government expenditure will not increase the money supply. But if the borrowing is provided by banks or building societies the expenditure will increase the money supply.

From 1987, the PSBR became negative, because taxation receipts exceed the expenditure of the public sector, and we then had a PSDR – public sector debt repayment. However, a PSBR of £28bn is likely to return for the financial year 1992/3.

3 The Bank of England is the UK's central bank, and works in tandem with the Treasury. The Treasury is the more powerful of the two 'monetary authorities', as they are known. The Bank has many functions:

(a) note issue;

(b) banker to the government;

(c) banker to the banks;

(d) issues gilt-edged securities and Treasury bills;

(e) acts as registrar of the national debt;

(f) maintains automated transfer and settlement systems for gilts, Treasury bills and other money market instruments;

(g) carries out monetary policy;

(h) provides sterling liquidity to the discount market;

(i) operates in the foreign exchange market, where it intervenes to alter the exchange rate of sterling from time to time;

(j) supervises the banking system;

(k) oversees the whole financial system;

(l) acts as a link between the government and the City;

(m) collects statistics;

(n) analyses the UK economy and publishes quarterly comment;

(o) has a liaison role with industry;

(p) maintains contacts with overseas banks and international institutions.

4 Monetary policy, which is implemented by the Bank of England on behalf of the Treasury, has certain *intermediate targets*. In 1992–3, the only measure of the money supply with a target was M0, with a growth rate of 0–4 per cent for the year to March 1993.

5 To achieve these targets, the authorities have *instruments*, such as the general level of interest rates. In the 1980s other instruments, such as portfolio constraints on the assets and liabilities of banks and building societies, were not used. Since October 1990, the exchange rate of sterling cannot be used as an instrument, since it *must* be kept within 6 per cent either side of its central rate in the ERM.

6 Monetary policy and fiscal policy are linked via the PSBR or PSDR and the source of the lending to finance a PSBR (or the recipients of the debt repaid with a PSDR).

7 The monetary counterparts – bank lending, PSBR/PSDR, finance of the PSBR/PSDR, and flow of sterling to and from overseas – provide an arithmetic framework showing the causes of increases in the money supply. Remember, please, that money in the hands of banks, the government and overseas residents is not usually included in the measures of the money supply.

8 Prudential regulation has nothing to do with monetary policy, being designed to ensure that banks act prudently and not recklessly.

9 The banks' mainstream business is regulated by the Bank of England under the Banking Act 1987. Their non-funds-based products are controlled by the Financial Services Act 1986. Other protection is afforded by the Deposit Protection Fund and the Banking Ombudsman.

10 Building societies are regulated by the Building Societies Commission under the Building Societies Act 1986.

■ SELF-ASSESSMENT QUESTIONS

1 Assess the effect on the UK's economy if interest rates were to rise substantially in:

(a) the USA;
(b) the Irish Republic;
(c) Germany.

2 How is liability management facilitated by the existence of wholesale money markets?

3 Which are the three main sources of finance for the public sector?

4 'The Bank of England's most important role today is to act as *prudential controller* of increasingly *innovative* financial markets.' Explain.

5 Why did the authorities announce the UK's intention to join the ERM at 4 p.m. on a Friday when the markets were still trading and *before* the application to join was formally submitted on the Saturday?

6 What is meant by the term 'parallel money markets'? Why are they important to commercial banks and building societies?

7 'The Bank of England can either control the supply of money or its price, i.e. interest rates. Like other monopolies, it cannot control both.' Explain.

8 Monitor the development of EFTPOS, *electronic funds transmission at the point of sale*. What other products do banks sell to help their customers make payments within the UK?

9 Explain what is meant by $MV = PT$ and classify some of the banks' main products as to whether they:

(a) help to finance T;
(b) facilitate V;
(c) are based upon M.

10 'Measures of *narrow money* seek to assess how much money is being supplied to meet the *transactions demand for money*.'

(a) Explain what is meant by the two terms in italics.
(b) Explain how the growth of 90-day term deposits is making M2 less reliable as an indicator of transactions balances.

11 Classify the various liabilities of banks into those which are money and those which are not.

12 Explain how GDP is calculated by the expenditure approach. What bank products help to finance this expenditure?

13 In 1955 a bank instructor told his class: 'Banks have three main functions: they pay, receive and transfer money; they lend money and they have a range of miscellaneous services.' How true is that summary today? In what ways have the functions of banks changed since then, if at all?

14 What is meant by the term 'quasi-money'? Why does it not include all the liabilities of banks?

15 Your manager has asked you to give a short talk to a group of business students on 'How the banks finance businesses'. Make a list of the various ways in which banks do this, to help you give the talk.

16 Your manager has asked you to give a short talk to a group of business students on 'How the banks finance exports and imports'. Make a list of the various ways in which banks do this, to help you give the talk.

17 Show how banks help to finance the gross fixed capital formation of:

(a) companies (in plant, machinery, buildings, etc.);
(b) people (in new houses).

18 'XYZ plc reports interim results next week, which are likely to reflect the impact of a weaker dollar, as 50 per cent of the company's earnings now come from the USA.' This sentence, from the FT, assumes that readers know whether profits are likely to be up or down as a result of the dollar's weakening. Explain, in everyday language, how a weaker dollar will affect the profits.

19 Your manager has asked you to talk to a group of GCSE students on 'Money in a modern society'. List the headings you would use to help you give the talk.

20 Have you enjoyed studying the course?

Answers to selected self-assessment questions

1 (a) only the banker; (b) both the economist and the banker. However, a banker would regard the purchase of an existing house as an investment.

2 USA, the 12 EC countries, Japan, Canada, Australia, New Zealand, Austria, Norway, Sweden.

3 Those countries which are neither very rich nor members of the former communist *bloc*.

4 Extra, or additional or incremental.

5 The difference between expenses and receipts per unit of output, e.g. profit margin.

6 Because the government feared that its nationalisation plans might be hindered by the City: controlling the Bank of England gave it control over the commercial banks.

7 Saudi Arabia, USA, Switzerland.

8 Chad, Ethiopia, Sudan, Niger, Bangladesh.

9 Apart from coal, it does not possess many.

10 UK, Ireland, Germany, France, Italy, Spain, Netherlands, Belgium, Denmark, Luxembourg, Portugal, Greece.

11 Most people regard distribution as transporting and selling goods, e.g. wholesale and retail distribution. Economists regard it as the way in which incomes are shared between people: in unequal shares. Strictly, it refers to the way in which the incomes of factors of production are allocated – wages (including salaries), profits and rent.

12 Interest rates and exchange rates.

13 Yes. Personal customers pay interest when they borrow and receive it when they deposit money; exchange rates affect them directly when they go abroad for holidays and indirectly when they buy imports or work for an exporter or importer. Business customers borrow larger amounts and are directly concerned with exchange rates whenever they export or import.

14 Not spending or consuming.

15 The total output of goods and services of a country.

■ CHAPTER 2

1 (b).

2 Unlimited (wants), limited (or finite) (resources).

3 As we consume more of an item, the extra satisfaction we obtain from each extra unit falls.

4 They are addictive: the more we consume, the more we crave. Certainly this is true for drugs.

5 Income; taste, fashion, religious beliefs; population – size, age and geographical distribution; advertising; prices of other goods and services.

6 Yes. Muslims require Halal meat and many people abstain from alcohol.

7 Most of the UK has a stationary population, but the inner cities have falling populations. East Anglia and the South West have rising populations.

8 It is likely to rise, unless you are addicted to coffee!

9 Prices rise – upwards!

10 Output (quantity) has to be moved from the seller to the buyer – usually in a horizontal direction!

11 Because we need to be 'bribed' into buying more by lower prices. These lower prices mean that we sacrifice less of other goods so as to continue to buy the cheaper good.

12 In the short run, only one factor of production is varied; the other factors are fixed. In the long run, all factors can be varied and firms can enter or leave the industry and even cease to trade altogether.

13 Returns to scale are the extra output derived from increasing the scale of production – for instance, doubling *all* the factors of production. The new output can be more than double or less than double the old output. Diminishing marginal returns refer to the extra output obtained by increasing one factor of production while holding the others constant. The extra output can be increasing (at first) and will later begin to diminish.

14 Increasing returns to scale means that if the factors of production are, say, doubled then output more than doubles. (We look at this concept in greater detail in Chapter 4.)

15 Falls.

16 Rises.

17 Market clearing (also equilibrium and, possibly, stable).

18 Because the goods cannot be sold on a Sunday (many supermarkets are closed) and by Monday they will be rotten. The choice is 'nothing then' or 'something now'. As the saying goes, 'something is better than nothing'.

Perishable goods such as cakes and bread.

19 In every sense. As workers we are part of the labour market; our salaries are the price of our labour.

■ CHAPTER 3

1 (a) *Copper*: S curve shifts to left (decreases). [Less will be available at each price, and the price will rise.]
Fibre optics: D curve shifts to the right (increases). [The price of copper having risen, fibre optics will enjoy an increase in demand.]
(b) S curve shifts to left (decreases). [Less vegetables available at each price.]
(c) D curve shifts to left (decreases). [Taxpayers have less disposable income available to spend.]
(d) *Coffee*: S curve shifts to left (decreases). [Less coffee available at each price. NB: had there been ample stocks, it might have been possible to maintain supply until the weather improved.]
Tea: D curve shifts to the right (increases). [The rise in the price of coffee will switch demand to tea.]
(e) S curve shifts to right (increases). [With no more storage available, the market is deluged with sugar.]

2 It is likely to fall.

3 Food in general; clothing; paraffin oil for heating houses; public transport.

4 Because it would now be profitable to begin production from more costly oil fields.

5 (b).

6 No. It was inelastic because the quantity sold fell by less than the increase in the price.

7 Probably the following would experience an increase in demand: cars, holidays, alcohol, petrol, dishwashers.
The following might fall: bus journeys, launderette usage.
Butter and margarine might be unchanged.

8 Cars – personal loans, motor insurance.
Holidays   – a major holiday – personal loans, travel insurance.
          – mini-breaks – budget account.
Food and drink, petrol – credit card, debit card.
Dishwasher – credit card (many personal loans have a £500 minimum).

9 Because the conditions of supply and demand are vastly different in the West End as compared to a cash and carry in the suburbs.

10 With all rides free in the theme park, queues soon develop for the most

popular. Notices are placed to guide people, e.g.:

- at this point, you queue for 30 minutes
- everybody leaving a queue must rejoin it at the end
- anybody pushing into a queue will be escorted out of the theme park.

To some extent, rules take over; it is not people's purchasing power that determines which rides they go on, but the length of the queues. It's not the price which puts us off a ride, but how long we must wait. It is very similar to life behind the former Iron Curtain – queuing for most things.

11 (a) Only those clearing banks with a branch there.
(b) A large number of banks and building societies with branches and subsidiaries in these 'offshore banking centres'.
(c) The clearing banks and building societies will have many branches here and the major merchant banks and some foreign banks will be seeking employees.
(d) Over 500 foreign banks are represented in the City – but not all will need a large workforce. The clearing banks will have many branches, and these are the principal offices of the merchant banks; there are also some branches of building societies.

12 Because they are sure of getting their revenue, as the quantity sold will not fall by very much.

13 Yes. Extra export revenue can be obtained by imposing a tax on this major product because the quantity sold will not change very much. The tax will be paid by foreign purchaser in foreign currency.

14 They are likely to move upwards as people decide to demand an existing fairly new house in preference to a new one. Sellers will raise their asking price too.

(a) Home loans are likely to be demanded for larger amounts.
(b) Greater insurance cover will be needed for the structure.
(c) This should rise, in line with house prices.

However, such a proposal if implemented in the late 1980s would have caused unemployment in the house-building industry, coming on top of very high interest rates. In the early 1990s, it would have caused house prices to have fallen even further.

15 Because goods with a price inelastic demand experience great fluctuations in their prices, although the quantity traded is fairly stable.

Goods with a price elastic demand do not experience fluctuating prices but are often slow to sell.

16 (a) Fashion could cause younger customers to move into interest-bearing current accounts. Custom/habit will mean that elderly customers will be slow to follow suit, retaining appreciable balances on which no interest is received.

(b) Unit trusts are affected by fashion – as share prices rise, so investors trend to buy more units. Custom/habit have little effect, apart from those unit-holders with regular contributions each month.

17 There is only one restaurant on each mountain; it is expensive to move the food to the top; tourists are often rich and always hungry!

18 TESSAs, annuities, investment management, PEPs.

19 Interest-bearing current accounts, budget accounts, personal loans, mortgages (home loans).

■ **CHAPTER 4**

1 (a) Economists regard all of them as firms.
(b) Bankers regard only partnerships as firms.

2 (a) Cost is the expenditure incurred by firms in production.
(b) Opportunity cost is the alternative forgone by the production or consumption of an item. The opportunity cost of more expenditure on the NHS might be less expenditure on education.

3 Premises, heavy machinery, insurance, salaries of office staff.

4 Power for machinery, raw materials, transport, wages of shop floor workers, packaging.

5 Marginal cost is the addition to total cost resulting from the production of an extra unit.
Average cost is the total cost of (say) X units divided by X. It is sometimes called unit cost.

6 When marginal cost is below average cost, average cost falls, because we are adding a smaller amount and dividing by a slightly larger total output. If average cost of 400 units is £40 (total cost is 400 x £40 = £16,000) and the marginal cost is £39, then 401 units have a total cost of £16,039. Divide by 401 and the average cost is £39.9975. If the marginal cost is £40, then the average cost is £16,040 ÷ 401 = £40. If the marginal cost is £43, then the average cost is £16,043 ÷ 401 = £40.01.

7 A small 'cottage hospital' may have one theatre, a surgical ward and a medical ward, plus an X-ray machine. Its market will be a county district. A large provincial teaching hospital will have a medical school, suites of theatres, a renal unit, a cardiology unit and facilities for chemo-therapy, plus dozens of wards specialising in various diseases. Its market may be as large as several counties.

8 Because time is limited (168 hours per week), if we specialise in one activity we have less time to do other things. Therefore, we rely on other people

to supply these items – car repairs for instance – to us. We 'buy in' these goods and services using money as a medium of exchange. Without exchange and money there can be little specialisation.

9 Falling average total costs of production as output rises.

10 Fixed costs spread over a larger output, specialisation, indivisibilities, increased dimensions, linked processes, better training, specialised management, savings from discounts obtained by bulk buying, new sources of finance.

11 Economy of information: trade journal.
Economy of disintegration: hiving off of various activities, e.g. farm secretarial agencies.
Economy of concentration: a pool of skilled labour.

12 These occur when average total costs start to rise. The technical economies are exhausted and the operation often becomes too big to control.

13 Small firms are important in service trades, which are growing in importance while manufacturing is relatively stationary.
The government (and banks) are providing schemes for advice and financial help.
Personal computers, fax machines and other recent developments mean that a one-man firm has most of the administrative machinery for office and design work that (say) ICI has. Hence, sole traders can specialise in doing (and selling) what they are good at. Distance is now no problem.

14 Printing at Watford, furniture at High Wycombe, caravans near Hull, breweries at Burton-on-Trent, pottery at Stoke-on-Trent, engineering consultants around Epsom.

15 Markets, raw materials and fuel.

16 Land, labour and capital. Some observers include management/risk-taking (enterprise) as a fourth.

17 Land – arable in East Anglia, sheep-farming on hills. Labour – shipyard workers in the North East, miners in a colliery village. Capital – textile machinery cannot be used for (say) assembling computers.

18 Difficult question. One person might be able to change more rapidly than a firm of several thousand people, but change may be too difficult for that person. Also, the person may not have the ability which is now needed.

19 In total, British Steel has fantastically high fixed costs – millions of pounds locked up in steel works, sinter plants and rolling mills. But, relatively speaking, the hairdresser, especially for a ladies or a mixed salon, may have to pay a greater percentage of his/her expenses for the premises, the hot water supply and the drying equipment.

■ **CHAPTER 5**

6 (a) Premises and computers. Retail banks have the cost of setting up the clearing system and keeping it up to date with 'state of the art' technology.
(b) Premises and computers.
(c) Premises, computers, advertising and postages.

7 Because they are all service trades where small firms can excel in giving personal attention.
There are probably more small firms in manufacturing than we realise because:

(a) they are not in high streets but in side streets;
(b) they supply bigger firms rather than the general public.

However, small firms cannot afford blast furnaces and expensive robots! But they can assemble intricate components.

9 Probably most are: selling motor spares, sweets, cassettes, flowers, sandwiches, barbecue fuel, etc.

10 The small branch gives little opportunity for specialisation. The larger one can give greater opportunities for full-time work by (say) an insurance clerk, but these days there are proposals for centralisation or regionalisation of securities work so that more attention can be given in the local branch to selling and customer contact, rather than on administration.

11 If there are economies of scale, firms will be quite large. They will then be able to influence market prices by their own actions. If they can do this then, by definition, one of the conditions of perfect competition is not met. Therefore there is no perfect competition.

12 It depends on the sizes of the two firms proposing to merge. If the merged firms were to have a market share in retail banking of more than 25%, it is likely that the proposal would be preferred to the Monopolies and Mergers Commission.

13 Yes, provided that the foreign bank is acceptable to the Bank of England. In 1992, the Bank of England raised no apparent objections to the bid by Hong Kong & Shanghai Banking Corporation for the Midland Bank. After 1992, any EC bank will be permitted to bid for a bank in any other EC country.

14 No, because of the high cost of the latest technology. Steel-making, car manufacture and telecommunications are industries likely to continue to be dominated by large firms.

15 Ability to use the largest mainframe computers, cheque sorting and reading machines, to apply the latest management techniques in controlling operations.

16 (a) Limit pricing is where a monopolist deliberately limits its price in order

to make less than maximum profits so as not to draw attention to its position. Possible competitors could pressure a government into allowing competition to occur.

(b) Dominant-firm leadership is where a very large firm sets the pace in market developments, e.g. charging for credit cards.

(c) Barometric-price leadership is where a small firm deliberately changes prices – usually a reduction – in order to drive up its market share. Eventually one of the bigger competitors may be forced to follow.

(d) Price discrimination occurs where different prices are charged for virtually the same product, e.g. a journey, a concert, a private ward rather than a public hospital ward. It can occur because the supplier has a monopoly and is aware of differing demand curves from different groups of its 'customers'.

(e) These show the percentage of the total market held by a certain small number (from two to seven, say) of the largest firms. Thus, a two-firm concentration ratio of (say) 40 per cent means that these two have 40 per cent of the market, leaving all the rest – which could be dozens – to share the remaining 60 per cent.

17 25 per cent, although in a recent report on brewing a market share of 15 per cent was thought to be significant.

18 First class have wider seats, more space, better meals and drinks, with a separate section. 'Club/Executive' class are not so well attended to. Economy class receive the least attention.

19 (a) In leaving the gilt-edged market, when their market shares were so small that they could not operate at low average cost.

(b) In paying interest on current accounts when two major building societies, with such accounts, began to make inroads into their market shares. Smaller numbers of cheques etc. would mean higher average costs.

20 No, they ceased in 1971 and 1983 respectively.

■ **CHAPTER 6**

1 (a) Income
(b) Expenditure
(c) Not included as part of GDP

2 Stable prices; low unemployment; high economic growth; exchange rate stability; some financial support for Third World. In addition, it is likely that environmental concerns will be included in these goals in the later 1990s.

3 Fiscal, monetary and, in some countries, indicative planning.

4 Yes, good economic growth should mean less unemployment (unless all the spending is on imports) but it could also mean an unacceptable rise

in prices. It is now considered that price stability is vital: if a country fails to have low inflation then none of the other goals can be achieved permanently.

5 An increase – because the wives' work did not feature in the statistics.

6 *Accelerator* – when trade has been very slack, its sudden resumption can come as a nasty shock.
Multiplier – my spending is somebody else's salary/profits.

7 No. It is better to use market forces to determine as many prices (wages are the price of labour) as possible.

8 No. In general, markets provide a better control. However, some prices are controlled, e.g. milk.

9 Yes. The market is not the best control here because the employer may have greater power than employees and both groups may be ignorant of some of the technical dangers involved.

10 Consumers' expenditure; government expenditure; gross domestic fixed capital formation; net export of goods and services; value of physical increases in stocks and work-in-progress.
Banks finance this spending by many forms of lending.

11 Wages and salaries; companies' gross trading profits; public corporations' gross trading surpluses; rent; self-employment; imputed charge for the consumption of non-trading capital (living in your own home!).
Interest-bearing current and savings accounts. Also, include life assurance policies and pension schemes, because these are contractual savings products.

12 Social security benefits – retirement pensions, attendance allowance, supplementary benefits, for example; pensions from former employers. These do not directly relate to current production and are financed by:

(a) taxation of profits and incomes;
(b) trading profits in the case of dividends, while ex-employee pensions are financed largely by dividends received from the investments of pension funds. So, there would be double counting.

BACS, cheques, bank giro credits. CHAPS and the Town Clearing have minimum charges which are too high for most of these transfer payments.

13 The sub-post offices would lose a lot of business and would have to rely on their stationery, food sales etc. Their cash flow would shrink, with credit balances at banks falling and borrowing rising.

■ CHAPTER 7

1 Central banks are usually responsible for monetary policy. Commercial

banks seek to make profits and usually have more customers than central banks. Commercial banks are often privately owned; central banks are often owned by their governments.

2 (a) Retail banks: Girobank, Abbey National, Midland.
(b) British merchant banks: Hambros.
(c) Japanese banks: Bank of Tokyo
(d) American banks: Citibank.
(e) Other overseas banks: Deutsche Bank, Banque Nationale de Paris.
(f) Not a bank: National Savings Bank.

3 Inter-bank, CD, local authority, finance house, commercial paper.

4 Treasury bills, commercial bills, local authority bills, CDs, CP.

5 Because loans and deposits, unlike financial instruments, are not usually bought and sold.

6 Financial intermediation occurs when specialist firms – such as banks and life assurance companies – come between ultimate depositors and ultimate lenders. Such firms take the transactions on their books, assuming the risks involved in the lending or the investment.

7 Their obligations – their deposits – act as money for the rest of the economy.

8 Colleagues at work borrowing from one another just before pay-day.

9 Because it produces services in an industry, seeking a profit (or a surplus for a building society) in competition with others.

10 (d)

11 CDs are issued by banks and building societies. Most CP is issued by large companies.

12 Unit trusts are bought and sold via the managers. Investment trusts have their shares bought and sold on the Stock Exchange.

13 (c)

14 High net worth individuals: (a) and (e)
Expatriates   (b) and (d)
Over 55s   (c)

15 Banking through a branch network, with money transmission products, and no serious limits – such as high minimum balances – on opening most accounts. Membership of APACS.

16 Banking through a treasury dealing room, relying on high minimum amounts to minimise administrative costs.

17 Retail banking is regarded as a saturated market, with high entry costs (premises, computers, etc.).

18 Because wholesale operations provide an additional source of funds/lending to those available via a branch network, and to compete with wholesale banks for a larger share of the business with large companies (corporates).

19 Lombard North Central is not a retail bank.

20 Products which do not directly involve lending or deposit-taking. Examples are unit trusts, life assurance.

■ CHAPTER 8

2 APR stands for annual percentage rate of charge. It is calculated in accordance with the Consumer Credit Act 1974, showing the interest and other compulsory charges paid each year expressed as a percentage of the average balance outstanding on the loan.
CAR stands for compounded annual rate, giving the equivalent rate of interest if interest were calculated only once a year and added to the balance instead of more frequently. For instance, 5 per cent p.a. with 'half yearly rests' is equivalent to a CAR of 5.25 per cent. At the end of a year £100 rises to £105.25.

3 Deposits raised from the branch network are stable, so that the quickest way to increase deposits is to bid for them in the inter-bank market. Here the rate paid by banks bidding for deposits is LIBID.

4 After Abbey National became a bank in 1989, no other societies have followed it. Most are content to stay as societies; one has even bought most of Girobank. But there may be changes before the end of 1992, when the European single market begins.

5 Oligopoly means competition is on most things *except* price.

(a) When the Bank England signals a change in base rate, the clearing banks have no option but the follow the signal.
(b) Banks will watch the trend of interest rates, their competitors, their own market share and the strong points of their products. If they seek a bigger market share they will be slow to raise their rates on lending products. However, if greater gross profit is sought and the product is good, then rates will be raised.

6 Marks & Spencer, Texas Homecare, Allders, B & Q, Mothercare, Next, Laura Ashley.
Longer opening hours, in prime retail locations (high streets and out-of-town locations). Shops can host receptions for cardholders to preview new ranges. Bank cards have far more outlets, and the use of ATMs in the UK and overseas. A storecard is limited to the store or group which issued it.

7 By 1990, the stampede had slowed down, with the occasional building

society or life assurance company buying a chain of estate agents. The agents had been 'powerless' because the purchase prices were over-generous! It was an offer the partners could not refuse!

9 Building societies and overseas banks, especially from the EC. In 1990, German banks were busy returning to their domestic market in the East, following German reunification but they are likely to look West again. Possibly British Telecom.

10 Because all *banks* are joint-stock banks. But building societies are mutual societies, so it may not be so old-fashioned after all.

11 Because home banking enables small banks and building societies to 'deliver products' without having a branch network.

12 In the early 1990s, pension mortgages were not being sold that much, because the banks and building societies were keen on protecting market shares by selling low-cost or fixed-rate mortgages.

13 Most are owned by the clearing banks. It is an example of vertical integration. As yet, there is no movement into HP companies by Japanese or other foreign banks.

14 Because most of its shops stocked only low priced goods, so that the profit per transaction was minimal.

15 Most banks have shareholdings in life assurance companies and unit trusts management companies. Most also own HP companies.

16 Interest and salaries are *current* costs. Computers and telecommunication networks are capital costs, spread over several years.

17/18 It's embarrassing when our customers know more about our bank's products than we do!

19 This approach is known as 'life cycle'. Briefly:

(a) students need sensible spending products, as do all the other groups;
(b) also need savings products;
(c) sensible spending products; } loans and life assurance/pensions
(d) savings products for any redundancy payment;
(e) savings products.

Briefly, life assurance is not suitable for people over 45 and loans are unsuitable for pensioners.

■ CHAPTER 9

1 (a) liability; (b) asset.

2 Because the borrower has a legal obligation to repay the loan, it is a liability and therefore a credit balance in the books of the borrower. The balance

is a 'mirror image', with the sign reversed, of the debit balance of the loan account in the books of the lending bank.

5 As a liability, perhaps included under 'Deposits'.

6 Liability management is where a bank (or building society) identifies a likely borrower or makes the loan and then bids for deposits to fund it. Asset management of a balance sheet is where banks (and building societies) take deposits and then arrange their assets so as to balance liquidity and profitability. Building societies face a 40 per cent limit on their wholesale funding under the 1986 Act.

7 *Nominal* rates of interests are those quoted in the lending contract. *Real* rates of interest are nominal rates *less* the rate of inflation. *APR* is the annual percentage rate of charge on the average amount borrowed during the period of a loan. *CAR* is credit interest – whether paid monthly, quarterly or half-yearly – expressed as an annual rate, to help customers make comparisons.

8 Gross interest, i.e. received and paid, will reflect monetary policy. The *net* interest earned will indicate the efficiency of the bank in lending and deposit-taking.

9 (a) rises by the amount of shares issued and paid for;
(b) rise by the same amount;
(c) unchanged.

10 (a) rises by the amount of the shares issued;
(b) unchanged;
(c) fall, by the amount transferred to share capital and issued as shares (same amount as in (a)).

11 Three per cent real growth of GDP is an *average* for the UK.

(a) likely to grow faster in SE, with congestion;
(b) likely to grow substantially more slowly than three per cent;
(c) would grow at about the same rate as UK average;
(d) —

12 A difficult question – depends on the cost of borrowing, i.e. mortgage rate, because few of us pay cash for our house. In 1987–8, the faster that house prices rose, with much lower mortgage rates, the greater was the demand. In the early 1990s, houses may seem to be cheaper but purchasers will need lower interest rates and certainty of employment plus wage rises at least in line with inflation.

13 The profit able to be earned from non-interest-bearing current account balances. It's disappearing because banks are paying interest on more and more current accounts.

15 Operational balances.

16 To some extent, yes. The more they can 'enhance their products' and 'segment their markets', the more they can raise their charges and practise price discrimination. Banks, unlike theatre owners, are new to price discrimination but they will become adept at it in due course!

17 Liabilities which fall due only if another event happens, e.g. a customer fails to fulfil a contract with an overseas government.

18 Insurance, pensions, PEPs, unit trusts should all be considered. Richer customers need asset management and investment products.

19 If they receive substantial lump-sum redundancy payments as compensation for the loss of their jobs.

20 Yes. Staff can be more profitably employed elsewhere. Premises can be sold and the cash used in (say) investment in computers, ATMs and telephone banking. The latter can overcome complaints about 'a long way to the nearest branch.'

■ CHAPTER 10

1 Banks argued that cheque and other payment products were available on current accounts, so that interest was unjustified. Building societies caused them to pay interest. However, some banks provide non-interest-bearing current accounts with cheaper built-in overdraft facilities than those available on their interest-bearing current accounts.

2 Notes and coin with the general public, in the tills, vaults and cash dispensers of banks; banks' *operational* balances at the Bank of England. None of these items earn interest for their holders.

3 Because interest was the only benefit available to depositors: building societies did not offer current accounts until given powers by the Act of 1986. However, the Cheltenham and Gloucester announced in September 1990 that it would cease to pay interest to all adults with balances of less than £100, because such small accounts are uneconomic for the Society.

4 Shipbuilding, aircraft construction, house building, and heavy industries such as boilermaking.
The replacement of these goods can often be postponed, so that demand for new ones can dwindle to nothing when there is no business to justify the owners replacing them.

5 Price leadership initiated by a *small* supplier. Their Gold Account paid high rates of interest and increased the society's market share. The society has just (*see* 3 above) become a market leader in *not* paying interest!

6 If the government borrows from a bank then bank deposits are unchanged until the government spends the money, when they rise. (Remember: the government's bank deposits are outside the money supply.)

If the government borrows from you or me, or a pension fund, then bank deposits fall (by definition) when the money is paid to the government. Deposits rise when the government spends the money. The *net* result is that the money supply is *unchanged* because the fall and rise cancel our each other.

7 In 1992–3, only M0 had a growth target – between 0 and 4 per cent over the year to March 1993.

8 Banks, building societies, pension funds, life assurance companies, unit trusts, investment trusts, finance houses and centralised lending institutions. Friendly societies and credit unions are smaller types.

9 The Act was the Building Societies Act 1986, which enabled societies to compete more effectively with banks for personal customers. Thus, bank and building society deposits became very similar. In addition, it gave societies the right to convert themselves into banks. When the Abbey National became a bank in 1989, one effect was to swamp some of the money supply figures, which comprised mainly bank deposits. Because building society deposits are already in M4, the statistics for M4 are unchanged and hence can still be used.

10 Because the cheque may be dishonoured. This is in spite of the use of cheque guarantee cards. Also, nobody really knows whether any particular cheque will increase a debit balance on a current account or decrease a credit balance. All the payee wants to know is 'Will it be paid?'

11 Loans and deposits are secured; the Bank of England supplies day-to-day sterling liquidity to the banking system via its operations in the discount market; it uses these operations to signal changes in short-term interest rates.

12 Loanable funds, liquidity preference.

13 Because they do not place the transactions on their own books, e.g. an estate agent merely acts for the seller and does not buy the house from him or her. Their incomes come from commissions and not interest.

14 Insurance is seen to be a major growth area, especially life assurance and personal pension business. Estate agents were making losses at the end of the 1980s but some insurance companies and banks were still buying them – if the price was right! The purchase of a house is usually the largest purchase a person ever makes, and so there are good opportunities to 'cross-sell' loans, life assurance policies and budget accounts.

15 Only their liabilities (bank notes and bank deposits) were accepted as money. Today, building societies' deposits are very important parts of M2 and M4, so their liabilities are virtually the same as banks' liabilities.

16 Scarcity, stability, portability (transferability), uniformity, durability, recognisability, acceptability, divisibility.

17 When deficit firms/households borrow *directly* from surplus firms/households. They do this in the inter-company market, while commercial paper (CP) issued by large companies is often bought by the treasuries of other large companies. However, CP can be bought by other financial intermediaries and banks.

18 Because (a) there are many types of borrowers, with many degrees of risk; (b) loans can be for many periods of time; (c) loans can be in many different currencies – not just sterling; (d) the tax treatment of loans can vary, e.g. MIRAS (mortgage interest relief at source).

19 A medium of exchange – 'round' money to pass from hand to hand! A liquid store of value – 'flat' money to be piled high!

20 Only if they have products into which the depositors are locked for a considerable period of time. Building societies are more likely to have such accounts for investors but competition is so fierce that most products have an encashment option, usually involving an interest-rate penalty.

■ CHAPTER 11

1 The English are becoming less inefficient at growing vines and more efficient at exploiting new tourist ideas.

2 All, except apples. Apples are a seasonal product and cannot be stored so a reduction in export sales could result in loss of part of a whole year's crop. Also, France is in the EC, so VERs cannot be requested.

3 In Munich it is a tourist receipt in the invisibles section of the German current account. In Manchester it is a merchandise import.

4 A small part of the sales price. In 'profits' of IPD or as a fee/royalty in 'services'.

5 Increase in UK's official reserves and an increase in external liabilities. In IPD, with a negative sign. (a) Receiving banker and share registration. (b) Share registration, collections or negotiations.

6 (a) Tourist receipts. (b) Service receipts. Both are invisibles in the UK's current account.
Bank products: (a) foreign notes, travellers' cheques, Eurocheques, credit cards; (b) negotiations, SWIFT.

7 Depreciation/devaluation of exchange rate (provided the country is not a full member of EMS); deflation, high interest rates, prices and incomes policy, export drive. Banks' credit expansion would be curtailed – except for export finance – and high interest rates could lead to more bad debts.

8 Banks should be able to expand their overseas operations, if they wish.

9 Asset sales and/or borrowing, in one form or another. UK banks, with big

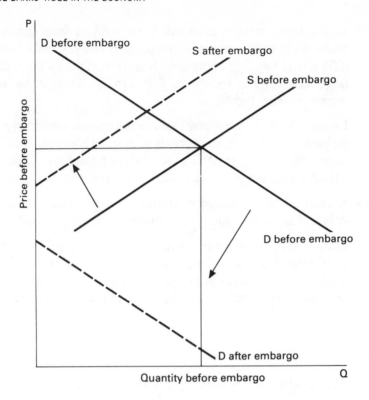

currency operations, can help with borrowing and advice/help with asset sales, as with privatisation.

10 Borrowing from IMF and World Bank. Indian banks, with only small overseas operations, would not be in a position to help, and the world's leading commercial banks have no wish to increase their lending to developing countries.

11 *See* diagram above.

The new D curve will shrink into the bottom left-hand corner of the diagram and S curve will move upwards to the left because Iraq cannot ship its goods. In this diagram, they do not cross, so there is no trade, but Iraq could subsidise its supply curve so that a small amount of trade occurs.

12 Future earnings from IPD will fall by the amount no longer received from assets. Reserves will rise.

13 Germany and the USA must borrow even more on capital account, while Japan merely invests part of its current account surplus.

14 It is a surplus. There could be problems – with either strained relations or a movement towards union.

15 Probably easier, provided they all traded equally with one another.

16   −200   +250   −50
       +200   −300   +100
         —   −50   +50

17 Very helpful. Country can then lend to overseas borrowers and invest in overseas assets, e.g. branch networks.

18 (a) Current account: visible earnings from oil exports would rise. IPD would on balance rise as UK oil companies made grater profits overseas. Inflation would curtail UK exports of manufactures, already hit by a rising exchange rate a sterling was bought to pay for oil.

Capital account: UK oil companies would invest more in overseas oil production, platforms, etc., but US companies would probably invest more in North Sea fields which were unprofitable until now. So, a net inflow of capital.

(b) A fall would result in the opposite effects.

19 Fall in the oil price; too much spending on imports; increasing payments to EC budget.

20 We do not need: GDP, budget deficit, total company profits and loans *outstanding* (that's the clue) to foreign banks.

	Rbn	
Exports	250	
Imports	−370	
Visible balance	−120	
Tourist receipts	15	
Other invisibles	78	(Invisibles (net) 70)
Net IPD	−23	
Current account	−50	
Net capital inflow	47	
Fall in reserves	3	(Transactions in external assets/liabilities 50)
	Nil	

■ CHAPTER 12

1 In Zimbabwe sterling is being quoted at £2.5 for Z$10.

2 Because the authorities (Treasury and the Bank of England) will raise interest rates to attract investors who will bid up the exchange rate.

3 (a) Tourists would be buying sterling with foreign rates, travellers' cheques and credit cards; exporters would need finance and payment products.
(b) Tourist trade and exporters would flourish. The public would be hit by a general rise in prices, as would the shopkeepers and importers.

4 Oil prices would rise, as would transport costs. The bank's heating costs and salary bill would increase.

5 Inflow of cash (a debit); increase in external liabilities as the assets are

owned by a foreigner (a credit). Its exports still count as UK exports, although it is now foreign-owned. Also, its dividends now appear as a debit in the IPD section.

The UK bank could lose remunerative international business, while still having to cash the weekly wages cheque!

6 Because inflation is higher or interest rates are lower than in other major countries.

7 To correct a current account deficit, a country will often devalue its exchange rate and begin to deflate the economy.

8 Finance comes from:

(a) increasing liabilities – borrowing from overseas;
(b) decreasing assets – selling assets located at home or overseas and/or running down reserves of foreign exchange.

9 (a) Make them more expensive in their export markets.
(b) Make their sterling value lower.

10 It would fall, so inflation should be less. Exports of oil will still be priced in US dollars.

11 To ensure that the deal is done at the current exchange rate and not at yesterday's.

To advise the dealers of movements in or out of a nostro account so that the correct balance can be maintained. This advice is still needed when exchange rates are fixed.

12 No. UK will need the agreement of all other EC members now that sterling is in the ERM.

17 Nostro accounts are kept with correspondent banks and are in foreign currencies. Vostro accounts are kept at our bank *by* correspondent banks and are in sterling.

Without the use of foreign currency accounts with banks abroad, this bank will have to convert all foreign currency transactions into sterling, passing them through its vostro accounts with its correspondent banks. This is a cumbersome process.

18 A theory that exchange rates reflect the comparative purchasing powers of the two currencies involved. If the purchasing power (at home) of one currency falls, as domestic prices rise, so then its exchange rate will fall.

19 Because the majority of foreign exchange deals are involved with finance and investment rather than trade in goods. Investors seek high interest rates, provided there is little risk of the currency they buy falling against their domestic currency.

20 Most likely by 1 January 1994.

■ CHAPTER 13

1 (a) The US dollar would rise, making UK exports more competitive in the USA. Sterling might fall, making UK inflation rise. The USA is *the* economic power.
(b) Ireland is about 1/75 the size of the USA economically and quite small in relation to the UK. The overall affect would be minimal.
(c) German interest rates lead the general level of interest rates in the EC. Under the rules of the ERM, the UK may have to raise interest rates if sterling falls substantially against the DM.

2 Banks and building societies are able to bid for large deposits to fund their lending. They do not need to rely on a branch network.

3 Borrowing from banks and building societies, from the private sector (including pension funds and life assurance companies) and overseas. And taxation! Strictly, receipts from the sale of nationalised industries are treated as a deduction from expenditure.

4 Prudential control ensures that participants in these markets do not act recklessly. The new financial instruments and their markets – such as commercial paper and derivatives – need to be understood before regulations can be introduced.

5 Because the authorities wished to 'test the water' by making the market's reaction to entry and a 14 per cent base rate. In the event, share prices and the exchange rate of sterling against most currencies rose.

6 The money markets which began after the mid-1950s – inter-bank, CDs etc. Loans and deposits are unsecured, unlike the discount market, and the Bank of England does not play a day-to-day role in them.
They provide wholesale banks with deposits and retail banks and building societies with an alternative source of deposits, not dependent on their branches.

7 If the Bank of England sets a limit to interest rates it loses control over the money supply. If it controls the money supply, then interest rates will rise dramatically. It has a monopoly over the money supply – but it cannot control both price and quantity.

8 EFTPOS seems to be dominated by credit cards and debit cards. Cheques, standing orders, direct debits, BACS, bank giro credits, CHAPS.

9 The equation of exchange: M = amount of money; V = velocity of circulation; P = price level; T = transactions (GDP)

(a) Loans and overdrafts.
(b) Those mentioned in the answer to Question 8.
(c) Current accounts, savings and investment accounts. CDs held by non-banks.

10 (a) Narrow money is money used as medium of exchange. Transactions demand is another name for the need to use money as a medium of exchange – for spending.
(b) Ninety-day deposits are well outside the one-month maximum for interest-bearing bank deposits in M2. However, many 90-day accounts have very easy withdrawal terms, e.g. no penalty if £10,000 remains in the account. Balances over £10,000 in such accounts could easily be used for day-to-day spending (i.e. transactions balances).

11 Money: deposits.
Not money: share and loan capital, reserves, taxation, trade creditors.

12 We add the following together:

(a) consumers' expenditure on goods and services;
(b) gross domestic fixed capital formation;
(c) government expenditure on goods and services;
(d) net exports of goods and services, i.e. we do not count imports because some other country produced them;
(e) physical increase in stocks.

The clue is in word 'finance'. Payment products are not wanted.

(a) personal loans, term loans, overdrafts, factoring.
(b) overdrafts, loans, leasing.
(c) — (the government creates the products, e.g. gilts)
(d) Loans, overdrafts, leasing, factoring, forfaiting, advances against bills, documentary credits, ECGD-guaranteed loans, etc.

13 Still true. Perhaps the balance between the functions has changed, with greater emphasis on insurance, unit trusts, etc. Also, more people have more than one bank account.

14 Assets which fulfil the liquid store of value function but not the medium of exchange function. Nearly all bank deposits fulfil both functions.

15/16 As shown in your studies for 'The Business of Banking'.

17 (a) Loans, overdrafts, leasing (for plant and machinery.
(b) Home loans (mortgages).

18 XYZ is a plc, so it is British with its accounts in sterling (the unit of account). Earnings in US$ will decline in sterling if the US$ falls, e.g. US$2 = £1, but when US$3 = £1 then US$2 = £0.67p.
Hence, the sterling equivalent of 50 per cent of its earnings will fall so that total earnings will be affected.

19 Functions; qualities; notes/coin, bank deposits, building society deposits, a single European currency.

Outline answers for selected activities

60 Front Street
Anytown
Tyne & Wear
NE76 4QT

20 October 199X

Dear Mrs Smith,

It was nice to see you at the Metro Centre the other day. I've been working at the bank since I left school, and was delighted to pass all three subjects in the Preliminary Section of the Banking Certificate.

However, this year seems much harder – accountancy, law and economics, which weren't taught at the High School. I can understand why we didn't do law and accounts, because they are very specialised and there weren't enough periods in the timetable. But economics is different: it seems to affect everything I do – and what everybody else does. We study people, firms, governments and, of course, banks. Some of these things are important at election time – our year will be on the electoral register soon and then we'll have to make up our own minds. By the way, did you know that Mr Major was a member of BIFU – that's our union – before he became an MP?

Economics is an interesting subject but it seems very hard. We're not expected to know facts but causes of things and possible outcomes. If we'd known just a little, it would have been a help. In short, what I'm asking is: can you and your colleagues ask the Governors to introduce a GCSE economics course? It would have been immensely helpful to me, and would benefit all those who leave school and work in commerce – and their numbers do seem to be increasing!

By the way, when I've sat the exams next May I'm going to run in the Great North Run in the autumn. Can you sponsor me, please? What with training *and* studying, I'm very busy, as I'm sure you'll understand.

Best wishes.

■ ACTIVITY 2.3

Your list might look something like this; but times and programmes are often changed.

Daily

(Mondays to Fridays)	0635-0655	BBC1	*Business Breakfast*
	2145-2200	Radio 4	*Financial World Tonight*
(*Note*:	2230-2315	BBC2	*Newsnight* carries some good economic news but is mainly political. Good for Budget night or if a Chancellor resigns!

Weekly

Thursdays	2240-2310	ITV	*The City Programme*
Saturdays	1200-1225	Radio 4	*Money Box* (mainly personal finance)
Sundays	1835-1915	BBC2	*The Money Programme*

■ ACTIVITY 3.1

Demand increasing – curve shifts to the right:

(a) prolonged heavy rain – more umbrellas, wellingtons, raincoats, meals in restaurants;
(b) heatwave – more ice cream, salads, soft drinks, swim suits, shorts, sun tops;
(c) cold winter – more tinned soups, overcoats, hats, boots.

Demand decreasing – curve shifts to the left:

(a) prolonged heavy rain – less ice cream, salads (in summer, for picnics);
(b) heatwave – fewer raincoats, wellingtons, tinned soups.

It seems that the demand for clothes could be more affected by weather than that for food, because so many households in the UK now have fridges and freezers.

■ ACTIVITY 3.2

Supply increasing – curve shifts to the right:

(a) prolonged heavy rain – supply is rather more likely to decrease (*see* below);
(b) heat wave – similar to (a);
(c) correct weather for a particular crop – wheat needs dry weather when sown, then some rain and then dry weather before and during the harvest.

Supply decreasing – curve shifts to the left:

(a) prolonged heavy rain – less vegetables if they rot in the ground; less wheat if there's too much rain at sowing or harvest-time;

(b) heat wave – some fruit crops may fail if there is a draught;
(c) cold winter – vegetables cannot be dug out of the ground;
(d) spring frosts – fruit blossom is killed, so fruit crop fails in the summer.

The supply of clothes is hardly affected by the weather.

■ ACTIVITY 3.3

Student: Let's take your last point first, because it is correct. There are a number of different ways of taking money abroad apart from travellers' cheques. Foreign currency and even sterling are straight forward alternatives but the development of plastic money has really changed things. Credit cards, Eurocheques with guarantee cards and even ATM cards are used today. Some ATMs have instructions in six languages! So, travellers' cheques have to be priced very finely if sales are to be maintained. Otherwise, people will use cash or plastic.

Senior colleague: I never realised that. I haven't been abroad for 20 years! Things certainly changed since I was your age.
But there's still the problem of falling sales after a rise in commission. Do all these new products mean less sales?

Student: Not exactly, because in very nearly every case, when a supplier raises his price, some people will no longer buy the product. When a bus company raises fares, some passengers will walk, especially those travelling a short distance. But they'll come back, when it rains or after they've had a big pay rise.
The important thing is: how many people will be driven away by the rise? If it's a lot, then total sales revenue will be lower after the rise than it was before, and that would be disastrous. And, if there are a great many substitutes, as there are with travellers' cheques, we must expect total sales commission to fall a lot, perhaps by more than the percentage increase.

Senior colleague: Well, I've learnt two things ...

■ ACTIVITY 4.2

Farming: Most operations are now mechanised:

(a) milking;
(b) sowing;
(c) harvesting;
(d) hedge-cutting;
(e) sorting fruit.

Apart from arable farms, however, most are still family businesses because that is the wish of the farmers and their families.

Motor car manufacturing: Highly mechanised but work on 'the track' is very monotonous. So, firms have introduced team-work but, more important, robots. Market is big, so firms are large – to get the economies of scale.

Hairdressing: Only partly mechanised, because it is such a personal service. Also, the market is very small – within a few miles' radius of the shop.

Solicitors: Office machinery and computers help, but the market for a firm is still small.

Banking: We now have note-counting machines, ATMs and cheque sorters, but the largest are miles away in computer centres. Most specialisation occurs in head offices, although it is possible in large branches (i.e. those with large markets).

Increased emphasis on selling rather than bookkeeping could place a limit on economies of scale.

■ ACTIVITY 5.1

Such petrol is usually slightly dearer. Why? Often, due to the lack of a nearby competitor. The petrol stations are found away from main roads as a rule, because the operators cannot afford the rents charged for the 'prime sites' on such roads.

■ ACTIVITY 6.2

	£bn	%
Consumers' expenditure	361	76.8
Central government consumption	61	13.0
Local authorities' consumption	39	8.3
Gross domestic fixed capital formation	100	21.3
Physical increase in stocks	3	0.6
	564	120.0
Exports of goods and services	123	
Imports of goods and services	142	
Net imports	(19)	–4.0
Gdp at market prices	545	116.0
Less taxes (plus subsidies) on goods and services	(75)	–16.0
	470	100.0

A 10 per cent rise in consumers' expenditure has apparently led to a 7.6 per cent rise in gross domestic product.

It is wrong to assume that all the other figures remain unchanged because:

(a) some of the consumers' spending will be on imports;
(b) much of it will bear taxes, so that –£75bn could become –£80bn;

(c) this extra tax revenue will be spent by the government, so that the £61bn will rise;

(d) businessmen, encouraged by the growth in consumer sales, may begin to invest more in new buildings, plant and machinery, so that gross domestic fixed capital formation will rise. Not only that, but the government, with extra tax revenues, may decide to do the same.

■ ACTIVITY 6.4

	Boom	*Recession*
Job advertisements in local papers	More	Less
Postcard notices in CTNs offering gardening and decorating services	More	Less
Empty parking spaces at factory car parks	Less	More
Empty shops and closing down sales	Less	More
Men under 65 shopping during the day	Less	More
New cars, with K or L registrations	A lot	Not as many

■ ACTIVITY 9.2

Three per cent over base rate is always higher than the interest rates available on liquid assets.

The reasons are that the banks' money is outstanding for a much longer period – a home loan, on average, lasts for eight to ten years – and the risk of default by the borrower is much greater.

Most liquid assets are funds lent to the government, which is unlikely to default, or to banks and building societies, which are closely supervised by the Bank of England and the Building Societies Commission, respectively.

■ ACTIVITY 9.3

(a) *See* balance sheet of XYZ Bank Plc on the next page.

(b) It is a wholesale bank because it has:

- only one office;
- a high management/staff ratio;
- low cash holdings;
- large deposits/advances in foreign currency.

■ ACTIVITY 10.1

Probably not, because a dictionary is concerned with everyday meanings of words. It is not a textbook of economics, or of anything else for that matter.

XYZ Bank Plc: Balance Sheet as at 31 December 199–

	£m
Share capital (paid up)	200
Capital reserves	400
P & L account	50
Sterling deposits	3800
Foreign currency deposits	3900
	8350
Notes and coin	2
Balance at Bank of England	14
Treasury bills	2
Money market assets	1146
Commercial bills	600
Gilt-edged securities	86
Advances (sterling)	3000
Advances (foreign currency)	3000
Investment in UK leasing company	500
	8350

■ ACTIVITY 10.2

This is an outline of your reply – remember you're talking.

This is a good question and a difficult one. We must go into quite a bit of theory.

First, UK retail banks are oligopolists, who respond to competition by devising new products rather than by drastic price changes.

Secondly, there is a 'liquidity spectrum' – from 'very liquid' to 'quite liquid' and 'not very liquid'; banks and building societies design their products to capture the funds which people seek to deposit with these liquidity requirements in mind.

Notes: When speaking, always begin a reply to a question with 'That's a good question' – it flatters the questioner and gives you time to think! But never use this beginning in a written answer or in a formal interview.

Also, although some French banks are nationalised, we shouldn't stress this point, because many Europeans think that UK banks are over-staffed and inefficient, in spite of their being privately owned.

■ ACTIVITY 11.3

1 (a) Credit exports – bigger visible trade surplus (or smaller deficit)
     Debit cash – larger foreign exchange reserves (external assets)
(b) Credit exports – as (a) above
     Debit buyer with the loan – larger external assets for the UK because of the loan.

Note: The sterling paid to the exporter by the UK bank making the loan to the importer will not feature in the UK's balance of payments. However, if the funds pass to the foreign importer then the UK's foreign exchange reserves will fall and then rise as the cash flows out and back.

Eventually, the loan will be repaid, so that the composition of the UK's external assets will change, with loans falling and foreign exchange reserves rising. In the meantime, interest will be credited to invisible exports and debited to the foreign exchange reserves.

(c) *Note:* Presumably the foreign buyer will not be paying for the goods for some time: otherwise, there would be no point in the UK exporter borrowing from a foreign bank.

Credit exports – as above.

Debit buyer with a trade debt – as above, except that it is not a loan from a UK bank.

Credit the foreign bank – with the amount of its loan, which is an increase in UK external liabilities.

Debit cash – as above.

Eventually, the loan will be repaid by the UK exporter, as the foreign buyer repays his debt. Thus, the UK's assets and liabilities both fall by the same amount.

Interest payments would roughly offset each other.

2 Credit external assets – as the total of portfolio investments fall.

Debit cash – as foreign exchange reserves rise as the proceeds are received.

Net result: UK external assets are unchanged in total.

Note: Credits on IPD in future years will be smaller by the difference between the dividends on the shares and any interest received on the holdings of foreign exchange.

Past examination papers

Answer **five** questions. Each question carries 20 marks. Time: 3 hours.

1 (a) What is meant by diminishing marginal utility? Can it be measured? [5]

(b) To the banks' and building societies' personal customers what is the utility of:

(i) current accounts with credit balances [3]
(ii) current accounts with authorised overdrafts [3]
(iii) the various types of savings accounts [3]
(iv) the various types of loan accounts [3]
(v) 'with profits' endowment life assurance policies. [3]

[Total − 20 marks]

2 (a) Distinguish between Marginal Cost, Marginal Revenue and Marginal Product. [8]

(b) Explain, with the aid of a table or a diagram, why two of the concepts discussed in (a) must be equal for a firm's profits to be at a maximum. [8]

(c) List four items which feature in the marginal costs of a retail bank. [4]

[Total − 20 marks]

3 Many UK retail banks have introduced bank charges for operating the accounts of clubs and societies.

(a) Demonstrate, by means of demand and supply curves, the likely results of these charges on the numbers of such accounts held by:

(i) a bank which imposed such charges [5]
(ii) a bank which did not [5]

(b) What factors are likely to influence a retail bank in deciding whether or not to introduce such charges? [5]

(c) State five other instances where banks have begun to levy charges in recent years. [5]

[Total − 20 marks]

4 (a) Why do countries engage in international trade? [10]

(b) Give examples of eight bank products, apart from sterling loans and overdrafts, which help to finance international trade and enable firms to make payments to their suppliers and buyers in other countries. [8]

(c) Do you think that the use of these products will increase or decrease when the European Community has a single currency? Give brief reasons for your answer. [2]

[Total − 20 marks]

5 (a) If interest rates remain unchanged, and the rate of inflation falls, what happens to the 'real rate of interest'? Who is likely to benefit from such a development? [5]

(b) What is meant by the statement that "real rates of interest were strongly positive in the UK in 1991"? Who suffers from positive real rates of interest? [5]

(c) For what reasons do banks – wholesale and retail - maintain similar rates of interest for similar products? [5]

(d) What is meant by the 'endowment effect'? Why is it of decreasing importance to UK retail banks in the 1990s? [5]

[Total – 20 marks]

6 Explain the effects of a sudden, sharp fall in oil prices, from their current levels; on:

(a) the current account of the UK's balance of payments [8]
(b) operating costs of UK firms [5]
(c) the coal mining industry in the UK [2]
(d) the real gross domestic product of the UK [5]

[Total – 20 marks]

7 (a) With reference to the functions of money, explain why it is impossible for an economy to progress or even survive without money. [16]

(b) Outline problems likely to arise during the introduction of a single currency for the European Community. [4]

[Total – 20 marks]

8 (a) Compare and contrast the effects of the economic recession of the early 1990s on banks and building societies in the UK. [10]

(b) What actions can the UK government take to bring the economy out of recession? How is such action constrained by membership of the ERM? [10]

[Total – 20 marks]

9 Each of the following four sentences about the Bank of England contains a fundamental error. Explain how and why each sentence is incorrect.

(a) Founded nearly 300 years ago the Bank of England has become one of the world's leading independent central banks. [5]

(b) In 1991 it controlled the quantity of money and credit in the UK by imposing restraints on the growth of balance sheets of banks, through the use of special deposits and reserve ratios. [5]

(c) It takes no part in the clearing of cheques, etc., because it has few commercial customers. [5]

(d) It is not involved in the management of the national debt, which is the responsibility of the National Debt Commissioners. [5]

[Total – 20 marks]

Outline answers
Question 1

(a) Utility is satisfaction or usefulness arising from consuming a product or service. It usually falls the more we use the item in question, so that the last unit consumed produces the least satisfaction.

    (b) (i)   means of payment

         source of cash

         accrues a little interest

    (ii) means of payment and source of cash

         smoothing the uneven flow of income or of payments

    (iii) liquid stores of value

         more interest than on current account

         ease of access often related to interest rate

    (iv) mortgages – buy a house over a long period

         personal loans – buy items with a fixed monthly repayment

         enhancing cash flow so to buy goods earlier

    (v) a means of saving over a long period

         can be used *as security* for a mortgage or for a straight loan *[bonus mark]*

Question 2

(a) Marginal cost is the addition to total cost resulting from an additional unit of output.

    Marginal revenue is the addition to total revenue resulting from an additional unit of output (assuming it is sold).

    Marginal product is the additional output resulting when one factor of production is increased by one unit with the other factors held constant.

    (b) The two concepts involved are MC and MR.

        TR less TC = Profit

        So profit is maximised when difference between TR and TC is greatest.

        At this point, MC = MR then profit is unchanged

           if MC > MR then profit falls

           if MR > MC then profit rises.

        Table needs output TC, MC, TR, price MR, Profit.

        One such table could be:

Units of output	TC	MC	Price	TR	MR	Profit (TR less TC)
	£	£	£	£	£	£
38	380		12	456		76
39	390	10	12	468	12	78
40	400	10	12	480	12	80
41	411	11	12	492	12	81
42	423	12	12	504	12	81
43	436	13	12	516	12	80
44	450	14	12	528	12	78
45	465	15	12	540	12	75

It demonstrates that, given these costs and a price of £12, that profit falls after 42 units are produced, when MC has become larger than MR.

Other tables could show: falling MC
rising MR
falling MR

Two possible diagrams are:

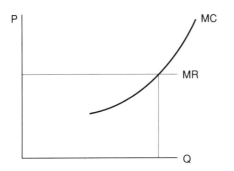

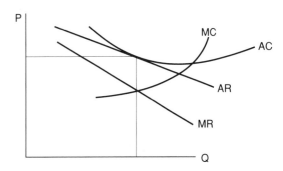

Constant MR   **Falling MR**

(c) Interest on deposits
Capital and liquidity costs of balance sheet expansion
Staff overtime
Advertising
(not: premises, salaries, computers)

Question 3

(a) (i) Bank imposing charges – bank loses accounts, depending largely on slope of D curve – greater the PED (price elasticity of demand) the greater the number of accounts lost.

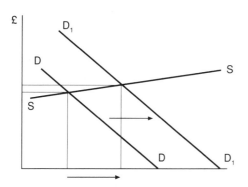

(ii) Bank not imposing charges – bank gains accounts, depending on size of its competitors' price rises. (See diagram on the next page.)

(b) Banks' profits – how they are being affected by:
● recession;
● competition with building societies;

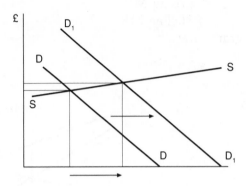

- payment of interest on most credit balances.
  Growing numbers of accounts for clubs/societies – a new part of the market.
  Estimates that PED < 1
(c) Stopping a cheque
  Duplicate statements
  Travel facilities
  Credit cards – annual charges
               – duplicate statements
               – change of statement date
  Letters re 'out of order' accounts
  Management time

Question 4

(a) To enjoy greater specialisation than is possible within a single country owing to differences of land (minerals), climate (agriculture), labour and capital. Thus, Western Europe imports bananas, rice and other agricultural products which it cannot produce efficiently.

Where countries *can* produce the same goods – e.g. motor cars or TVs – then the country(ies) with the greatest productivity will tend to specialise in its production, with greater total output.

Even if a country has an absolute advantage in (say) two products vis-a-vis another country then specialisation is still possible, with each country specialising in the item where it has the greater comparative advantage or lesser comparative disadvantage.

(b) Drafts, SWIFT, TTs, LOCs, ECGD – guaranteed loans in foreign currencies; forfeiting, advances against bills, negotiations, collections; foreign currency accounts, factoring, leasing.

(c) Within the EC, these products will vanish, as there is only one currency. But for EC exports to non-EC countries their use should increase, because these exports should increase. However, the overall use of these products is likely to fall.

Question 5

(a) Real rate of interest is the nominal rate of interest (expressed in current prices) less the inflation rate (or RPI). If inflation falls against stationary nominal rates, then the real rate of interest will rise. This will benefit savers, who will find that their interest receipts will purchase more goods and services than previously.

[Bonus mark for stating that real rates can be positive or negative.]

(b) Inflation was well below most interest rates, so that borrowers found their interest payments represented a greater loss of purchasing power than before. Personal and corporate borrowers suffered, especially those with large debts.

(c) Because competition forces them to maintain very similar interest rates.

For wholesale banks competition in the money markets is akin to perfect competition.

For retail banks, most of which are oligopolists, competition to attract new business comes from non-price (non-interest rate) competition, so they tend to charge similar rates.

[Bonus mark: some banks have increased margins, thereby charging a premium interest rate.]

(d) Current accounts paid no interest on credit balances so the banks' average cost of funds was lower. When rates rose, the average cost of funds rose proportionately less than the interest earned on assets and vice versa. Today banks pay some interest on most current accounts.

Question 6

(a) Oil export revenues will fall
    PED < 1
    oil import payments will fall
    PED < 1
Interest, profits and dividends from oil companies will fall.
Sterling could fall, giving UK exporters a further competitive advantage.

(b) direct − energy costs from oil-based fuels would fall
             − road transport costs would fall
    indirect − most domestic input costs would fall
             − but fall in sterling would cause domestic cost of imports to rise.

(c) Cheaper oil would make many of the remaining UK pits unprofitable leading to closure and to further unemployment for coal miners.

(d) GDP at first would be unchanged, since it is unaffected by price changes but later, as industries grow and contract and foreign trade changes, the total of GDP will change.

Examples from above:

Contracting	*Expanding*
coal	exports
	road transport
	oil (PED<1)

Question 7

(a) Money has four functions, each of which is vital to economic growth:
medium of exchange leads to specialisation, economies of scale, so output rises.
liquid store of value savings and investment are done by different people so that much more capital investment is possible than if it had to be financed by retained profits.
standard of deferred payments which provides the legal structure for loans – money is used as the basis on which repayments will be made rather than real goods or index-lined money.
unit of account here money is used for profit determination; resource allocation; budgeting; and forecasting.

(Bonus point: money featuring in monetary policy to achieve policy aims. Societies without a cash economy have lower living standards than those with money.)

(b) There are eight characteristics of money, so students can choose any four likely to cause problems or write about the actual changeover
For example:
- (i) portability – establishing an EC/ECU clearing system
- (ii) acceptability – by people and/or machines
- (iii) recognisability – by people
- (iv) changing legal documents, vending machines, bank balances, rental agreements, etc.

Question 8

(a) *banks*
- personal customers defaulting on
  - mortgages (repossessions)
  - overdrafts
  - personal loans;
- corporate failures, especially among small firms but also larger companies;
- lack of demand for new borrowing;
- high cost of redundancy payments in P/L account.

[Bonus marks for mentioning high cost-income ratios of banks.]
- distress lending to corporates
- self imposed constraints on lending via capital adequacy ratios.

building societies
- personal customers defaulting on mortgages (repossessions);
- not really involved in business lending;
- not many redundancies (lower cost-income ratios);
- some societies forced to merge with larger societies when values of houses repossessed fell below loans outstanding against such properties.

(b) *fiscal policy*
- reduce taxes;
- increased government spending.

monetary policy
- lower interest rates;

- expand credit;
- devalue the exchange rate.

ERM membership required UK to use monetary policy to maintain DM 2.95 bilateral central rate, in order to contain inflation and to converge with EC.
[Bonus mark for possibility of realignment.]
    Interest rates used firstly to support the DM 2.95 rate and then to ease the economy out of recession, once UK left the ERM.

Question 9

Errors corrected:

    (a) Bank of England is not one of the world's most independent central banks:

- monetary policy – base rate and, until ERM, the exchange rate – is in the hands of the Chancellor of the Exchequer.
- Bank's role is to advise and caution and then to implement the Government's decisions.

    (b) Bank does not control the quantity of money and credit in this way:
[Bonus mark: last time such controls used was 1980/1.]

- instead, it relies on the level of interest rates to control credit and thus the growth of the money supply.
- apart from MO – with a target growth of 0–4% to 3/92 – there are no other monetary targets.
[However DM 2.95 can be so regarded – bonus mark.]

    (c) Bank of England takes a very important role in the clearings because:

- it is the government's banker, so payments to the government are payments out of the operational accounts;
- the clearing banks settle their clearing outstanding balances by drawing on their operational accounts;
- as registrar of the national debt it uses BACS to pay interest to stockholders;
- Bank of England's operations in the discount and foreign exchange markets require it to be an active member of the clearing house.

    (d) National debt management is a most important function:

- Bank sells debt on behalf of the government and repays debt when it matures;
- will conduct open market operations in gilts, re-paying stocks before maturity so as to smooth the government's cashflow and selling tap stocks.

■ MAY 1993

Answer **five** questions. Each question carries 20 marks. Time: 3 hours.

1 (a) Explain what is meant by price elasticity of demand.   [7]
    (b) If a large retail bank were to double its charges for cashing cheques for non-customers – e.g. where supported by a cheque guarantee card – show diagrammatically the effects of the increases where:

(i) demand is price elastic [4]
(ii) demand is price inelastic. [4]
(c) Why should a bank wish to turn away customers of other banks by a large increase in charges? Does it make commercial sense? [5]

[Total – 20 marks]

2 (a) Explain how perfect competition is not possible in an industry where there are significant economies of scale. [10]
(b) To what extent can banks compete with each other by:
(i) price competition
(ii) non-price competition. [10]

[Total – 20 marks]

3 (a) Describe the ways by which a country's total output of goods and services is measured. [12]
(b) How does a government seek to achieve a sustainable increase in UK's total output of goods and services? [8]

[Total – 20 marks]

4 (a) Distinguish between fixed and variable costs, giving examples from manufacturing. [10]
(b) Distinguish between fixed and variable (floating) rates of interest, giving examples from the UK. [6]
(c) Explain briefly the impact of rising interest rates and falling sales on the profits of a manufacturer with large fixed costs and substantial borrowings at variable rates of interest. [4]

[Total – 20 marks]

5 (b) Explain the mechanism by which changes in bank and building society sterling lending lead to changes in M4. What other major causes can lead to changes in the money supply? [14]
(c) Why did the increases in this sterling lending, and hence the increases in M4 become much smaller in the early 1990s? [6]

[Total – 20 marks]

6 Your branch has an active bureau de change (foreign currency till) dealing with tourists from the USA, Japan and fellow member states of the European Community. It has a large sub-branch in an industrial estate where there are many company customers owned by US and Japanese multinational firms.
(a) What would be the effects on the UK economy and on your branch's operations and profits of:
(i) the introduction of a single European currency
(ii) a substantial fall in the value of sterling. [14]
(b) What events affecting the UK economy might cause the US and Japanese companies to close down their factories and warehouses on the industrial estate? [6]

[Total – 20 marks]

7 (a) What is meant by inflation and how is it usually measured in the UK? [4]
  (b) What are the effects of a high rate of inflation on:
      (i) firms and businesses   [3]
      (ii) banks and building societies   [3]
      (iii) the economy of a country?   [4]
  (c) How can governments lower the rate of inflation?   [6]

[Total – 20 marks]

8 (a) Define fiscal policy.   [4]
  (b) What is meant by 'tight' fiscal policy?   [2]
  (c) Distinguish monetary policy from fiscal policy and outline how they interact.   [10]
  (d) State four ways in which the commercial banks can lend money to the UK government.   [4]

[Total – 20 marks]

9 (a) Distinguish between a central bank and a commercial bank.   [10]
  (b) For what reasons and in what ways does the Bank of England control and influence the commercial banks of the UK?   [10]

[Total – 20 marks]

Outline answers

Question 1

(a) Measures the responsiveness of quantity demanded to small changes in price. It is measured by dividing the percentage change in the total demanded by the (small) percentage change in price, viz.

$$\frac{2\% \text{ increase in sales}}{1\% \text{ fall in price}} = 2 \text{ (usual negative sign is generally omitted)}$$

when demand is said to be price elastic.

$$\frac{1\% \text{ increase in sales}}{2\% \text{ fall in price}} = \frac{1}{2}$$

when demand is said to be price inelastic.

with $\dfrac{1\% \text{ fall in sales}}{1\% \text{ rise in price}} = 1$ price elasticity of demand is said to be unitary (or unit elasticity)

(b) Elastic demand: number of cheques cashed falls drastically.

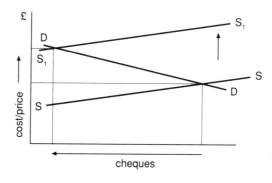

233

Inelastic demand: number of cheques cashed falls slightly.

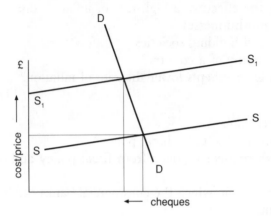

(A bonus mark might have been awarded for noting that PED refers to small price changes, whereas Q refers to doubling of the charge.)

(c) ATM withdrawals are not charged.

Such people are unlikely to change their bankers, and merely clutter up the banking halls for the bank's own customers – who are delayed.

More important, they take up the time of counter staff, who could be cross-selling products to existing customers.

Question 2

(a) Perfect competition requires many small firms, each unable to affect market price by its own actions. Hence, each firm can produce as much as it can, until its MC rises to equal price (=MR). In other words, MC is the constraint on output, coming into operation long before the firm becomes large enough to influence market price.

Economies of scale mean that MC and AC both fall over long ranges of output, so that firms can grow to a size at which they can influence market price.

(b) Price competition is limited because the general level of interest rates (the price of loans) is determined by the government's monetary policy. Competition is found in fractionally different rates of interest and commission charges.

Eventually, most banks step into line, e.g.

- annual charges on credit cards;
- payment of interest on current accounts.

Non-price competition is legendary in retail banking – oligopoly. For example:

- colour;
- image;
- location;
- branding of services;
- quality of service.

Question 3

(a) *Income* from:

- employment (wages/salaries);
- trading profits
  - companies
  - public corporations;
- rent;
- self employment.

Expenditure:

- consumers' expenditure;
- gross domestic fixed cap formation (investment);
- government consumption (goods/services);
- increase in stocks;
- net exports (deduct net imports bonus).

Output:

- indexes by industry of output at constant factor cost (accept constant prices).

Bonus mark: GNP = GDP + net factor income from overseas.

(b)
- Devaluation of exchange rate;
- Stimulating expenditure by a budget deficit
  - either increasing government expenditure
  - or reducing taxes
  - or increasing subsidies;
- Supply-side measures to assist farmers, small firms, etc and to provide training;
- Lowering interest rates.

(b) (i) Price stability has the cornerstone, to be achieved *before* any of the other goals can be achieved over a long period. At present this requires a tight monetary policy.

Price stability is targeted as 1–4% p.a. rise (RPI less mortgage interest or RPI–MIP).

(ii) Supply side methods, especially training.

(iii) Fiscal policy is currently (September 1993) not used to stimulate the economy, but merely respond to increased social security payments and a slow growth in tax receipts by moving to a £37bn PSBR for 1992–93.

Question 4

(a) Fixed costs do not vary with output (but they can change over time), for example: premises (rent), uniform business rate, interest on long-term loans, administration costs including staff salaries, publicity, advertising. They are sometimes known as 'overheads or 'indirect costs'.

Variable costs are those which vary directly with output, for example: wages, overtime, fuel, raw materials, transport.

In the long-term, all costs are variable because the firm can cease production.

(b) Fixed rates are fixed for the life of the loan/instrument, e.g:

- a gilt coupon;
- NSCs;
- personal loans.

(Possible bonus marks for mentioning the first 2–3 years of a fixed rate mortgage offer.)

Floating rates change from time to time, e.g.

- base rate;
- mortgage rates;
- LIBOR.

Causes of changes are: market conditions, conscious decisions of governments and banks.

(c) High fixed costs + falling sales > lower operating/trading profits.

These lower trading profits will have to service larger interest payments on the borrowings. So net profits will fall drastically.

Note: There was no need to distinguish between net and gross profits.

(Possible bonus mark for referring to gearing.)

Question 5

(a) Unless used to buy imports or pay taxes, every loan creates a deposit.

If loan is taken in cash, then M supply rises as cash with public rises (deposits are unchanged).

Changes in interest rates, quantitative and qualitative controls, portfolio constraints affecting bank lending and hence money supply.

M4 includes building society deposits, as building societies deposits are increasingly similar to those of the banks.

Other influences are:

- large PSBR not funded by government borrowing from non-banks and non-building societies (debt sales);
- flow of funds into UK, e.g. credit account surplus.

Note: M4 counterparts not required, but a possible bonus mark for mentioning it. Also a possible bonus mark for mentioning gilt sales to banks (redefinition of funding in March 1993 budget).

(b)

- decline in real GDP – industry needing less to finance its trading;
- reluctance of banks to continue distress lending to firms;
- fall in house prices and number of house sales leading to smaller new lending for house purchase;
- reluctance to take on new borrowing, etc, by both consumers and businesses.

Question 6

(a) (i)
- more vouchers in the new Euro-clearing;
- diminution of forex profits as the 11 EC currencies and sterling merge;
- intra-EC financial transactions should become much cheaper;
- long-term growth in EC exports and tourism;
- USA and Japanese transactions unaffected;
- UK loses all chance of devaluing against the EC countries.

(ii)
- Foreign tourists would increase – in numbers and total spending – as the dollar (more business for and profits for the foreign section) bought more pounds.
- Exports would increase, as sterling became cheaper.
- UK imports would become more expensive and their total value should fall.
- Inflation would increase.
- More export business means less imports for foreign section (depending on price elasticities of demand).
- Current account of UK balance of payments should improve (possible bonus mark for J curve).
- Inward investment into subsidiaries in UK should increase as UK becomes more competitive. This should bring more business to the whole branch.

(b)
- if UK costs (labour, interest rates) rose faster than those in other parts of EC;
- if UK entered 'outer zone' of a two-part EC;
- if UK left the EC;
- if EC engaged in a trade war with USA and Japan;
- if events outside UK made other areas more attractive;
- if there were shortages of skilled labour in UK;
- overall, if the UK lost its comparative advantages;
- strikes increased.

Question 7

(a) Steadily rising general level of prices measured by a price index, usually the General Index of Retail Prices, although other indices (or adjustments of the RPI) are used.

(b) (i) Easier to make profits when prices are rising on domestic market, although profits will be affected if costs rise faster than output prices, especially for exports in face of competition from non-inflating countries. If prices rise too fast, sales may drop and profits fall.

(ii) Customers prefer to borrow rather than to lend (deposit), so interest rates may be raised to adjust the supply and demand of funds. If business borrowers face falling profits, then some may cease trading, leaving banks – but not building societies – with bad debts.

Possible bonus marks for mentioning: uncertainty, distortion of price signals, reallocation of resources.

(iii)
- Exports sales may be harder to achieve, and imports may begin to increase leading to a worsening of the visible balance.
- Exchange rate may fall – if floating – or come under pressure if fixed.
- Borrowers benefit at expense of lenders and those on fixed incomes.

Possible bonus mark for mentioning indexation.

(c)
- prices and incomes policy;
- ERM 1990–92 in UK;
- high exchange rate;
- high interest rates 1988–90 in UK;
- low budget deficit or even budget surplus;
- extra direct taxation;
- lower indirect taxes (massaging the price index downwards).

Question 8

(a) Refers to government spending, government income (largely from taxation but also privatisation) and government borrowing to finance the balance (PSBR).

(b) 'Tight' refers to reducing or containing the size of the PSBR, with few tax increases or increases in spending – not a giveaway budget.

(c) Monetary policy has the same goals as fiscal policy – low inflation, sustainable growth etc, but uses the prices and quantity of money and credit to achieve them.

It works through the exchange rates and interest rates (external and internal price of money) and the quantity of money and credit.

Often targets – published or unpublished – are set, or portfolio constraints (asset/liability ratios and ceilings) are used.

Fiscal policy also uses targets but most are published in the budget and Autumn statement. It works via the taxing and spending of the government to achieve the same goals as monetary policy. It tends to use legal penalties far more frequently than monetary policy, although the latter does use legal controls, e.g. if exchange controls are in force.

The two interact in the size of the government's borrowing (PSBR) and how it is financed. If the government borrows from banks, the money supply will be increased, so it avoids this if at all possible.

(d) *Direct*

- treasury bills – in sterling and ECUs;
- gilts;
- holdings of banknotes.

Possible bonus mark for Euro-currency loans, especially to support sterling in September 1992.

Indirect

- money at call to discount market – secured on Treasury Bills.

Question 9

(a)

Central bank	Commercial bank
Usually owned by government	Usually privately owned (Plc)
Government is major customer	Government is minor customer
Few private customers	Most customers are from private sector
Bankers' bank	
Non-profit seeking	
Responsible for monetary policy	Follows monetary policy
Non-profit seeking	Most are profit seeking
Responsible for note issue	Usually do not issue notes
Smaller than largest commercial banks	Largest ones are bigger than their central bank
Often responsible for prudential regulation	
Only one in a country	Usually many in each country
Operates exchange equalisation account	
Oversees financial system	

(b) UK: *Implementing monetary policy* (decided by Treasury to achieve government's economic goals)

- changes interest rates, viz. base rate directly;
- indirect effect on other interest rates;
- could resurrect a wide range of controls (portfolio constraints) which have been dormant since 1981.

Prudential controls (to prevent commercial banks from acting recklessly)

- licenses banks under 1987 Act;
- capital ratios – *Minimum* of 8% of risk-weighted assets;
- liquidity ratios – confidential to each bank;
- large exposures – % age of capital;
- foreign exchange exposure;
- controllers/directors must be fit and proper persons;
- continuous dialogue/interviews;
- discussions with auditors;
- Deposit Protection Fund.

Postscript: Black Wednesday and its results

OBJECTIVES

After studying the Postscript you should be able to:
- recall the events of the late summer of 1992;
- explain why these events occurred;
- describe what happened after 16 September;
- state the problems facing the UK Government for 1994 and 1995.

■ THE EVENTS

In 1992, the UK experienced a financial crisis comparable to that of 1931 when the UK had to leave the gold standard. This time the UK left the ERM. In addition, Italy also left and Spain devalued while Spain (again) and Portugal later devalued their currencies against those remaining in the ERM. Early in 1993, the Irish punt was devalued.

To try to raise the exchange rate, the UK authorities raised base rates by 2 per cent on the morning of 16 September. When that increase had no effect whatsoever, the authorities announced in the early afternoon that base rates would be increased by a further 3 per cent to 15 per cent, with effect from the next day, 17 September. This, too, did not stop the selling of sterling.

Shortly after 7.30pm, the Chancellor announced, in front of the TV cameras, that the UK was temporarily suspending its membership of the ERM and that the increase of 3 per cent in base rates would not be implemented.

Most observers have named that day 'Black Wednesday'.

■ THE REASONS FOR THE CRISIS

The UK had joined the ERM in October 1990 to bring down the rate of inflation, which was then about 10.5 per cent p.a. Unfortunately, sterling was linked to a currency (the DM) whose economy was booming as a result of the unification of the two halves of Germany – and the UK was then entering a recession. Instead of Germany pulling the UK out of the recession, the German authorities – largely its central bank – raised interest rates slightly in order to prevent their inflation rate from rising.

From the autumn of 1990 until the summer of 1992, the UK authorities had been able to lower interest rates as inflation fell. However, by that summer, UK interest rates were roughly level to German interest rates and could be reduced no further. The reason was if they were below German interest rates, then sterling would not be able to keep within $\pm 6\%$ of DM2.95.

The problem was two-sided:

- that the UK needed interest rate cuts desperately, so as to prevent unemployment rising and output falling;
- that the UK dare not raise interest rates to bring the DM exchange rate anywhere near the DM2.95 bilateral central rate, for fear of causing the worst recession this century.

The situation can be likened to soldiers defending a town with one gun, which is so dangerous that, if they fire it, the whole town is destroyed.

The speculators spotted the UK's weakness and pounced. They borrowed sterling at about 12% a year (about 1% a month), sold the sterling for DM at about DM2.80 and waited. When sterling fell to around DM2.55 they bought sterling with their DM, repaid their loan and kept the balance of the DM sale as profit.

This is the arithmetic of the deals (ignoring commission and expenses).

(say)
10 September   Borrows £100m @ 12% a year
                  Sells this for DM @ DM2.80 = £1
                  Obtains DM2.80m from this transaction

(say)
24 September   When sterling falls to DM2.55 buys £100m for DM2.55m
                  This repays the loan of £100m, leaving the speculator with DM25m out of which he has to pay the interest for 14 days on the £100m loan. At DM2.55 to £1, DM25m equates to £9.8m, and the interest is £460,274 ($^{14}/_{365} \times 12 \times$ £100m = £460,273.97). Net profit of £9.34m in a fortnight!

This speculation was profitable because the UK and Germany were at opposite ends of the economic cycle – UK striving to come out of recession and Germany striving to keep inflation down.

The speculators forced the UK out of the ERM.

The problems of that summer were not helped by three other factors:

- The central banks had begun to assume that the ERM was, by then, a system of virtually fixed exchange rates. They forgot that it is still possible to change the rates in the ERM;
- There was a failure, it seems, of communication between the UK, France, Germany and Italy. The Italians were agreeable to a devaluation of the lira, but the French wished to keep their central rates unchanged against the DM;
- France chose to ratify the Maastricht Treaty by means of a referendum on 20 September. By the end of August, the opinion polls were forecasting a very close vote – in fact, the French voted 'yes' by about the same narrow majority as the Danes voted 'no'. As the vote approached, so the speculation against sterling increased.

■ THE RESULTS OF THE CRISIS

- Firstly, the UK was able to 'do its own thing' in economic policy and within six months, there were fairly clear signs that the recession was ending. Base rates were down to 6% p.a. in the early part of 1993;
- Secondly, the UK had to construct an entirely new monetary policy, because the ERM had gone and the ERM had been the foundation of the old monetary policy;
- Thirdly, the devaluation of sterling against other ERM currencies, as well as against the UK dollar and the yen, increased potential inflationary pressure for the UK – via higher import prices.

■ WHAT IS MONETARY POLICY NOW?

It took the Government three weeks to reconstruct its economic policy after the UK quit the ERM on 16 September. The major points of this policy are:

- A definite target for inflation, measured by the RPI minus mortgage interest payments. This measure is termed *underlying inflation* and the target is to be between 1% and 4% p.a. for the lifetime of this Parliament which could be until April 1997. "I believe by the end of the Parliament we need to be in the lower part of the range", said the then Chancellor Mr Norman Lamont.

  However, there is an escape clause, in that the target might have to be exceeded if there were price movements resulting from sharp changes in the terms of trade – particularly through commodity prices.
- A long-term target for inflation of 2% p.a. – presumably into the next century.
- Continuing the existing 0–4% monitoring range (formerly named a target) for the annual rise of MO.
- Using interest rates to contain inflation, after monitoring;
  (a) monetary aggregates (MO, M4, etc.) (but see below);
  (b) asset prices, including prices of houses, shares and gilt-edged securities;
  (c) the exchange rate.
- Committing the Government to explaining fully to Parliament and the markets the reasons for any failure to achieve these targets and detailing how to get inflation back within its target range.
- Using judgement, rather than automatic rules, as the cornerstone of policy (as before joining the ERM in October 1990).
- No target for the exchange rate.
- 'Monitoring ranges' for M4, which are between 3% and 9% per annum. If M4 grew at a rate outside these ranges there would be increasing case for concern. The same would apply if MO grew outside its monitoring range.
- A tight fiscal policy, but with little reference to replacing the ERM as the cornerstone of economic policy with a new Medium Term Financial Strategy. In fact, the cornerstone of monetary policy appeared to be the inflation target.

- Great openness in monetary policy, involving:
  (a) publication of a monthly monetary report submitted to regular meetings of the Chancellor and the Governor of the Bank of England;
  (b) the Bank of England publishing a quarterly Inflation Report, commenting on progress towards achieving the inflation target;
  (c) appointing a Panel of (seven) Independent Forecasters, to meet three times a year to submit their own forecasts to the Chancellors. Dubbed the 'Seven Wise Men', they could be regarded as advisers (on what to do on policy) rather than forecasters. Their reports, too, are published.

In late May 1993, Mr Lamont was replaced by Mr Kenneth Clarke as Chancellor of the Exchequer, who outlined his views on economic policy in a speech about three weeks later.

The new Chancellor restated most of the above policy guidelines but he added that low inflation, while crucially important, was of little use unless it was accompanied by economic growth – rising output – and falling unemployment.

Three new developments need to be mentioned:

- The possibility of greater independence for the Bank of England is likely to be discussed openly, partly because Mr Lamont mentioned it in his statement to the House of Commons after he ceased to be Chancellor. He stated that he regretted that he had not been able to convince the Prime Minister of the merits of his proposal. A second reason for discussing the Bank's possible independence is because many other EC countries are giving their central banks greater freedom in the run-up to Economic and Monetary Union.
- In future, the UK's budget will be announced in late November or early December each year, for implementation in the following April. This gives students (and teachers) over five months in which to learn about any major changes of economic policy.
- The UK's PSBR for 1993/94 is very large – £50 billions – and many observers believe that it must be reduced substantially if inflation is to be kept within its target range. Substantial cuts in Government spending and/or big tax rises are very likely in the next two budgets.

Finally, once Germany has ratified the Maastricht Treaty, EMU is likely to be discussed again, and there is a slim chance that the UK could rejoin the ERM. But rejoining the ERM is highly unlikely if the UK is booming and the rest of the EC is in recession, i.e. the UK and the continent are still at opposite ends of the economic cycle.

ACTIVITY

Obtain recent data for unemployment, output and inflation, and compare the figures with those before 'Black Wednesday'. Do the figures support those people who say that the name for 16 September 1992 should be White Wednesday, because leaving the ERM enabled the UK to move out of recession?

Index